PORTRAIT OF A CITY

LINCOLN, NEBRASKA,

at the Turn of the Twentieth Century

BRUCE F. PAULEY

University of Nebraska Press
LINCOLN

The University of Nebraska Press is part of a land-grant
institution with campuses and programs on the past, present,
and future homelands of the Pawnee, Ponca, Otoe-Missouria,
Omaha, Dakota, Lakota, Kaw, Cheyenne, and Arapaho Peoples,
as well as those of the relocated Ho-Chunk, Sac and Fox, and
Iowa Peoples.

Library of Congress Cataloging-in-Publication Data
Names: Pauley, Bruce F., author.
Title: Portrait of a city: Lincoln, Nebraska,
at the turn of the twentieth century / Bruce F. Pauley.
Other titles: Lincoln, Nebraska, at the turn of
the twentieth century
Description: Lincoln: University of Nebraska Press, [2023] |
Includes bibliographical references and index.
Identifiers: LCCN 2022055981
ISBN 9781496234124 (paperback)
ISBN 9781496237118 (epub)
ISBN 9781496237125 (pdf)
Subjects: LCSH: Lincoln (Neb.)—Social life and customs—20th
century. | Lincoln (Neb.)—Civilization—20th century. | BISAC:
HISTORY / United States / State & Local / Midwest (IA, IL, IN,
KS, MI, MN, MO, ND, NE, OH, SD, WI)
Classification: LCC F674.L7 P38 2023 | DDC
978.2/293031—dc23/eng/20221122
LC record available at https://lccn.loc.gov/2022055981

For Marianne: The love of my life for sixty years.

Contents

List of Illustrations | xi
Preface | xiii
Acknowledgments | xvii
A Note on Terminology | xix

1. Revisiting the Past | 1
   Everyday Life on the Eve of Modernity | 1
   Pioneer Lincoln, 1867–89 | 5
   Progressive Reforms | 15

2. Electronic and Transportation Revolutions | 22
   A Decade of Inventions | 22
   World Fairs: "No Greater Sensation Than . . . Electricity" | 24
   From the Omnibus to Electric Streetcars:
       "The Welcome Stranger" | 29
   Interlude: The Brief but Spectacular Popularity of Bicycles | 35
   Here Comes the "Devil Wagon"! | 38

3. The Athens of the West | 51
   Public School Education in Nebraska:
       Compulsory in Theory | 51
   Beyond the Struggle to Survive: The University of
       Nebraska | 56
   The Denominational Schools: Nebraska Wesleyan,
       Union College, and Cotner College | 66

4. The New Woman | 75
   New Jobs for the New Woman: "An Unwomanly Desire"? | 75
   Turn-of-the-Century Fashions and Sports for Women | 82
   Downsizing and Modernizing: New Houses, Kitchens,
       and Bathrooms | 93

5. Feminine Reformers | 99
    The Revolt against the "Two Spheres" Ideal | 99
    Cigarettes: "A Plain Case of Self-Destruction" | 103
    Saloons and Prohibition: "The Vanguard of Progress"? | 107
    Women For and Against Suffrage: "Masculine
       Womanhood"? | 113

6. Amusements for All | 123
    The Increase in Leisure Time | 123
    Highbrow Entertainment: Opera, Opera Houses,
       and Theaters | 124
    Respectable Entertainment: The Chautauqua Movement | 131
    Risqué Entertainment: Vaudeville and Silent Movies | 134
    Dancing: "A Moral Graveyard"? | 140
    Vacations by Rail, Amusement Parks, and Circuses | 143
    The State Fair and Buffalo Bill's Wild West Show | 149

7. College Football: Birth Pains and Reforms | 152
    School Spirit and a Controversial New Sport | 152
    A Game "Fit for Savages"? | 154
    Changing the Rules: "An Outdoor Game of Basketball"? | 157
    From "Bugeaters" to "Cornhuskers" | 163
    From Obscurity to Fame: Bummy Booth and the
       Stiehm Rollers | 167
    The "Secrets" of Success | 175

8. Minorities and Immigrants | 178
    Lincoln's Black People: "Ambitious Improvement,
       Not Yet Realized" | 178
    Volga Germans: "Thrifty and Independent" | 187

9. World War, "Aggressive Patriotism," and the Spanish Flu | 199
    The "Great War" and "Scientific" Propaganda | 199
    Profiles in Courage: Bryan and Norris | 206
    Ethnically Cleansing German Culture: "America Does Not
       Want You" | 208
    The Campaign against Foreign Languages | 213
    "A Strong Aggressive War Spirit" | 215
    The Spanish Flu: "Not an Unusual Epidemic"? | 219

10. Reaction, Prosperity, and Depression | 227

    Ending War and Making Peace | 227

    The League of Nations "Menace" and the Conservative

        Reaction | 230

    The Roaring Twenties | 232

    The Declining Interest in Reforms | 238

    Postwar Nebraska | 242

11. Enduring Gains and Disappointing Setbacks | 248

    Notes | 257

    Bibliography | 287

    Index | 299

Illustrations

1. "I Grow Hair in One Night" | 3
2. Lincoln circa 1870 | 6
3. First state capitol, 1867 | 7
4. Railroad maps of Nebraska revealing explosive growth after 1890 | 8
5. Young lawyer William Jennings Bryan | 12
6. Carnegie library, built in 1902 | 18
7. Street view of O Street looking east circa 1900 | 21
8. Second state capitol, 1900 | 23
9. Omaha's Trans-Mississippi Exposition of 1898 | 28
10. Checkerboard map of Lincoln circa 1920 | 30
11. World Bicycle advertisement | 35
12. A new symbol of status | 40
13. "A Joy Ride" | 43
14. My father and grandfather in Yellowstone National Park in 1915 | 47
15. The new Lincoln High School in 1922 | 55
16. Collage of "Old Mains" | 57
17. Looking east on O Street circa 1926 | 82
18. "This Line of Best Fitting Corsets" | 86
19. "New Spring Suitings" for 1907 | 87
20. "Get Your Fall Suit Now" | 88
21. The 1905 University of Nebraska women's varsity basketball team | 91
22. "Leave It to Camels!" | 106
23. Advertisement for *Richard III* and *Othello* at the Opera House | 127
24. ROTC cadet band circa 1895 | 129
25. Advertisement for *The Birth of a Nation* | 137

26. Advertisement for *Passion's Playground* at the Rialto | 139
27. "Opening Announcement of the Castle School for Dancing" | 141
28. "Florida Best Reached by the Magnificent Train Service of the Louisville & Nashville Railroad" | 144
29. "Capital Beach, Nebraska's Beautiful Resort on the Lake" | 148
30. "The 'New Down' Added to Football" | 158
31. "There's a Big Black Cloud a Threatening" | 161
32. The 1915 University of Nebraska football team | 171
33. "Professor: 'You will disappear'"; "Sambo's Soliloquy"; "Couldn't Trust Him" | 183
34. "The Finest Sleeping Cars in the World" | 186
35. Volga Germans arriving in Lincoln (undated) | 193
36. "Make Your Choice Now!" | 203
37. "Lest We Forget" | 212
38. "Do You Measure Up to That?" | 216
39. "Mopping Up" | 218
40. "Their First Chance at a Real Square Meal" | 228
41. "Look Under the Lid!" | 250
42. "June Is Dress Month" | 251
43. Football fans pack uncompleted Memorial Stadium | 254

Preface

Historians have focused on the great men of history—be they emperors, kings, generals, or perhaps philosophers—ever since Herodotus and Thucydides in fifth-century BC Greece. It is only in our time, beginning in the late twentieth century, that historians have begun to turn their attention to the lives of ordinary people such as farmers, shopkeepers, and workers. When European and American cities began to explode in population in the second half of the nineteenth century, previously forgotten men and women could no longer be so easily ignored.

I argue in this book that the pace of change for ordinary people, particularly in cities, increased dramatically during the last third of the nineteenth century through the beginning of the Great Depression in 1930. First in the United States, and soon thereafter in western Europe, Australia, New Zealand, and Japan, the everyday lives of people were drastically impacted by the change from manual labor to work that was increasingly performed by machines. Power was no longer provided primarily by horses, wind, or manual labor, but by engines powered by steam or electricity. Housework, jobs for women, transportation, heating and lighting, education, entertainment, fashion, and medicine all changed drastically in little more than a single generation.

These changes provide an overview of society at large. In studying them we also gain a new understanding of the lives of our ancestors and the customs and habits we have inherited from them. However, unless those ancestors were among the few who left behind a memoir, diary, or a large stack of correspondence, it is unlikely that we will learn more than their birth and death dates, the names of their spouses, and when they came to this country, including, perhaps, on which ship.

I have attempted in this book to create a picture of these enormous changes. I have highlighted my hometown of Lincoln, Nebraska, but only as an example. To be sure, Lincoln was unusual, although certainly not unique, in being a state capital and home to the state's only major university. However, in most respects it was typical of many medium-size cities, especially newer municipalities in the central and northern plains around the turn of the twentieth century. On the other hand, I have not hesitated to provide an overview of the period immediately preceding the 1890s, a time when Lincoln and many other cities were founded and struggling to create a livable environment. Nor have I neglected to mention the reaction to reforms after the First World War.

Among the many surprises I have discovered was that Lincoln was never a "Wild West" city like those fictitious towns we still see portrayed in old movies and the black-and-white television programs of the 1950s and 1960s. On the contrary, Lincolnites, especially women, were busy establishing literary societies, musical organizations, and encouraging the establishment of theaters. By 1890 Lincoln had ornate theaters filled with patrons watching grand opera brought to them by trains from New York and other big cities. And little more than three decades since its founding, the University of Nebraska had become the fifth largest public university in the country and one of the best both academically and in football.

My other big surprise was how many controversies of the late nineteenth and early twentieth centuries are still with us today, albeit in different forms, of course. Are women treated equally with respect to jobs, sports, and health? How many people should we allow to immigrate into this country each year and from what countries? Who should be given the vote and for what purpose? Should high schools and colleges prepare students simply to get a job upon graduation or should they try to enrich their lives by teaching the humanities and fine arts? How can football and other sports be made safer? Should people be required to wear a mask during an epidemic? Should we continue our dependence on gasoline-powered cars for transportation, or should investments be made in high-speed trains, electric cars, bicycle paths, and urban light-rail systems?

When Lincoln was founded in 1867, the territorial phase of Nebraska's history had just ended. The city had few trees or natural surroundings that would appeal to anyone coming from settled areas east of the Mississippi River. But come they did, especially young people, who were eager to make Lincoln a political, educational, and cultural center. Lincolnites were not merely interested in populating a new city; many also wanted to help create a more enlightened society where women could be something more than the "weaker sex," content to remain forever in their "separate sphere."

Nearly sixty distinct subjects are covered in this book. I don't pretend to have covered any of them in exhaustive detail. My hope is to give readers at least an impression of the fascinating lives of their ancestors, as well as the astounding changes that occurred over a relatively brief span of time. By so doing I wish to provide some insight into the origins of their values and customs and the controversial issues of our own day.

Acknowledgments

A book is seldom, if ever, the product of an unassisted individual, and *Portrait of a City* is certainly no exception. Numerous friends, colleagues, and family members were all indispensable in this five-year enterprise.

Donna Shear, then director of the University of Nebraska Press, encouraged the pursuit of my project almost from the outset. Likewise, Dr. Connie Lester, editor of the *Florida Historical Quarterly* at the University of Central Florida (UCF), was helpful early in my research by suggesting secondary sources related to the Progressive Era and by commenting on parts of the first draft. The interlibrary staff at UCF was instrumental in obtaining important books on everyday life throughout the United States at the turn of the twentieth century.

On topics specifically related to the history of Lincoln, Jim McKee gave me a list of hundreds of articles he had written about the capital city and published in the *Lincoln Journal* and *Star* over several decades that proved to be of utmost importance. Micaela Fiker of the *Lincoln Journal Star* helped me find newspaper articles published as early as the 1880s. Katie Jones of the Archives and Special Collections section of Love Library at the University of Nebraska–Lincoln deserves to be singled out for her crucial work in locating and forwarding parts of rare books and long-forgotten MA theses and PhD dissertations.

A UCF colleague, Dr. Tom Morgan, read the entire draft of the manuscript and saved me from numerous mistakes. The same is true of my former roommate at Grinnell College, John Roy Price, the author of *The Last Liberal Republican*, who provided particularly helpful observations on turn-of-the-century train travel. Kenneth Rock, professor emeritus of history at Colorado State University and a specialist on Volga Germans, was especially valuable for his insights concerning Lincoln's largest minority around the turn of the twentieth century. My older son, Mark, provided invaluable technical assistance, especially concerning illustrations, and he meticulously proofread the entire manuscript. Bridget Barry, the editor in chief of the University of Nebraska Press, and Emily Casillas were helpful in myriad ways but particularly regarding the reproduction of illustrations. Jennifer Boardman's copyediting was superb, Erin Greb created fine and important maps, and Nathan Putens selected an appropriate cover for the book.

Special recognition must be given to professor emeritus Harl Dahlstrom, a former graduate school colleague of mine at the University of Nebraska–Lincoln, longtime specialist in Nebraska history at the University of Nebraska–Omaha, and coauthor of *Upstream Metropolis: An Urban Biography of Omaha and Council Bluffs*. Professor Dahlstrom made indispensable suggestions about obscure sources on the history of Lincoln as well as Nebraska and saved me from numerous factual errors and dubious conclusions.

I cannot close without mentioning my wife of nearly sixty years, Marianne, who meticulously proofread all seven of my books and has given me unstinting encouragement. None of my accomplishments could have been achieved without her love and support.

A Note on Terminology

It should be admitted at the outset that there was no agreed upon definition in 1890 of what was "west." During the three decades that are the centerpiece of this book, the demographic center of the forty-eight contiguous states was in southern Indiana. So far as educational institutions and their football teams were concerned, however, the "West" was anything west of the Alleghany Mountains. At other times, for example during Omaha's "trans-Mississippi" world's fair, the Mississippi River was the dividing line. However defined, Nebraskans considered themselves part of the West especially in the nineteenth century. The term "Midwest," so far as I have been able to determine, was never used until well past the turning of the new century.

The original language used in newspaper cartoons contained in figure 33 has been retained to avoid censoring the historical record and to illustrate the popularity of racist commentary in the early twentieth century.

PORTRAIT
OF A CITY

1

Revisiting the Past

Everyday Life on the Eve of Modernity

This is a book about changes in the everyday life of Americans around the turn of the twentieth century using my hometown of Lincoln, Nebraska, as an example. Recreating a portrait of everyday life as it existed more than a century ago is challenging to say the least. Not only has the generation that lived through this period long since died out but so too have their children. Even most of the grandchildren of turn-of-the-twentieth-century Lincolnites have passed from the scene, or at best did not have the good sense to systematically quiz their grandparents about life before electricity and automobiles.

I fall into this latter category. When I was an instructor of history at the University of Nebraska in 1965–66, I lived across the street from my paternal grandmother. She had been born in 1888 and moved with my grandfather to Lincoln in 1915, where he established the Pauley Lumber Company. She could have been a goldmine of information about the "olden days." But like most historians at that time my historical interests were limited mostly to traditional topics like politics and war and did not include the daily lives of any Americans let alone Lincolnites.

Long after the death of my grandmother in 1984, I did have a remarkable opportunity to interview a survivor of the early twentieth century. While strolling through the historic district of Fort Collins, Colorado, in the summer of 1994, my wife and I noticed an elderly lady enjoying the evening on her front porch. After I praised her charming home, she noted that she had been born there one hundred years earlier! Together with an old friend, a history professor at Colorado State University, we interviewed

Lydia Hoffman Morrison for about an hour and a half the next day. My last question was, "Do you think people are any happier today than when you were young?" Her initial response was an emphatic, "No." However, after a moment's reflection, she said, "But I do like the automatic washing machine."

This cryptic response in many respects is the central theme of this book. What inventions and social changes have given us a longer life expectancy, made physical work much easier, and increased our overall happiness? And on the other hand, what changes have resulted in growing social isolation, a less healthy lifestyle, and a deteriorating environment?

It is no secret that changes in everyday life have been constant in the lives of each generation since colonists came to North America in the early seventeenth century, and indeed in the lives of all humans since Neolithic farmers established cities in Mesopotamia in the fourth century bc. During our own lifetimes we have witnessed improvements in television reception, medicine, automobile and airplane safety, and especially in telecommunications. We have marveled that the lights in our houses and our furnaces can now be remotely controlled.

I attempt in this book to take the reader back to the time when heat came from a fireplace and lights from kerosene lamps; when municipal transportation was by foot or pulled by horses; when streets were unpaved and hospitals were places where people went to die; when doctors and lawyers did not need a license to practice; when washing clothes took all day and ironing another day; and when motion pictures and radios were not even imagined. In 1890 automobiles did not exist and only a few hundred wealthy people in Lincoln owned a telephone. Not only had airplanes not been invented, but most people were convinced that humans would never fly except in hot air balloons. Within the span of just three decades, everyday life changed drastically and would be in many ways quite recognizable to us if we could magically go back to the 1920s.

Major changes in the lifestyles of Americans and people living in other technologically advanced countries were drastically accelerated by the Industrial Revolution. It began in Great Britain toward the end of the eighteenth century and spread to the northern and

"I Grow Hair in One Night."

A Famous Doctor-Chemist Has Discovered a Secret Compound That Grows Hair on any Bald Head.

SEND FREE TRIAL PACKAGES TO ALL WHO WRITE.

Discoverer of This Magic Compound That Grows Hair in a Single Night.

1. "I Grow Hair in One Night." *Lincoln Star*, January 19, 1904, 6.

western parts of Europe and the United States in the second quarter of the nineteenth century, a period when steam produced by burning coal replaced wind to power transatlantic ships and railroad trains. Steam power made crossing the Atlantic Ocean and the North American continent relatively easy, thus vastly increasing immigration and the settlement of the states west of the Appalachian Mountains.

Great as these changes were, it was not until the last third of the nineteenth century that most Americans began to witness vast changes in their everyday lives. Machines were rapidly replacing manual labor, electric lightbulbs were used instead of kerosene lamps, and wood-burning fireplaces were replaced by coal-fed central-heating furnaces. Municipal transportation by foot or by horse-drawn buggies gave way to streetcars and automobiles.

No group was more affected by the profound changes of the turn-of-the-century decades than women of all classes, especially those living in cities. They were entering the workforce in huge numbers and into professions that had previously been closed to them or had not even existed. At the same time, they gained the right to vote in all elections local or national. The years between 1890 and 1920 saw an enormous increase in leisure time that affected all classes both urban and rural. Automobiles and electric lightbulbs affected Americans of all social classes and incomes in profound ways in their everyday lives unequaled by any other period of history. Of the modern conveniences we take for granted today, only steamboats, trains, and the telegraph were well-established before 1890.

The United States as a whole had just 31 million people in 1860, two years before the Homestead Act of 1862, but nearly 63 million by 1890. After that date, for all practical purposes, there was no longer a sizeable region of the United States that was not inhabited by people of European descent. Although more than half of the country's population still lived on farms or in small towns, the lure of free or inexpensive land that had proved so attractive to landless farmers and peasants from western, northern, and central Europe no longer existed. The census of 1920 exposed an equally shocking fact for a country that had been overwhelmingly agrarian since its beginning: out of a total population of nearly 106 million, most Americans now lived in towns or cities of more than 2,500 inhabitants.[1]

Raw numbers only tell a small part of the monumental changes that took place around the turn of the twentieth century. These changes were so broad that it is hard to say which one was the most important. Certainly the application of electricity to everyday life would have to be at or near the top. It is difficult to overstate how dramatic the change was from candles and kerosene lamps to the incandescent electric lightbulb that could illuminate a room with the flip of a switch. When applied to trams, electricity drastically reduced, almost overnight, the need for horses in cities. They remained useful on farms well into the twentieth century, but once replaced by tractors, their feeding grounds, which in 1890 encompassed around a quarter of all agricultural land in the United States, were now available for producing food for humans.[2] In the 1880s the discovery of germs as the cause of many illnesses, and thus the subsequent need for cleanliness, drastically reduced death by disease.

In 1900 automobiles were virtually nonexistent in the United States. Little more than twenty years later, they were beginning to replace streetcars in cities and almost nowhere more so than in Nebraska, which claimed in 1913 to be second only to California in the per capita ownership of cars.[3] By 1920 airplanes had captured the imagination of Americans, especially during the First World War, although it would not be until well into the 1950s before they even began to seriously compete with trains for cross-country transportation and ships for international transportation.

Pioneer Lincoln, 1867–89

When Lincoln was designated the state capital in 1867 it had few natural advantages. Unlike the nearby capitals of Missouri, Iowa, and the two Dakotas, it was not on the banks of the Missouri River, or any other important, let alone navigable, river. It was simply the product of a dispute between two of Nebraska's oldest towns, Omaha and Nebraska City, which both wanted the distinction. To resolve the controversy, the state legislature appointed a three-person commission that picked Lancaster—a village founded in 1859 and had only thirty-four souls in 1867—to be the capital and to bear the name of the recently assassinated president. Lincoln's only clear advantages were its equal distance from Omaha and Nebraska City and its proximity to the western edge of land then considered suitable for agriculture. Not apparent at the time, Lincoln would become and remain to this day near the demographic center of the state. Fortunately the people of Omaha, the capital of the territory of Nebraska since 1854, were not outraged by the

2. Lincoln circa 1870. Courtesy of History Nebraska.

choice because their town had already become Nebraska's leading commercial center and headquarters of the Union Pacific Railroad.[4]

Lincoln's only distinguishable physical characteristic was Salt Creek, which was not even a reliable source of drinking water or even a supplier of commercial salt. However, it did provide sustenance for elms and cottonwood trees, the only trees in the area. Starting at least as early as 1889, it also provided saltwater for large numbers of bathers. That the first areas of the city to be settled were bereft of trees is all too obvious in pictures of Lincoln in its early years. The nearest railroad stations were in Omaha and Bellevue, both more than fifty miles away, which made building Nebraska's first capitol a difficult and haphazard project. It was rushed to completion in 1869 before the state legislature could change its mind about the location of the capital city. Even the stone used for the project was untested and turned out to be sandstone, thus requiring a second capitol to be built on the same site just twenty years later. One of Nebraska's premier authors, Bess Streeter Aldrich, described the first capitol in its early days as "a cumbersome-looking affair, top-heavy with dome. Paths cut diagonally across the meadow toward where it stood in solitary grandeur, a miniature Rome with all roads leading to it. The grounds

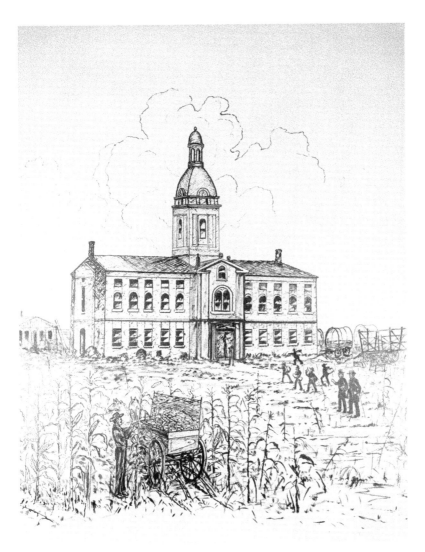

3. The first state capitol, 1867. Courtesy of History Nebraska.

surrounding it were treeless virgin prairie on which the cows of the neighborhood munched the early spring grasses."[5] However unimpressive the building was, it was put to good use for conventions, balls, and theatrical performances.[6]

Towns needing close railroad service in the nineteenth century resembled towns needing nearby interstate highways in the 1960s and major airports in the twenty-first century. In other words transportation was essential for any settlement that hoped to have a

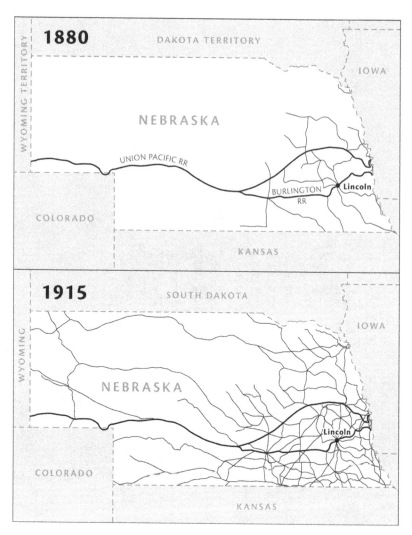

4. Railroad maps of Nebraska revealing explosive growth after 1890. Maps created by Erin Greb.

future. The problem was resolved for Lincoln in 1870, when the Burlington and Missouri Railroad reached the city, which put an immediate end to stagecoach service, until then the only public way to reach Lincoln. The Burlington was soon followed by several other railroad lines ending with the arrival of the Rock Island Railroad to Lincoln in 1892, which helped increase railroad mileage in Nebraska from 1,868 in 1880 to 5,144 in 1890. It was the

Burlington and Missouri River Railroad, however, with its 2,500 miles of rails in the state and its six lines radiating from Lincoln, which made the city a railroad hub for commerce, agriculture, and entertainment. Every day in 1889, "800 men handled from 1,000 to 2,000 cars, and thirteen passenger trains and fifty to seventy-five freight trains left the city."[7]

In the meantime a high school was built allegedly large enough to house all the state's high school students in 1872. Two years later Lincoln acquired a public library, a full-time fire department in 1877, two small department stores in 1880, and water works the next year. A telephone exchange was established in 1880; by 1889 Lincoln had 615 telephones.[8] By 1890 there were more than eighteen miles of water lines throughout the city along with 168 hydrants, which, like other American cities, was about two decades after such facilities were available in western Europe.[9] Filtered water was crucial to the reduction of waterborne disease. The census of 1880 listed the city's population a respectable thirteen thousand, easily passing Nebraska City as the second largest in the state, a status it retains to this day.[10] However, its streets only started to be paved in 1887; until then they were full of mud in the winter and spring and dust in the summer. Sidewalks were even slower to be built. Not until the turn of the century did they appear in residential areas, and then only due to private owners who used bricks and stones, the city declaring that wood was no longer an option.[11] Gasoline streetlights came only in 1888. A sewage system, commonplace in the Roman Empire, did not yet exist. Streets had names, but houses did not have numbers until 1882, making life considerably easier for mailmen.

Lincolnites and other Nebraskans could not count on reliable help from physicians whose training came mostly from apprenticeships, medical diplomas not being required until 1881.[12] Lincoln was hardly alone in this predicament. Prior to 1890 hospitals throughout the United States were widely regarded as mere dumping grounds for the lower classes or poor immigrants.[13] This attitude began to change soon after 1890. Whereas in 1870 there had been 120 hospitals in the whole country, by 1920 there were around 6,000.[14] Not until 1889 did the city gain its first public hospital, St. Elizabeth, whose patients were known as "inmates."[15] Most

Lincolnites feared and hated hospitals, regarding them as places to die. People stayed at home unless they were very sick; doctors came to them if need be.[16] This practice was still common when I was a youngster in the 1940s. I can remember a doctor coming to my bedroom with his big bag and taking my temperature after vigorously shaking his thermometer. The usual prescription was to take a couple of pills and drink lots of liquid.

Although early Lincoln's natural surroundings were anything but impressive, the city did soon have several distinct advantages. The state legislature made Lincoln the home of the state's only university in 1869. Much less esteemed, but still a source of reliable employment and income, was Lincoln housing the state's insane asylum and penitentiary. By contrast, in neighboring Wyoming, these three institutions were divided between Cheyenne, Laramie, and Rawlins. Moreover insurance companies were established that would later lead to Lincoln being known as the "Hartford of the West."[17] None of these institutions made Lincoln rich; however, they did help avoid drastic rates of unemployment. Consequently the city's distribution of wealth and leisure remained relatively even.[18] The absence of abject poverty and big-city slums assured Lincoln's middle-class status, which it retains to this day. Unlike major cities like Boston, New York, Philadelphia, or even Omaha, Lincoln was never the home of anyone who belonged to the super-rich class, who owned a private railroad car or a mansion requiring twenty-four servants as described in Thorstein Veblen's 1899 classic work, *The Leisure Class*.[19]

Lincoln was unusual in being planned. From the outset its streets were laid out in grid formation just as the Romans had done two millennia earlier. Four square blocks were set aside for the state capitol and an equal number for the university. Today's capitol occupies the same space, but the University of Nebraska has long since spilled over its original boundaries. Starting in 1882 streets running west to east were labeled with the letters of the alphabet from A to Z, with O Street presumably having the honor of being in the exact middle of the alphabet as well as becoming the center of the business district. (Whoever came up with this idea was not a great speller; even by excluding the letter I to avoid confusion with the numeral 1, the middle of the alphabet should have made N Street the city's central avenue.) First Street was next to the railroad tracks, and the newest streets to the east had the highest numbers.

As late as 1880 most of Lincoln lay between the state university on the north and the state capitol to the south. But well before 1890, A Street also lost its designation as the city's southern boundary, being replaced by South Street, then Van Dorn, and after World War II, by Highway 2. Dakota Street, where much of my childhood was spent, was three blocks south of Van Dorn. When my home was built in 1929, Dakota was one of the last streets in Lincoln built on the grid plan.

When considering living conditions in Lincoln prior to 1890, one must assume that the city appealed only to the most hardy, young, adventurous, and ambitious people, like the future presidential candidate William Jennings Bryan. In 1880 the governor of the state was thirty-two, and the average age in the legislature was thirty-four. Only the chancellor of the university was a relatively "elderly" fifty.[20] The earliest residents were not only young but also remarkably well educated and cultured. They brought along "their tapestries and oriental rugs, their fine linen and china, pianos and libraries. . . . These were the pioneers not of land but of commerce and the professions: judges, lawyers, merchants, publishers, railroad builders, professors. . . . They did not come to Nebraska to build a different world; they wanted the kind of society they had always considered desirable—but they wanted it here, where success (so they thought) was quick."[21]

They refused to be discouraged by the locust and grasshopper plagues in the mid-1870s, which could obscure the midday sun and wipe out a crop in a day. The city endured a railroad strike in 1873 and a depression that did not end until 1878. Lincoln lacked a sewage system and paved streets. Houses were small and usually made of wood. Yards were generally large enough for a garden, a horse, some chickens, a cow, and sometimes a pig, although they were not permitted to run loose.[22] There was no zoning, so large and expensive houses could stand side by side with more modest ones. Haystacks and piles of manure were commonplace because horses were the only means of municipal transportation other than walking because there was no public transit until 1883. Almost need-

5. The young lawyer William Jennings Bryan. Courtesy of History Nebraska.

less to say, there was no central heating, and light was provided
by stoves and oil, kerosene, or gas lamps, all of which polluted the
air.[23] Streets were wide but unpaved, unpoliced, and unlighted. As
previously mentioned the city did acquire an impressive new high
school in 1872, and the library was established the same year. However, the University of Nebraska remained tiny, and its continued
existence was still very much in doubt during the 1880s. The sta-

tus of medical education in the 1870s was so low and the cleanliness of hospitals so bad that the average Nebraskan was better off living in a rural area as was confirmed by physical examinations during the First World War.

Many of these deficiencies were at least partially rectified during the 1880s, including public transportation, streets, sidewalks, and vegetation. Just a few years after the founding of the city there was a vehicle known as an "omnibus," or a "herdic carriage."[24] Invented in the 1830s and pulled by a horse, it was roughly the size of a stagecoach. These vehicles moved about three miles per hour on unpaved streets—about the same as a moderately fast walker. They were used in Lincoln between about 1870 and 1883 to carry passengers and their luggage from a train depot to hotels, concerts, and the state capitol. Even their modest speed was often hindered by four- to six-inch-deep mud. This problem was resolved by rails that greatly reduced friction, enabled one horse to do the work of two, and allowed the vehicle to travel at five miles per hour.[25]

Although rails helped increase the speed of Lincoln's public transportation, potential passengers were still faced with the daunting task of crossing a muddy or, at best, dusty street just to board an omnibus. Lincoln's horrific streets became the center of attention in the last few years of the 1880s. After watching four horses attempt to pull a loaded wagon out of a bad place on West O Street in 1887, a leading businessman told a reporter that "there is not a city in the whole country that needs paved streets so badly as this. . . . We will never be any more than an overgrown country town until we get them. . . . Hardly a merchant or businessman in the place but has lost money directly on account of our villainous streets ever since the middle of February."[26] The street situation had not improved the following December when O Street was impassable for two months causing many shoppers to take their business elsewhere.[27] The *Nebraska State Journal* commented that "there was mud on everything yesterday. . . . The unpaved part of the city was simply a morass. Even the paved streets looked discouraged enough to throw up."[28]

A problem closely related to unpaved streets was the lack of sidewalks in Lincoln, a problem that continued as the city kept growing. Four-foot-wide residential sidewalks were required to be paved in the 1890s, but there was great latitude in the type of paving permissible: brick, stone, asphalt, tar, iron, or two-inch planks were all permissible.[29]

In 1890 there were already thirteen churches in the city, four daily newspapers, and twelve weeklies. The Lincoln Telephone Exchange was established in 1880, and by 1889 615 phones were in use in the city connecting to fifty-seven towns in Nebraska and sixty-six towns in Iowa. The city, as well as the rest of the state, benefited from above-average rainfall that lasted throughout the decade, which contributed to an enormous increase in the population of the city and state. A new, larger, and sturdier state capitol was completed in 1888 on the site of the old capitol, although it too had to be replaced in the 1920s.

By the latter part of the 1880s, Lincoln was no longer the nearly treeless, frontier outpost that it had been at the beginning of the decade. Instead it was covered with a "forest of shade trees which line[d] the streets and the green lawns decorated with flowerpots and shrubbery."[30] In fact some two million trees, mostly elms, were planted in the city's first twenty-five years.[31] Only 7 of the city's 750 miles of streets were paved by 1889, all of them with red cedar blocks, which tended to float away when it rained. The city also had twenty miles of water lines and sewers, thirty-five miles of street rail lines, forty churches, four daily newspapers, and twelve weeklies.[32]

Indeed the city was mature enough in 1887 for the promising twenty-seven-year-old lawyer William Jennings Bryan and his wife, Mary Elizabeth, to come to Lincoln from Illinois to establish a new home and practice and for a good place to raise children.[33] However, it was still far from modern in the way we define the word today. On the other hand, Lincoln was never a "Wild West" frontier town so frequently depicted in movies and on television, especially between the 1930s and the 1960s. There were, to be sure, thirty saloons in 1889, but also thirteen temperance societies as well as forty churches and synagogues, twenty-six periodicals, and four daily newspapers.[34] Although no statistics are available, poverty and crime were most likely well below the national average. Nor was Lincoln bereft of serious cultural outlets. Quite the opposite, as will be seen in chapter 6, Lincoln had a flourishing cultural life almost from its founding.

The first author of a comprehensive history of Lincoln boasted that by 1889 "the city was beautified, verily transformed from a raw-looking western town, with sidewalks full of ups and downs, and a general evidence of disorganization and lack of system. Now the city is as beautiful as any place of its age in the United States. . . . In brief, Lincoln is in a condition to continue its prosperity, and afford such enjoyment to its inhabitants as only a completely built city can do, possessed of such ample improvement and acquirements in the way of education, commercial, social, and religious facilities."[35]

Despite this fulsome praise, if we could somehow visit the Lincoln of 1889, the city would seem strange. Not only did the modern conveniences already mentioned not yet exist, but almost no public buildings still survive today aside from the former city hall built in 1879.[36] Families were large, but life expectancy was still short. Except for wealthy families who could afford servants, life was hard, especially for women. Almost every house had a vegetable garden and often chickens and a cow or two as well. The University of Nebraska had scarcely five hundred students, and an intercollegiate football team existed only in the minds of some impatient students. On the other hand, Lincoln already had an astonishingly active and varied cultural life. Just thirty years later, most of Lincoln's homes had been electrified and enjoyed central heating, and a substantial minority of families owned a car.

Progressive Reforms

The decades between 1890 and 1920 were not only marked by a blizzard of society-altering inventions but were also profoundly affected by laws influencing everyday life. Progressives wanted government to reform almost all aspects of the state, economy, and society including laws regulating food and medicine. They wanted to abolish the sale of alcoholic beverages and to grant women the right to vote in all local and national elections. Women played a huge role in bringing about these reforms. However, not all women supported them, and just as certainly, not all men opposed them.

Progressives, wanting to improve social conditions through government action, were able to advance their agenda through the enormous growth in the circulation of books, newspapers, and magazines during the last two decades of the nineteenth century. The explosive growth resulted from the expansion of public education, more efficient means of production, the increase of mass advertising, and growing literacy. In the words of one Nebraska historian, "Reading became virtually a national obsession. Everyone was urged to read. Americans read alone; they read aloud to one another; they read to improve themselves morally and materially; and they read to acquire culture."[37] A bookcase filled with bound volumes became a sure sign of middle-class status. This passion was abetted by mass-produced magazines typically costing just 10 cents a copy, and newspapers, including the *New York Times*, sold for a penny a copy starting in 1898 (today it costs $4). Circulation was increased still more by "muckraking" articles that revealed political corruption and horrendous social problems. Upton Sinclair's book *The Jungle* was particularly influential in revealing horrendous conditions in the meatpacking industry and was instrumental in leading to the Pure Food and Drug Act of 1906.

Not surprisingly middle-class women were especially concerned about public health care for mothers and children and were particularly eager to ban child labor. The latter was more difficult than one might imagine because many poor families desperately needed the income provided by their own children. Some children also preferred working in factories and mines to the strict rules and harsh punishments doled out in many public schools.

In 1890 only Wyoming had granted women the right to vote in national elections. In 1920 the Nineteenth Amendment granted suffrage to all women. For better or worse, women were also the primary drivers of the amendment to abolish the sale of alcoholic beverages. The *Ladies Home Journal* led the attack against patent medicines by refusing to advertise them after 1892 and exposing their ingredients in a series of articles it published in 1904–5.[38] Of monumental importance was the support women gave to the enactment of the Pure Food and Drug Act. The role of young women in primary education, already strong in 1890, was overwhelming three decades later. By 1920 they were nearly as likely as men to attend college, although few of them could become professors and be married at the same time. The invention of the typewriter enabled women to replace men as office workers but did nothing to elevate them to higher positions in the business world.

Most of the progressives' support came from middle-class women and professionals such as lawyers, teachers, physicians, ministers, and businesspeople. However, even some millionaires, who had numbered only about one hundred in the 1870s but had grown to four thousand in 1892 and to sixteen thousand in 1916, supported hospitals, colleges, medical research, museums, libraries, and opera houses. Steel magnate Andrew Carnegie was the most generous of all the superrich by helping found around three thousand libraries in the United States, Canada, and Britain along with other English-speaking countries. Lincoln acquired its own handsome Carnegie library in 1902, which was in use until 1960. Progressives, who could be found in both major parties as well as a third Populist Party, passionately believed that humankind could improve their natural and social environment and turned to experts in those fields to help them bring about the changes they sought. Progressives, in short, wanted to make the world a better place in which to live. In this endeavor they were aided by the emergence of political science, history, and economics, achieving the status of academic disciplines in regional and national organizations.

Progressives' support was weakest among first- or second-generation immigrants, who often turned to bartenders and local politicians for advice in getting a job. German Americans often viewed the attack on alcoholic beverages, especially beer, as an assault on their way of life, which included family gatherings in beer gardens. Attacks on breweries, many of which were owned by German Americans, were also viewed with suspicion.

Between 1890 and 1920 by far the most *enduring* politician in terms of national prominence was William Jennings Bryan, whose support had been critical in Woodrow Wilson winning the Democratic nomination for president in 1912, thus leading to Bryan's post as secretary of state. Known as the "Great Commoner," Bryan was in many ways quite different from the three presidents who came after the assassination of William McKinley in 1901: Theodore Roosevelt, William Howard Taft, and Wilson. Although he

6. Carnegie library, built in 1902. Courtesy of History Nebraska.

agreed with the presidents on constitutional reforms, he was an anti-imperialist, anti-militarist, and Anglophobe. On the other hand, like Wilson, he favored conciliation and collective action for maintaining peace.[39] Elected to the U.S. House of Representatives in 1890, Bryan was still mentioned as a serious candidate for the presidency in 1920. A Lincolnite from 1887 until he moved to Florida in 1916 because of his wife's health problems, he holds several noteworthy records. His nomination for the presidency by the Democrats in 1896 when he was just thirty-six makes him to this day the youngest nominee of any major political party. He was also the only person to win the nomination three times; the other two campaigns being in 1900 and 1908. Although he was immensely popular in Lincoln as a public speaker, he never succeeded in winning "his own precinct, ward, city, and county all at once and usually couldn't carry any one of them."[40] Bryan was strictly conservative in his religious fundamentalism and his support of prohibition but was a progressive in his belief in the central role of government as well as science and technology to improve society. His beliefs played a major role in transforming the Democratic Party "into a modern party that favored using the power of government to reform American society."[41] These principles were probably derived in part by an eleven-month cruise around the world beginning in September 1908 in which he visited eighteen countries where he encountered new ideas about the role of government already being practiced in Europe.[42] Thereafter he became an advocate of a national minimum wage, free textbooks, a reduction of tariff rates, the regulation of railroad rates, income and inheritance taxes, an eight-hour workday, and the rights of labor to organize and strike, all foretastes of President Franklin Roosevelt's New Deal of the 1930s.[43] He was not the decisive supporter of any of the constitutional amendments that took place during his career, but his endorsement of all of them proved helpful in their passage. He was particularly influential in his advocacy of the rights of labor, reform of big business, enfranchisement of women, and progressive taxation while being a staunch opponent of imperialism and militarism.[44] Ironically his anti-imperialism in 1900 became far more acceptable a few years later.[45] He favored prohibition but did not hesitate to campaign in saloons and buy all its patrons a beer.[46] His opposition to imperialism in the Philippines in 1898 and to U.S. entry into the First World War when he was secretary of state, as well as his resignation in 1915, have appeared more and more farsighted with the passage of time. Although he has had his critics—especially about his religious fundamentalism, both during his lifetime and since his death in 1925—his reputation among historians has generally been favorable.[47]

Bryan was by far the most popular orator of his day, or perhaps of any time in American history. Over time his speaking ability enabled him to make as much as a thousand dollars a speech—an enormous sum at a time when the dollar was worth twenty-five times what it is today. He became wealthy enough to give up his law practice and build a large house on Fifty-Sixth Street in Lincoln in 1902 called "Fairview" because of its unobstructed views to the west. The house no longer has the view it had in Bryan's time owing to Lincoln's growth but has been preserved as a museum. In Bryan's time it was the site of many important meetings with famous people including President Wilson.

Bryan delivered around six thousand scheduled addresses starting at age four, which made him even more precocious than Mozart, who did not compose his first work until he was five. His speeches were delivered to a great variety of forums including college and high school commencements and religious revivals. He had a booming, melodic voice, capable of reaching an audience of thirty thousand, which worked to his advantage at a time when loudspeakers did not yet exist.[48] The importance of oratory around the turn of the twentieth century can be seen in the fact that it was a required subject in schools with a speech being obligatory for both high school and college graduations.[49] Bryan wrote his own speeches but did not read them while speaking. He was always careful to include a joke or two to put his audience at ease. Some historians think he would have been elected president if radios had existed at the time to give him vastly larger audiences. One of his most recent biographers has noted that in "speaking common truths to millions of common people [Bryan] persuaded himself that he was doing God's work by defending the interests of suffering humanity. . . . Pious democrats such as himself should dedicate their lives to reforming both their own society and the world."[50]

His most important speeches probably occurred during presidential campaigns when few candidates thought it necessary to actively campaign for the presidency. He did so when campaigning against McKinley in 1896 by traveling 19,000 miles on chartered trains for his "whistle stop campaign" in which he gave 599 speeches, establishing a tradition lasting into the 1950s.[51] Previous candidates, including William McKinley, campaigned from their front porches. Bryan, in fact, was the first presidential candidate to openly seek a presidential nomination. When it came to race relations, he was not much more progressive than Wilson. He did speak out forcefully against lynching but did not challenge Jim Crow laws, believing with many, if not most, white progressives at the time that Black people, for historical reasons, had not yet evolved to the point where they could be trusted with the vote and would suffer less violence if they were segregated.[52] The widespread support for segregation among whites is best illustrated by there not being a single Black congressman

7. Street view of O Street looking east circa 1900. Courtesy of History Nebraska.

in the House of Representatives in 1900. Before Jim Crow acts were implemented, there had been twenty Black representatives and two Black senators.[53]

Despite the real progress that Lincoln had made in just two decades since being a frontier village of thirty-four residents, the city was far from modern in the sense we understand the word today. Before the new decade began, the University of Nebraska's enrollment was still little more than five hundred, and there was no football team. Automobiles were not yet even a dream. Above all, the magic of electricity, except for telephones, had not yet reached any household or street in Lincoln. The capital city was about to begin a huge transformation.

2

Electronic and Transportation Revolutions

A Decade of Inventions

The huge social and economic transformation was accelerated in spectacular fashion just two weeks after the start of the 1890s with a charity ball. Proclaimed by the *Nebraska State Journal* as

> the greatest social event ever held in Lincoln took place in the recently completed second statehouse. Four or five hundred of the *best people* of Lincoln showed their interest in the great cause. . . . Festoons and rings of evergreen and holly were hung between the windows and joined the columns. The windows were covered with lace and tapestry and the window panels were decorated with clusters of evergreen and flowers. Large flags defiled the corners of the hall. . . . The effect of the *incandescent lights was magnificent*. The dancing, which consisted of waltzes, Virginia Reels, and Polkas, lasted until three o'clock in the morning.[1]

On the same day a large audience of German-speaking Lincolnites enjoyed an evening of German vocal music performed by the Germania Maennerchor (men's choir). Smoking was "verboten."[2]

The year 1890 was monumental for Lincoln and the whole country. As previously noted, the beginning of the new decade witnessed the election of William Jennings Bryan to the House of Representatives and the start of his remarkable thirty-year career as the most enduring and perhaps the most consequential Democratic politician in the country. A much more spectacular and lasting development of the new decade was the relatively sudden emergence of electricity as a source of power for an almost endless number of new and useful inventions. Foremost among these inventions for city dwellers were the incandescent electric lightbulb and the electric streetcar.[3] The *Lincoln Evening Call* predicted

8. Second state capitol, 1900. Courtesy of History Nebraska.

that "electricity promises to bring about a regular revolution in domestic affairs. . . . If electricity does not solve the servant question, then nothing can."[4] The *Lincoln Herald* was equally ecstatic in proclaiming that the "coming year of grace, 1891, will be the greatest in the history of Lincoln. [There will be] electricity on every [street]car line in the city, a grand union depot, viaducts at all dangerous crossings, factories, and businesses without number."[5] Two weeks later the Lindell Hotel on Thirteenth and N Streets bragged that it had "all modern improvements: Steam heat and electric lights in every room."[6]

Before the dawning of the new decade, there were only three common means of illumination, none of them either safe or powerful: candles, kerosene lamps, and gas lights, all of which, as noted in chapter 1, polluted the air. The incandescent lightbulb, invented by Thomas Edison in 1879, eliminated the air pollution caused by gas and kerosene lamps. The latter needed to be periodically cleaned and their wicks trimmed. Electric lights produced no soot and required no ventilation, although skeptics feared possible fires, explosions, or even electrocutions. Kerosene lamps, which dated back to the 1850s, needed daily filling, wick trimming, and regular washing of shades and chimneys. Gas lights were cleaner but considerably more expensive.[7] Perhaps most important of all, a 100-watt bulb provided twelve to fifteen times more illumination than a kerosene lamp. (However, in Lincoln during the 1910s, most electric lightbulbs had a strength of 25 or 30 watts, although even that strength produced far more illumination than kerosene lamps.) It was also quickly realized that as a source of power, electricity was cheaper and more reliable than either wind or water-power.[8] In short, electric lights made houses cleaner, housework easier, and eliminated interior darkness after sunsets. Few if any inventions have been so enthusiastically and quickly received and so readily described as "indispensable."

Popular as they were, however, electric lights were merely one invention that used electricity. The countless others included household appliances, most of which were related to traditional female household jobs: washing machines, stoves, refrigerators, vacuum cleaners, heating pads, toasters, radiators, and fans, all of which will be discussed later.[9] What can be noted here, however, is that all these appliances were far more expensive than lightbulbs and did not become commonplace in some cases until late in the second quarter of the twentieth century. For example only 8 percent of American homes owned an electric refrigerator in 1930.[10]

World Fairs: "No Greater Sensation Than ... Electricity"

Lincolnites and other Nebraskans, especially those living in Omaha, were fortunate in having easy access to an almost infinite number of marvelous new inventions displayed at the World's Columbian Exposition (Chicago World's Fair) in 1893 and the Trans-Mississippi and International Exposition in Omaha in 1898. The first truly international, and perhaps the most famous of all world fairs, was housed at the Crystal Palace in London in 1851. Named for its innovative glass and steel construction, it was so popular that it became a model for future world fairs.[11] There had been fairs displaying handmade and manufactured products as early as the Middle Ages, but they attracted only nearby artisans and casual visitors. By the middle of the nineteenth century, railroads and steamships, primitive and slow as they were, made it possible for manufacturers and visitors from as far away as Australia and the United States as well as from western and central Europe to be represented. The world's fair held in Paris in 1889, to mark the centenary of the French Revolution, was especially remarkable for its 1,024-foot-high Eiffel Tower. The two American fairs of the 1890s sought not only to display the latest manifestations of technology in more than two hundred buildings but also to entertain as many people as possible by providing an escape from everyday life and by appealing to every class.

Chicago had already established itself as the most important railroad hub in the country and was not terribly far from major metropolitan cities to the east. Omaha was relatively accessible by train from every city and most small towns west of the Mississippi including the most remote areas of Nebraska. Special overnight trains could take Lincolnites to Chicago and back. The Northwestern Line, for example, sold special round-trip tickets for $22.65, or $616 today ($1 at the time would be worth $25 today), with the train leaving Lincoln at 5:25 p.m. and arriving in Chicago the next morning at 9:30. In both Chicago and Omaha, fairgoers were met by electric streetcars, which took them directly to the fairgrounds. Those people traveling long distances may have found their trips more comfortable and enjoyable, and in some cases even faster, than a similar trip would be today. Expenses in Chicago were reasonable if you avoided big hotels. A comfortable room at a good hotel cost a dollar, and a shave—do-it-yourself safety razors had not yet become widespread—was a quarter at a big hotel and a dime at a Black barbershop![12] However, even the 50-cent entrance fee to both fairs was enough to keep out the poor, especially since it did not include food, drinks, rides, and midway shows.[13] The entrance fee of $109 per day per person in 2022 at a theme park like Walt Disney World in Orlando has the same exclusionary impact. It was probably of some importance that one of the visitors to the Chicago fair was Walt Disney's father, Elias, who told his son many stories about the fair.[14]

The Columbian Exposition, celebrating the five hundredth anniversary of the discoveries of Christopher Columbus a year late, had a spectacular first night. President Grover Cleveland, who attended the opening of the fair along with 286,000 fairgoers, by pressing a single button illuminated much of the park with more than ninety thousand incandescent electric lights, caused pumped in water to begin rushing, and started the revolving wheels of what was then the world's largest Ferris wheel.

The exposition was often referred to as the "White City" because of its uniformly painted neoclassical buildings. The *Lincoln Star* summarized the importance of the exposition by saying that "there can be no greater sensation here than the exhibit of electricity. This is the electrical age, and Americans are the leaders of the world in the new art. Of this there can be no doubt. American inventors have produced nine out of ten of the important electrical inventions of the times. . . . The strong feature of the exhibit is that it is more than a mere display; it is in use; it furnishes the light and the power, the beauty and the spectacularism."[15] One exhibit that was especially promising was Edison's kinetoscope, a forerunner of motion pictures. More mundane but more useful were displays of the first zippers and the first all-electric kitchen, which included a dishwasher. That the eyes of the world were truly on the exposition could be seen in the thirty thousand American and Canadian newspapers as well as five thousand foreign newspapers that covered it. The publicity helped persuade twenty-seven million people to attend the fair.[16]

The exposition was far more than a display of the latest inventions. Like both earlier and later world fairs, it was an escape from everyday life for people of every social group or class.[17] Its midway had performances and rides, which were, in theory at least, to educate visitors about cultures around the world but were entertaining as well. For example roller coaster rides were made to look like scenic railways in foreign lands; exotic villages were made to look like life among primitive tribes.[18]

Of special interest to what was then called the "gentler sex" was an exhibit devoted to "Women and the Home," which was dedicated to an "elevated womanhood." Designed by a woman and with the displays organized by a board of women, it was seen as

an opportunity to demonstrate the skills of women in the various industries of arts and professions as may convince the world that ability is not a matter of sex. Urged by necessity, she has demonstrated that her powers are the same as her brother's and that like encouragement and fostering care may develop her to an equal point of usefulness. . . . We advocate, therefore, the thorough education and training of women to fit her to meet whatever fate life may bring, not only to prepare her for the factory and workshop for the profession and arts, but more important than all else, to prepare her for presiding over the home [Applause].[19]

Despite its overall success, the Chicago exposition was not without its controversies. Sabbatarians vigorously objected to the park being open on Sundays. However, the *Lincoln Star* noted that they were at least partially "disarmed of their most effective arguments against a seven-day fair by several clauses in the rules adopted. One of these provide[d] for holding religious services at the park each Sunday" in halls holding up to seven thousand people and led by eminent ministers.[20] This tactic ultimately failed, however, which meant that many people whose only day off was Sunday were unable to attend the fair without missing a payday.

Organized by a group of Omaha businessmen, the Trans-Mississippi and International Exposition of 1898 in Omaha was designed to revive trade and advertise returning prosperity following a long depression, which started with the Panic of 1893 and lasted until 1897. The exposition managed to attract only 2.6 million visitors but, unlike most expositions, was a financial success for a city having somewhere between 100,000 and 140,000 residents.[21] Attendance was likely hurt by the distraction of the Spanish-American War. Located two miles from downtown Omaha but easily accessible by streetcars, Omaha's exhibition, like the Chicago fair, featured twenty-one white, plaster-of-Paris buildings in classic and Renaissance style that encircled a two-thousand-foot lagoon. Promoters claimed that their grounds had more lights than Chicago's. For the visitors who came from small towns in the West, the fair was their first opportunity to see electric lights or anything else powered by electricity. Like the Columbian Exposition, the lights were turned on by the president of the United States, but this time the president was William McKinley, who was in Washington DC, not at the fair (although he was later to visit it).

Most visitors were enthusiastic about the fair but not all Lincolnites were pleased. Once again the issue was the exhibition being open on Sundays. A group of forty-three Lincoln ministers, repre-

9. Omaha's Trans-Mississippi Exposition of 1898. Courtesy of History Nebraska.

senting eleven denominations, adopted resolutions objecting to the Sunday openings. Attempting a new tactic, the Lincoln ministers claimed that Sunday closings would increase attendance because pious Christians in surrounding states would have no reason to boycott the exposition.[22] Baptists were especially incensed by the prospect of the Omaha exposition being open on Sundays. Dr. Rowlands of First Baptist Church in Lincoln charged that "the opening of the exposition on the Sabbath . . . [would offend] the religious consciences of thousands of Christian people . . . and would mean the paralysis of interest in a great many people who would otherwise . . . attend. The youths of our towns and farming communities [will be in a city] given over to the saloon with its accompanying drunkenness, debauchery, and all manner of corruptions."[23]

Much more advantageous publicity resulted from a certain Lt. Dorothy Maurer of the Salvation Army, who climbed to the top of the wings of the arc of states and hacked one of the arms off a nude figure. Reports of that unique spasm of ultra-morality and pious fervor were telegraphed far and wide, and newspapers gave it great prominence because of its novelty.

Like Chicago almost certainly the most popular part of the exposition was the midway, which purportedly sought to educate visitors about cultures around the world but again did much more to entertain than to educate. Among the performances were "male and female negroes of the Old Plantation Company."[24] One must wonder just how entertaining life was on the old plantation. In addition there were sword fighters, dervish dancers, and make-believe Egyptian street scenes.

From the Omnibus to Electric Streetcars:
"The Welcome Stranger"

The expositions in Chicago and Omaha were especially dependent for their success on railroads. The whole period between 1890 and 1920 was the golden age of American trains, at least as far as accessibility was concerned, although not yet speed—at only around forty miles per hour—or comfort. By 1916 there were 254,000 miles of rails in the United States, which was one-third of the world's total. Nebraska alone had 5,144 miles of rails in 1890 and 7,879 in 1910.[25] Without the trains overland travel was entirely horse driven—stagecoach or covered wagon—just as it had been in the days of the Oregon and Mormon Trails from the 1840s to the completion of the transcontinental railroad in 1869.

If the application of electricity to illumination was spectacular at the two world's fairs of the 1890s, Americans had to be patient before electricity powered other everyday inventions. As late as 1900, only 3 percent of American homes were using electricity.[26] Nationally the average American home in 1929 had only enough electricity to power a 100-watt bulb, or its equivalent, for five hours, with no electricity remaining for anything else including a refrigerator or even a radio.[27] In some towns women were asked *not* to iron on Tuesdays, the traditional ironing day, to avoid monopolizing available electricity. Electric refrigerators, which my generation still commonly called "ice boxes" well into the 1950s, did not sell well until the 1930s because of their cost and the shortage of electricity. My father, who had what was probably a slightly

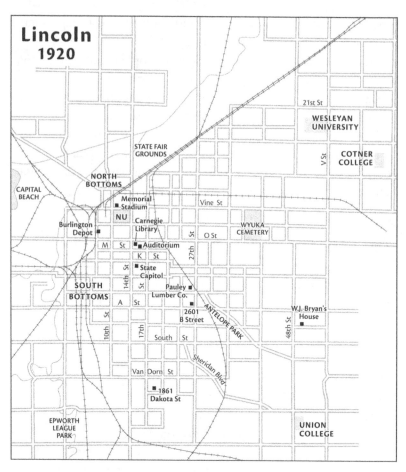

Lincoln 1920

21st St

WESLEYAN UNIVERSITY

STATE FAIR GROUNDS

V St

COTNER COLLEGE

NORTH BOTTOMS

CAPITAL BEACH

Memorial Stadium

Vine St

Burlington Depot

NU

Carnegie Library

M St

Auditorium

27th St

O St

WYUKA CEMETERY

K St

State Capitol

14th St

SOUTH BOTTOMS

Pauley Lumber Co.

A St

2601 B Street

ANTELOPE PARK

W.J. Bryan's House

10th St

17th

South St

48th St

Sheridan Blvd

Van Dorn St

1861 Dakota St

EPWORTH LEAGUE PARK

UNION COLLEGE

10. Checkerboard map of Lincoln circa 1920 showing most relevant sites. Map created by Erin Greb.

above average income at the Pauley Lumber Company in Lincoln, did not buy an electric refrigerator until sometime after he married my mother in 1933, and then only after dropping a large block of ice on his foot![28]

One of the most obvious impacts on everyday life in the 1890s and well into the first decade of the twentieth century was the electric streetcar. Its growth was explosive from the time it began service on the streets of Lincoln in 1891. When operation commenced on July 1 from downtown Lincoln to the suburb of University Place, streets along the way were lined to see "the welcome stranger go whizzing by."[29] This route, which was favored by the merchants of Havelock, at the time a separate town, did not go unchallenged. University Place businessmen, the Methodist Church, the faculty of Nebraska Wesleyan University, and the Women's Christian Temperance Union all objected to the extension on the grounds that Havelock allowed saloons, which would enable Wesleyan students to imbibe. Despite the dynamiting of a streetcar bridge, the service to Havelock began in July 1898.[30]

The omnibuses were, for the most part, sufficient until the early 1880s, because Lincoln was small enough to make walking practical. When the capital city reached the population of around thirteen thousand in 1880, however, walking was no longer realistic, particularly if the city hoped to expand its boundaries. Having existed in big eastern cities since the 1830s and '40s, omnibuses were rapidly replaced by horse- or mule-drawn streetcars or trams. By the 1880s there were more than five hundred such transit systems in the United States. Omaha began building a system of its own as early as 1868.[31] Operating on rails, which made the ride smoother and less noisy, they could move at a comparatively speedy six to eight miles per hour; they were also safer than omnibuses because they had brakes.[32] Even the modest increase in velocity made it possible for Lincoln to expand its boundaries and for residents living in the outskirts to reach the downtown business district in a reasonable time.

An improvement as they were, horse-drawn trams had plenty of problems of their own.[33] The first was the most obvious: the fact that each horse used in the system left in its wake an average of twenty-two pounds of manure and a gallon of urine per day did nothing to improve the smell, cleanliness, or hygiene of the city. Moreover they were slow, could not negotiate hills, were susceptible to diseases, and were a threat to public hygiene after they died and before their carcasses were hauled away. Because they lacked electricity, heat and interior lighting by kerosene lamps were far from satisfactory. Horses were expensive to maintain and had a working life of only four or five years.[34] They also sometimes ran away on their own pulling the car with them. The seats, being no more than wooden benches paralleling the sides of the car, were hard and uncomfortable.[35] By 1890 there were around two hundred horses in Nebraska's capital city pulling thirty-seven cars on eighteen miles of track. However, few, if any, Lincolnites regretted their passing, although the last horse to pull a streetcar in their city was not retired until 1906.[36]

Electric streetcars represented a huge improvement in mass transit. Their acceptance was so fast and widespread that it would not be an exaggeration to say that, along with the electric lightbulb, they belonged to the most rapidly accepted inventions in the history of technology.[37] They could easily go ten to twelve miles an hour and did not start or stop with a lurch.[38] Their interiors were finished in polished hardwood and were heated and electrically illuminated. Their seats faced forward and were upholstered.[39]

The first city to have a complete system of electric streetcars using overhead "trolleys" on poles that were attached to wires was Richmond, Virginia, beginning in 1888. Within three years the system had spread throughout the country including to Lincoln. By 1895 there were nearly nine hundred streetcar companies throughout the United States using this trolley system. Their very existence helped mark a city as "modern" and "metropolitan." Across the country urban transit reached its peak in 1925, when there were 383 rides per person.

The economic impact of streetcars on Lincoln was huge and emerged even before they started operating in 1891. Construction companies boasted that new residential neighborhoods such as Lincoln Heights would soon double in value because of their view of the city and nearness to an electric streetcar line. Knob Hill would likewise be near the new electric streetcar line, which extended as far south as the state penitentiary and would operate from five o'clock in the morning until midnight and cost 15 cents, or around $4 in today's valuation. Such suburbs were now within easy reach of downtown Lincoln, the state university, and railroad depots.

Construction companies and prospective homeowners were not the only ones to welcome the new electric cars and their extended lines. Lincoln's longest line, six miles, was completed to Havelock in 1898. A somewhat shorter but more popular route went from downtown Lincoln to College View starting in 1891, at first by way of Twelfth Street and after 1908 along Seventeenth Street, South Street, and Sheridan Boulevard. Other extended lines carried 110,000 passengers north to the State Fair Grounds in 1891. Another well-used route was to Wyuka Cemetery on Thirty-Sixth and O Streets to the east. At a time when Lincoln still lacked public parks, a streetcar trip to the campus of the newly founded Seventh Day Adventist Union College in the suburb of College View was a pleasant Sunday afternoon outing made all the more enjoyable by the absence of windows in the summer and by the smell of freshly roasted peanuts sold by vendors along the route.[40] The "highline" route to College View became particularly popular after 1908, when part of it followed the scenic new Sheridan Boulevard with its beautifully landscaped median and impressive houses.[41] Like College View, Havelock was a separate town at the time but was now also accessible from downtown Lincoln by a streetcar line and became a popular destination, especially after 1909, when saloons were banned in Lincoln but not in Havelock.[42] The conductors were not among the beneficiaries, however, because they were required to continue wearing their warm uniforms.[43]

Lincoln's streetcars had a variety of uses. The first and most obvious was to take businessmen, salespeople, and clerks to and from their downtown jobs and students to their school or college. They also brought shoppers to recently established department stores like Miller and Paine on Thirteenth and O Streets. Churches and landlords renting apartments next to a streetcar line were eager to inform prospects of their proximity to public transit. In the summer streetcars could take them to Lincoln's amusement park—at first called Burlington Beach, later Capital Beach—northwest of town. For special events like operas, circuses, Fourth of July celebrations, baseball games, football games, and most of all the state fair, several cars could be linked together and were independent of normal streetcar runs. Theatergoers could take a streetcar to or from a stop next to their destination without any need for a parking place for their buggy or automobile.

Unfortunately electric streetcars in Lincoln ran into controversies almost from the beginning. A major issue was that there was not just one streetcar company but as many as thirteen in 1893, each one competing against the others to gain the upper hand and profit at the expense and goodwill of its customers.[44] Meanwhile

San Francisco, Detroit, Cleveland, Seattle, and even Fort Collins, Colorado, switched to municipal ownership. In Lincoln such a move was decisively rejected. Progress was made in 1909, when the separate streetcar companies were merged into a single "Lincoln Traction Company." Even then, however, the company was hit by strikers, who objected to their ten-hour, forty-five-minute workday, which was finally reduced to nine hours in 1922.[45] Like American railroads, streetcar companies were responsible for repairing their tracks. Lincoln's buses, on the other hand, paid a mere 1 percent of gross revenues for using city streets.[46]

Profitability for the Lincoln Traction Company reached its peak in 1916, when it operated on sixty-five miles of rails. But in 1922 there was a 14 percent decline in ridership over the previous year, probably in part because of the strike.[47] As elsewhere throughout the United States, the increasing number of automobiles and buses, which were not limited to certain fixed routes, were enough to ruin most North American streetcar companies. By 1929 five out of six families in Nebraska and Iowa, the highest in the country, owned motorized vehicles.

The demise of Lincoln's streetcar system was in part due to it enabling urban sprawl. From its very outset Lincoln was an overwhelmingly middle-class city where people wanted a single-family home with a yard or garden (or both). The city had few factories and not many high-density apartment houses; those that it did have were often close to the state capitol and the downtown business district where walking was still possible. When the city grew to the south beyond South Street and east of Wyuka Cemetery, streetcars could not compete with automobiles, especially after the First World War.

In our age of global warming caused in part by the burning of oil, the decision to discontinue streetcar service in Lincoln seems at least questionable. Many North American cities such as Toronto, San Francisco, New Orleans, and Fort Collins have retained streetcars either as part of their heritage or as part of their mass transit system. More importantly, with drivers tired of long and time-consuming commutes with their cars, streetcars—now often called "light-rail"—are currently experiencing a renaissance and operate

11. World Bicycle advertisement. *Nebraska State Journal,* July 3, 1900, 8.

in more than thirty American cities, with more being considered (including in Omaha), planned, or under construction.[48]

Interlude: The Brief but Spectacular Popularity of Bicycles

The only partial challenge to the dominant position of streetcars in the 1890s was the "safety bicycle," so called because, much like today's bicycles, it had two wheels of equal size and was powered by pedals and a chain. Bikes, which reached their popularity in the late 1880s and early to mid-1890s, were unusual at the time for being popular with both genders.[49] Their use in Lincoln probably had something to do with the paving of Lincoln's streets in the late 1880s.

The first commercially successful, two-wheeled machine steerable and propelled by a human was invented in 1817 by a German named Baron Karl von Drais. Thousands of these velocipedes—often called "hobby horses" in Britain—were sold in western Europe and North America, but their popularity was short-lived because the difficulty of steering and stopping made them dangerous. They were useless going uphill and dangerous going downhill. The velocipede, now pedal driven, made a huge comeback in the late 1860s as a bicycle, a French word that came into usage in the 1870s. The seat was high in the air and was attached to a front wheel, which was far bigger than the rear wheel. Much faster speeds were now attainable, but the risk of serious injuries was obvious. This type of big-wheel bicycle was popular only with well-to-do young men and was rejected by women, in part because it was difficult to ride while wearing a dress.

The safety bicycle was invented in 1885 and by the end of the decade had completely replaced the "high wheelers." Often called a "roadster," like today's bicycles it had two wheels of equal size—both soon pneumatic—and was powered by pedals attached to a chain, which in turn was attached to the rear wheel. By 1890 it was enormously popular with both genders especially after the invention of a "step through frame," which enabled ladies, with their long skirts, to get on the seat, although long skirts, or "furbelows," could still be a problem for women, particularly when it was windy.[50] No longer was the bicycle regarded as a dangerous toy for young men alone.[51] The new, safer, and more rideable bicycle was not without its critics, especially conservative clergymen, who believed that the new machine would lead to far too much unchaperoned mingling of the sexes and hence to moral degradation.

In 1882 Americans (virtually all males) owned twenty thousand bicycles. Ten years later, a million peddled vehicles having one to four wheels were ridden by males and females. In 1900 the count had reached ten million.[52] When Americans were not riding themselves, they watched other Americans racing with bicycles.[53] During the 1890s the annual sales of bicycles rose from one million in 1890 to ten million by the end of the decade.[54]

During its heyday at the beginning of the twentieth century, every town and city in the United States had a bicycle club that sponsored cross-country rides on summer evenings. Racing and long endurance runs were also popular. Bikes were recommended for health and physical development. But as early as 1902 "the special interest and comradeship connected with wheeling in its earlier days ha[d] entirely disappeared." By 1910 the sale of bicycles nationwide was in steep decline because of the growing popularity of automobiles.[55] However, as late as 1907 Lincoln's bicycle dealers claimed that they were selling as many bikes as ever, the cost ranging from $25 to $55.[56] As a means of entertainment, bicycles were replaced to some degree by motorcycles, probably because of their speed, which excited spectators watching them race at the Nebraska State Fair.[57] However, like the increasingly popular automobile, their noise was not appreciated by many Lincolnites.[58]

In the meantime, however, bicycles enjoyed a variety of uses besides pure pleasure. In Lincoln they were used to get to work by people from every walk of life including businessmen, professionals, and letter carriers. For women of any class, bicycles were a welcome activity. Other sports like croquet, horseback riding, tennis, and golf were enjoyed primarily by wealthier women, who did not work outside the house during the day.[59] After moving from his hometown of Harvard, Nebraska, to Lincoln in 1915, my paternal grandfather rode a bike from his home on Twelfth Street to his office fifteen blocks away on Twenty-Seventh Street. However, after purchasing a house at 2601 B Street, just three blocks from work, he "decided a bicycle was not the proper mode of transportation for a man at the head of a thriving business." Consequently he substituted a Buick for his bicycle, the latter being passed on to my twelve-year-old father.[60]

My grandfather's decision regarding his bicycle typified the United States in the 1920s, when the bicycle went from being a useful means of adult transportation to becoming largely a children's toy. When I went to Lincoln High School in the early 1950s, bicycle racks were plentiful—but empty. They had apparently been used during the Great Depression when people could not afford to buy a car, or during the Second World War when gas was severely rationed and new cars were not being manufactured after February 1942. But by the early 1950s teens wanted to drive *cars*, not ride bicycles. Today bicycles, like streetcars, are making a comeback, and many cities are building lanes exclusively for bikers and hikers. The impact of the COVID-19 pandemic is likely to increase this trend. In the meantime, bicycles, like streetcars, have never gone out of fashion in Europe or China for any age group, especially in densely populated cities. The *New York Times* published an article in 2019 stating that 49 percent of the population of Copenhagen shopped and went to work or school on a bicycle.[61] Amsterdam could not have been far behind.

Here Comes the "Devil Wagon"!

Bicycles and electric streetcars made horse- and mule-drawn trams obsolete almost overnight. However, it took about fifteen years for the automobile to make an almost equally negative impact on streetcars. Remarkably the supremacy of the automobile vis-à-vis streetcars was predicted by a no doubt self-serving article from the *Automobile Magazine* published in the *Nebraska State Journal* in 1900, the same year the first automobile appeared on the streets of Lincoln: "The cheapening of the motor vehicle will naturally prove an important factor in the extension of its use as a competitor of the streetcar. . . . Once started the encroachments of the automobile on the field of municipal transportation will be rapid. The new vehicle may also be expected to displace street cars in many auxiliary services, such as the conveyance of the mails and the transportation of farm products in the rural districts."[62] Indeed only sixteen years after the first cars were seen on the streets of Lincoln in 1900, streetcars reached the peak of their profitability; by 1922, as we have seen, the patronage of Lincoln's streetcars began to decline, with automobiles, and to a lesser degree buses, being the perpetrators.

In view of the number of useful inventions that North Americans made in the late nineteenth and early twentieth centuries, it is somewhat surprising that Americans had relatively little to do with the invention of the automobile. This is obvious by the sheer number of French words associated with the automobile, such as "carburetor," "differential," "chauffeur," "limousine," "chassis," and "automobile" itself, although the word was not used in print until the *New York Times* did so in 1901: "The 1901 Mercedes has been described as the first modern motorcar in its essentials and had a maximum speed of fifty-three miles per hour" in a race in Nice, France.[63] However, as early as 1769 Nicolas-Joseph Cugnot of France had built a heavy, steam-powered tricycle, which had a speed of 2.25 miles per hour, hardly a speed that would have given it much commercial value.[64]

From the beginning European car manufacturers emphasized quality over quantity because the demand for cars on the Continent was relatively limited. The people of the most industrialized and urbanized parts of Europe in 1900 already had excellent transportation networks both between and within their cities. Small towns were compact enough that people could easily get around on foot or with a bicycle. The transportation situation in the United States around the turn of the century was quite different. Small towns in the United States were relatively sprawling, and farmers were often far removed from the nearest town, especially in sparsely populated states like Nebraska. Overall Americans were also wealthier per capita than Europeans in the early twentieth century. The cheapness of raw materials as well as the vastness of the American market ultimately gave the United States a huge advantage in the production and sale of automobiles and most other manufactured products. Purchasing on the installment plan also helped increase sales in the United States.[65] Consequently by 1920 there were more than eight million motorized vehicles in the United States, far more than the rest of the world combined.[66]

By no means was every American enthusiastic about the arrival of what was often called the "devil wagon," "horseless carriage," or "tin can on wheels."[67] One can only imagine how surprised and fearful the manufacturers and sellers of horse-drawn carriages, or buggies, were at the arrival of the automobile.

Although we can now look back on them as hopelessly old fashioned, horse-drawn carriages had several advantages over cars until "improved" dirt and gravel highways began to be built across Nebraska in the 1920s. For one thing they cost only a fraction as much as an automobile until Henry Ford began mass producing his Model T Ford in 1908. Ford's philosophy was to increase sales by producing cheap but reliable cars without "frills" such as a speedometer, bumpers, temperature and gas gauges, and spare tires.[68] In 1905 prices in Lincoln ranged from $65 for a two-seat buggy ($1,820 in today's money) to $250 ($7,000) for the biggest and finest carriages.[69] An advertisement in the *Lincoln Star* in 1903 claimed that you could get a basic, two-seat roofless automobile for $750. A 1907 Cadillac would set you back $850.[70] Being lightweight because it had no motor, and having a high road clearance,

12. A new symbol of status. *Nebraska State Journal*, March 14, 1915, 25.

a buggy could, with relative ease, be pulled out of deep, muddy ruts by a horse. They were also much less likely to break down or need to be fixed by an experienced mechanic. Most important of all, horse-drawn carriages were obviously cheap compared to the early automobile.

An article in the *Lincoln Star* in 1903 predicted that "persons who are waiting to buy an automobile when it becomes as cheap as a horse are not likely to make such an investment soon. It is more than doubtful if that dream ever will be realized. . . . When it comes to maintenance, well, you can keep quite a stable on what you would spend for repairs. . . . You can count on from $500 to $1,000 a year for repairs on a fine machine."[71] It was not until 1914 that the sale of automobiles in Nebraska outnumbered that of carriages and wagons.[72] But by 1927 automobiles outnumbered horse-drawn vehicles nationwide by a ratio of nearly 50-to-1.[73] However, there were still nine blacksmith establishments in Lincoln in 1930, and carriages were still being manufactured. Yet in the early 1930s "the care and management of horses" was dropped from the curriculum at the University of Nebraska.[74]

Once Henry Ford's assembly line was working at top speed in 1913, horse-drawn vehicles had no chance of competing with automobiles.[75] It had taken more than twelve hours to assemble a Model T in 1908. In 1914 the same car could be produced in ninety-three minutes. A Model T that had cost $850 in 1908 sold for $360 in 1916.[76] Meanwhile the frill-less Model T Ford of 1908 had, by 1915, added headlights, windshields, a top, a horn, and a speedometer as standard features.[77] By 1920 nearly half the cars on American streets were Fords.[78] In less than two decades automobiles had gone from being a luxury, affordable only for the wealthy or the mechanically inclined, to a *perceived* necessity by anyone with a moderate income.[79] This trend was accelerated when Henry Ford increased sales by making his cars more affordable for his own workers by paying them the astounding wage of $5 an hour for an eight-hour workday.[80]

Fords and most other American cars were fueled by gasoline. A crank had to be used to start them, gears had to be shifted manually, and cars were noisy and smelly. Avoiding all these problems was the electric car invented around 1890. It was so popular in Lincoln by 1907 that demand outstripped supply.[81] It could start with the turn of a key, had no gear shift, was clean, odor free, and quiet, and required no tools or mechanical knowledge to be driven. It was popular with women—perhaps in part because they could accommodate huge hats, and women did not need to wear any sort of protective clothing—that it came to be stigmatized as a "woman's car." It was also popular with physicians.[82]

By 1915 "the modern Detroit electric [car] had plenty of power to climb steep hills and with its top speed of twenty to twenty-five miles per hour was well above Lincoln's eighteen miles per hour speed limit." Nor was range a problem within Lincoln, where many charging stations were available and when 98 percent of all trips were less than sixty miles.[83] As long as rural roads in Nebraska remained virtually impassable, range was not a major issue. With the improvement of Nebraska's roads, however, range did *become* a major consideration, particularly in rural areas in Nebraska and other sparsely populated states where electricity was often unavailable until the 1930s or even later.[84] In the meantime, however, cost became the most important problem. As early as 1912 a gasoline car could be purchased for $650 at a time when an electric car typically sold for $1,750.[85] By the early 1930s electric cars had virtually disappeared in Nebraska and elsewhere around the country.

Among the few holdouts for horse-drawn carriages after about 1910 were heads of states. For example Franz Joseph, the emperor-king of the Austro-Hungarian monarchy between 1848 and his death in 1916, was often criticized by his contemporaries and later by historians for being hopelessly old fashioned in part because of his refusal to ride in an automobile. However, he was not alone. Theodore Roosevelt, who has rarely if ever been accused of being a retrograde, believed that it was "undignified" for an American president to be seen in any formal setting riding in an automobile. President Kennedy's hearse was horse-drawn in 1963. And up to her death in 2022, Queen Elizabeth II rode in an elaborately decorated coach whenever she attended a formal ceremony like a speech to Parliament or a royal wedding.

The reactions of Nebraskans to the new contraptions in the first decade of the twentieth century were mixed at best. The response of farmers was initially a combination of fear and ridicule. They hated the new machines for scaring their horses and other farm animals and were amused when drivers appealed to them for help getting their car out of mud or for repairs. On the other hand, as the cost of cars went down and their reliability went up, farmers realized that automobiles would enable them to escape their isolation and reach towns in a fraction of the previous time. Their knowledge of farm machinery also made them more adept at repairing cars.[86] Before long the Model T's high road clearance caused them to be known as a "farmer's car." Indeed as late as 1915 more than half of all automobile sales in Nebraska went to farmers or other people living in remote areas.[87]

When cars first appeared in Lincoln in 1900 the initial reactions of a good many people were also negative. They especially

A JOY RIDE! –:– –:– By NELL BRINKLEY

13. "A Joy Ride" complete with a cupid in the rumble seat. *Lincoln Star*, March 14, 1915, 11.

hated the recklessness with which many drivers drove and the noise from their electric horns, which the *Lincoln Star* described as "such a voice as might be produced by a hippopotamus, a walrus, and an angry baboon . . . all in one."[88] Almost certainly the people most favorably impressed by the new machines were physicians. In an age when physicians made house calls, including ones late in the evening, even for minor afflictions, it was far easier to go by car than by streetcar. Even among physicians, however, there was some disagreement. When a group of them met in 1902 to discuss the relative merits of buggies versus cars, one doctor came out in favor of a buggy. The reason: if a house call were late at night, his horse could find his way home while the doctor was sound asleep![89]

Despite the mixed reception given to automobiles, the number of the new vehicle began a rapid increase almost immediately in Lincoln. By 1905 the *Lincoln Star* reported that "the automobile industry has surpassed all expectations. . . . Machines by the dozens have been sold in Lincoln. There are automobile repair shops; retails stores, warehouses, carloads of automobiles, and a new branch of business has sprang [*sic*] up in Lincoln as if by magic. . . . The age of the automobile is at hand."[90] That prediction appeared to come true in 1908, when the city's first auto show was held in Lincoln's auditorium on Fourteenth and M Streets. It was such a huge success, particularly among farmers, that it was predicted to be an annual event.[91]

Practical reasons were not alone in inducing people to purchase automobiles. Especially in the early days of the automobile age the *status* of owning an expensive vehicle was alone an inducement in addition to the newfound freedom to go wherever and whenever one pleased, road conditions permitting.[92] However, in Lincoln cars were often driven for pure pleasure on a summer evening or on weekends.

Noise was not the only reason why automobiles received a mixed reception in Lincoln and elsewhere. Reckless driving, sometimes called "joy riding," and automobile accidents—some of them fatal— were among the reasons for hostility toward the automobile until at least 1920. Until shortly before that date, nearly every driver was a novice. At first there were no driver's licenses or age limitations. If you could see over the steering wheel and reach the pedals, you could drive, although in Lincoln few parents allowed their children to drive.[93] (The *Nebraska State Journal* claimed that "little girls and boys can be seen guiding electric vehicles in and about the crowded streets almost everywhere in big cities.")[94]

There being no driving classes, the only instructions drivers were likely to get were from a salesman, and they were limited to how to start the car, how to change gears (almost unknown to our generation of automatic gear shifting), and how to stop. There were no driving tests, stop or warning signs, or speed limits. The first markers on the Lincoln Highway—later designated as Highway 30—out of Lincoln were small cards attached to telephone poles.[95] Stoplights did not appear on Lincoln streets until 1913, when the city had eight hundred cars, three hundred of which had been purchased the previous year.[96] Lincoln's first filling station opened the next year.[97]

If there was no "Wild West" period in Lincoln's history in the Hollywood movie sense of the term, the first two decades of the twentieth century were an almost lawless period so far as automobile driving was concerned. In Omaha drivers "sped along streets, smashing into buggies, wagons, and pedestrians. In many cases drivers fled the scene rather than faced the consequences."[98] The *Lincoln Star* astutely predicted that "poor driving caused by external factors causing accidents like wind and weather . . . can only be fairly mastered as the result of lengthy experience."[99] Therefore it should come as no surprise that the number of fatalities per passenger mile caused by motorized vehicles increased in the United States every year from 1901 to 1931; the year of greatest increase was 1907, when it was 68.6 percent higher than the previous year.[100] Drivers, all of whom were called "chauffeurs" at the time, were not always to blame for fatal accidents. Also at fault were pedestrians crossing busy streets without looking in both directions, engrossed in reading a newspaper or talking with a friend—in fact doing almost anything except paying attention to where they were going.[101]

Not until 1911 did the state legislature set high fines for drivers causing injuries or death, and a minimum driving age of sixteen was established. It was only in 1913 that the Official Road Book of the Nebraska State Automobile Association set speed limits at ten miles an hour in business districts, fifteen miles in residential areas, and twenty miles elsewhere. The speed limit in downtown Lincoln was ten miles per hour in 1906. However, most accidents in that area were not caused by drivers of automobiles but by "delivery wagons" often driven by "irresponsible boys."[102] In 1912 the speed limit in Lincoln's residential areas was twelve miles per hour, six in the downtown area, and twenty-five in the countryside.[103] In 1918 the speed limit in Lincoln was raised to twelve miles per hour in the commercial area and eighteen miles per hour in residential districts of the city where the limit had been fifteen. Six was the limit at intersections, and passing was not permitted.[104]

It is reasonable to wonder how the police were able to estimate speed at a time when radar could not even be imagined. The method was simple, at least in cities where intersections were a block apart, or exactly one-twelfth of a mile. If it took less than five seconds to drive a block, twelve blocks at the same speed could be covered in less than sixty seconds, or sixty miles an hour.

Needless to say, speed limits in Lincoln were not always observed, not even by the mayor Francis Brown, who in 1907 was not stopped when driving at "fully twice the maximum allowed" while showing visitors the sights.[105] A young man from Beatrice was not so lucky. Expecting a fine of $1 for "scorching" down a residential street in Lincoln at more than twenty miles an hour where the limit was nine, he nearly fainted when fined $50 (about $400 today). His plea that he was "discriminated against" because his friends were also racing did not impress the judge.[106] Unfortunately the huge fine did not stop racing. In 1912 Eleventh Street became a veritable speedway. The *Lincoln Star* reported cars driving at least fifty miles per hour between nine and twelve in the evening when it was too dark for the police to see license plates.[107] Speeding, however, was not the only cause of accidents. Most accidents involving cars in Lincoln occurred between eleven and noon in the morning and five and seven in the evening.

The police were not the only counterweight to reckless and careless driving. Lincoln's Automobile Club, founded in 1908, played a significant role in influencing legislation beneficial to motorists by establishing road signs and helping improve country roads. Any owner of a car was eligible to join; membership automatically also made them members of the American Automobile Association (AAA). By 1912 there were sixty such clubs in the state.[108] In that year Lincoln's club erected seventy-five guideposts around Lancaster County, which gave directions and distances to major towns.[109] The club also tried to educate novice drivers and advocated improvement of country roads.

Not until 1926 did Nebraska get its first official numbered highway marker.[110] Still absent, however, were mileage markers and directional signs.[111] Interestingly enough the best drivers tended to be bicyclists, who were at least experienced in negotiation turns and avoiding pedestrians.[112]

The number of cars in Nebraska grew at an almost unbelievable rate. By 1905 there were 571 in the state, more than 11,000 in 1910, around 100,000 in 1916, and more than 200,000 in 1920, second only to Iowa in cars per capita.[113] By 1929, 90 percent of American households in the United States owned a motor vehicle. So popular were cars that if "Middletown," Indiana, can be used

14. My father and grandfather in Yellowstone National Park in 1915. Note the two spare tires. Author's collection.

as an example, more families had access to an automobile than to a bathtub in the 1920s.[114]

As the number of cars in Lincoln rose, the number of bicyclists declined (except for motorcycles) as did the number of blacksmiths, a trade that had been around since the beginning of civilization if not before. Saddle makers also nearly disappeared. By 1915 cars were getting easier to start, were more comfortable because of balloon tires, were much less likely to break down, and had become a cheap mode of transportation for families. They were also a great way of beating summertime heat. Nebraskans, especially farmers, were beginning to view them as necessities.[115]

Until the 1930s long-distance travel was more of an unpredictable expedition than a carefree adventure. In 1914 only 1.5 percent of Nebraska's roads were classified as "improved."[116] Lincoln's Automobile Club made its first run of the season in 1911 by driving forty-two miles to Beatrice, having lunch at a hotel, and starting back at 2:00 p.m. With the help of a pilot car, they hoped to maintain an average speed of fifteen to twenty miles an hour. Rain and mud postponed this great expedition three times.[117]

When my father and his parents vacationed in Yellowstone National Park in 1915, their car had a soft top, weak brakes, and, of course, no seat belts or other security devices we now take for granted. The next year a Lincoln couple, Edward and May Gehrke, dared to take an adventuresome trip to western Nebraska and back. There being no hotels outside of cities, they slept in city parks and ranchers' fields. When their car got stuck, only a rancher and team of horses could get them out. By the time they returned to Lincoln they had driven more than eight hundred miles in thirteen days, or a little more than sixty miles a day.[118]

Nebraskans would have to wait well into the 1920s before they would encounter even halfway tolerable driving conditions. Federal assistance for highway construction began with the Federal Aid Road Act of 1916.[119] More than $3 million from federal and state sources were available for new roads in Nebraska in 1919, but none of those roads were to be paved, and all of them went through, not around, towns.[120] Federal highways per se were not under construction until 1921.[121] Some improvement of country roads came in 1923, when they started to be graveled, a product that was readily available in Nebraska.[122] The difficulty of cross-country travel was brought home in 1919, when it took a military convoy, averaging six miles an hour, sixty-two days to travel from Washington DC to California after breaking down numerous times.[123]

My father drove with his parents from Lincoln to the West Coast in 1925 when he was sixteen. Except for the first six miles west of Lincoln, they encountered paved streets and roads only in California, and then only occasionally. Even the busiest highway in the state, between Lincoln and Omaha, now six lanes wide, was not paved until the end of 1935. In 1925 he and his parents "camped out in a tent-like contraption my mother had made and cooked most of our meals over an open fire. Sometimes a city or town would boast a campground and we would take advantage of this luxury; but many times, we put up our tent beside the road or even in someone's back yard (with their permission). [In Wyoming] we drove for long periods without seeing a house or even another car. . . . Several times we had to inch our way through cattle and sheep herds that were grazing unhampered by a fence."[124] Long distance travel by road was made all the more difficult because tires were thin and often blew out.[125] My father noted that during the 1920s "one never went on a trip of more than a few miles without two spares, and it was lucky for us that we adhered to that practice. I well remember one day in western Wyoming when I changed tires three times."[126]

My grandfather had to return early from their trip to California because he learned that the Pauley Lumber Company had burned down, leaving my father and grandmother to return to Lincoln on their own. On the last day, my father drove from Ogallala, starting at 5:00 a.m., and arrived home sometime after midnight, having driven about 280 miles on dirt and gravel roads at an average of thirteen miles per hour. It was a personal record that lasted for many years.[127] (The same trip today would take just over four hours.)

As the third decade of the twentieth century began, the results and promises of modernization were mixed with city dwellers benefitting the most. By 1920 only the poorest Lincolnites had not yet benefitted from electrification as far as their homes were concerned. Streetlights were plentiful, especially in commercial areas, and streetcars could take them all over the capital city and its suburbs like College View, University Place, and Havelock. We will see in chapter 6 how even poor Lincolnites were able to enjoy varied and inexpensive forms of entertainment. A high percentage of farmers in Nebraska were becoming automobile owners, which was to spell the end of their traditional isolation.[128] By the end of the 1920s, they could drive into the nearest town or take trains to virtually anywhere they could afford to go. Nevertheless paved roads remained a rarity not only in the 1920s but far into the 1930s and beyond as well.

Although automobiles proved to be a convenience for many Nebraskans, there were downsides as well. For many people, at least in "Middletown," Indiana, the tendency to buy on an installment plan increased, causing some buyers to fall seriously into debt.[129] Before the World War buying "on time" had been limited to such items as pianos. A sure sign of middle-class status, they numbered 32,000 in 1890 and 374,000 in 1904.[130] Other items that were "charged" were sewing machines and expensive furniture purchased by wealthy people on terms of one-third down with the balance paid within three years. After the war "the installment plan was to consumer credit what the moving assembly line was to the automobile industry."[131] By 1925 roughly three out of four new cars were purchased "on time" through credit.[132]

Preachers complained that Sunday morning rides were decreasing church attendance. By 1920 automobiles, especially those with tops, led to an increase in sex crimes and babies born out of wedlock.[133] An inevitable result of automobiles was a decrease in walking for pleasure or even to the nearest streetcar stop.[134] Ultimately, of course, cars produced traffic jams, polluted air, garish signs, and urban sprawl on a scale that hardly could have been imagined in 1920 as well as the near extinction of passenger trains outside the Northeast Corridor.

3

The Athens of the West

Public School Education in Nebraska: Compulsory in Theory

The year 1890 not only marked the promised arrival of electricity, but it was not long before Lincolnites began calling their city the "Athens of the West."[1] Although the phrase undoubtedly contained more than a little boosterism, it was also by no means without some foundation. It is quite possible, as one Lincoln newspaper claimed in 1890, that "no city of its size had more educational facilities."[2] The 1890s marked the time when the University of Nebraska became a real university as we recognize one today, with a rapidly growing enrollment and a reputation for excellence. The decade was also when Nebraska Wesleyan University, Union College, and the ill-fated Cotner College had their beginnings. By 1915 Lincoln also had two business colleges, three music conservatories, and finishing schools for both boys and girls.[3]

From the founding of the University of Nebraska in 1869, it was obvious that its growth and quality depended on the standards of the state's high schools. With fewer than 123,000 citizens in the state in 1870, it is not surprising that for a long time many people from all over the state questioned whether Nebraska even needed its own university.[4] We should at least be grateful that Nebraska, unlike its neighboring states (except Wyoming and Missouri), never established a Nebraska A&M (agricultural and mechanical) university to compete for scarce financial assistance from the state. Consequently until the twentieth century, all the state's allocations for higher education went to a single university, which enabled it to compete academically and athletically with the best universities in the country.

The number of qualified students was just one dilemma facing the new university. Lincoln had a new high school with eight teachers when it opened in 1872.[5] However, outside the capital city, Omaha, and a few of the larger Nebraska towns, the level of formal education was still checkered until the end of the century and resulted in a high drop-out rate at the university.[6] As late as 1890 there were a mere 9,029 teachers for 6,243 school districts in Nebraska. Because of farming needs, only slightly more than half of the districts held classes for even six months.[7] There were 440 districts with no schools of their own. Nevertheless it is impressive that the United States was second only to Prussia in establishing free public schools for all children.[8] And if the United States was not the first country to establish free public schools, it may have well been, in the words of one Nebraska historian, among "the world's most enthusiastic proponents of public schooling."[9] Equally enlightened was the requirement that school children be vaccinated for communicable diseases such as smallpox as early as 1882.[10]

In 1890 the number of sod house schools, or "soddies," reached its peak at 792.[11] The one-room schoolhouses could also be used for debates, meetings of literary societies, spelling bees, and box socials.[12] The teacher's only responsibility was to teach the three "R's": reading, "riting," and "rithmatic." The schools often had wood floors and plaster walls and were relatively warm in winter and cool in summer. However, there could be anywhere from a handful of students to thirty or more, all taught by one teacher as young as fourteen with little or no formal teacher training. Often the teacher's highest qualification was being the son or daughter of a school board member.[13] My grandfather Pauley, who graduated from Harvard High School first in his class at the age of sixteen, was relatively well prepared when offered a teaching position in the Harvard School District (which he declined).[14] Bigger schools made of wood, brick, log, or stone were called "grade schools"—of which there were 250 in Nebraska in 1890—that were large enough to be divided into rooms for separate grades established by age and ability and taught by different teachers.

In 1887 the Nebraska State Legislature made education compulsory from age eight to fourteen, and students were provided with free textbooks for the first time. Four years later the law was changed to require students to remain in school until they were sixteen. However, education was compulsory more in theory than in practice because strict enforcement proved impossible. Many parents were not cooperative, believing that learning how to read and write was sufficient; thereafter their children should work for the welfare of the family.[15] This feeling was especially true among immigrant parents, who also feared, with good reason, that more education, accompanied by Americanization, would drive a wedge between themselves and their own children. Teachers also viewed the new school leaving age with mixed feelings as they were often not much older than their students and were frequently smaller. The new law was also a headache for truant officers whose number of cases doubled. All in all compulsion did little to increase attendance.[16] Nevertheless by 1910 Nebraska, along with Iowa and Indiana, was one of the states outside of New England to have the highest graduation rates from high school in the country.[17]

The year 1890 marked the end, or at least the death rattles, of classical education in the United States, having been around since the founding of Harvard University in 1636.[18] Its emphasis was on the classical languages of Greek and Latin, ancient history, theology, and law. Other languages, the natural sciences, and modern history were badly neglected. On the eve of the First World War, Europeans—and Americans, if they had any historical knowledge at all—were more likely to know about the Peloponnesian War of the fifth century BC than about the Balkan Wars that had just occurred. Consequently it is easy to understand how otherwise intelligent people on both sides of the Atlantic were so confused about the causes and issues that were involved in what was then called the "Great War." It is also unsurprising that young men who were not training for the ministry or law considered higher education to be irrelevant. This attitude included businessmen, who before 1890 saw no need for their sons (let alone their daughters) to be educated beyond high school.

However, the emphasis on the classics was clearly being challenged in Lincoln's schools in the early twentieth century when Latin and Greek were dropped as required courses and replaced by German and several vocational courses.[19] The battle over the curriculum was not just fought within the University of Nebraska and at the more conservative private colleges in Lincoln and throughout the country. By 1890 educational authorities in Nebraska were tired of being told by University of Nebraska admission officers what courses their high schools should offer, which included four years of Latin and three years of mathematics and science.[20] The basic problem was that in 1869, when the university was founded, and for a long time thereafter, high schools of any quality were rare throughout the state; therefore few graduates were qualified to enter the University of Nebraska without first attending the university's preparatory school—for up to two years.

Nebraska had the nation's second-highest high school graduation rate after Iowa.[21] But as late as the academic year 1885–86, the University of Nebraska's catalogue listed only Beatrice, Grand Island, Kearney, Lincoln, Nebraska City, Omaha, Plattsmouth, and Tekamah as having fully accredited high schools with nine others, including Harvard, receiving minor accreditation.[22] In a magazine report published in 1891, superintendents in Omaha and Wymore concluded that "the number of well-organized high schools in the state comes very much short of one hundred."[23] In some districts there were no teachers, and it was not uncommon for students to live four or five miles away from the nearest elementary school.[24] Students wishing to attend a high school might be more than ten miles away.[25] I have often wondered how the history of the Pauley family would have been different if my grandfather had not lived just a mile away from Harvard's school, a handsome new building housing all grades through high school. Graduating from high school was still a rare and celebrated event for girls (who comprised most of the graduates) all wearing white dresses, a practice that lasted until 1917.

After 1890 and even more so after 1900, the attitude toward education at both the secondary and university levels changed drastically and resulted in a huge increase in enrollment in Nebraska high schools, at the University of Nebraska, and around the country.[26] In 1910 many public-school teachers, especially in rural areas, were poorly trained and paid and taught for an average of just three years. As late as 1911 there were about 7,000 school districts in Nebraska, but only 179 of them had high schools accredited by the

15. The new Lincoln High School in 1922. Courtesy of History Nebraska.

University of Nebraska. Given these circumstances it is no wonder that so many Nebraskans were not able to enroll at the University of Nebraska without taking preparatory courses.

For the few students attending high school, being among the
6 percent who finished was far more prestigious than graduating from college is today, when just over 33 percent of Americans
over the age of twenty-five hold a bachelor's degree. At the turn
of the twentieth century, a high school diploma qualified one for
entry-level jobs as bookkeepers, salesmen, managers, or cashiers.[27]
A generation later a college degree would be needed for many of
these positions.

An enlightened innovation taken by the management of Lincoln public schools in 1891 was to provide night schools, which
proved popular for both men and women. Students under the age
of twenty-one paid nothing for tuition or textbooks. Older students paid only a dollar or less. By the end of the year, four hundred people had taken advantage of this opportunity. Among this
group were many foreign-born girls, who worked as servants during
the day and studied English in the evening.[28]

Although Lincoln High School was very much a preparatory school for the University of Nebraska, like other American high schools of the early twentieth century, it also strove to be both traditionally academic and vocational. In 1914 a new high school replaced the city's second high school that had opened in 1898. The new building was near Antelope Creek and the proposed Antelope Park.[29] It was also to be within walking distance of the Pauley Lumber Company after it was established in 1915. The neoclassical high school building was very impressive for its time. Lincolnites thought the new school was on par with the most advanced high schools in other Midwestern cities such as Minneapolis, Chicago, and Kansas City.[30] Although it has been enlarged many times over the years, the original section of the building is still impressive today.

Beyond the Struggle to Survive: The University of Nebraska

The growth in the number of high school graduates in Nebraska's larger towns with college-preparatory credits was a major factor enabling the University of Nebraska to grow both in size and academic quality during the 1890s, despite the bleakness of the economy. Lincoln's earliest citizens were thrilled to have the laying of the cornerstone of the university's first building, University Hall, on September 25, 1869. It was celebrated in a banquet with a thousand attendees. The lowlight of the evening was evidently a speech by the attorney general Seth Robinson, who said much about Greece and Rome but very little about Nebraska. Evidently more entertaining was a dance lasting from ten in the evening until four the next morning, with music provided by a brass band imported from Omaha.[31]

When the University of Nebraska was first open for classes in September 1871, it was a university in name only. Its charter provided for five colleges; in practice it had but one. The sole College of Literature, Science, and Arts had a scant 8 fully accredited college students out of the university's total of 130; 11 students were classified as irregular, and the remaining 110 students were in the Latin school and would need six years to earn a college degree.[32] In 1870 colleges and universities throughout the United States were tiny; most of them consisted of no more than a few hun-

16. Collage of "Old Mains." (*above*) Nebraska Hall in 1890, 520-299-0142, Archives and Special Collections, University of Nebraska–Lincoln Libraries. (*below*) Nebraska Wesleyan in 1915, courtesy of History Nebraska. (*next page, top*) Cotner College circa 1900, courtesy of History Nebraska. (*next page, bottom*) Union College in 1900, courtesy of History Nebraska.

Union College,— College View, Nebr.   C.A. Skinner, Photo.

dred students. The University of Nebraska, being in a state capital and future metropolitan city, made it unusual at a time when most colleges were denominational and located in small towns in rural areas, far from the secular temptations of big cities. This was even true of many Ivy League schools such as Princeton, Dartmouth, and Cornell.[33]

From the middle of the nineteenth century until about 1885, an argument raged among educators as to whether the purpose of college was training for mental and moral power or for the accumulation of knowledge.[34] Up to 1885 college presidents rated their faculty on their moral character, which depended closely on their religious beliefs. Scholarship was not ignored but was not the primary criterion.[35] Administrators kept a close eye on the morals of both their faculties and their students. This attitude could be found most readily in the Lincoln area's newest colleges, Nebraska Wesleyan University, founded in 1887, Cotner College, established in 1889, and Union College, which held its first classes in 1891. However, by 1889 the University of Nebraska, in the words of the Lincoln historian Alan Hayes, had "passed safely through the period of sectarian intermeddling, and the dangerous reaction which followed. The spirit which controls its management [is] one which, while recognizing the Christian element which pervades all our institutions, is broad and tolerant."[36]

Not until the 1890s did enrollment at the University of Nebraska begin to look respectable. Even so enrollment for the academic year 1889–90 was a meager 349, and of those 170 were Latin students, not undergraduates or graduate students.[37] Thereafter enrollment at the university surged as indeed it did across the country. In 1900 there were around 2,500 students; in 1919–20 there were nearly 7,000 students. Little if any of the increase during the 1890s was due to population growth. Nebraska's population in 1900 was officially only about five thousand more than it had been in 1890. Unofficially it is more likely that the state's population had declined because the 1890 census, as we have seen earlier, was notoriously inflated. Nor can the increase in enrollment be attributed to a booming economy. Nebraska was hit hard by the Panic of 1893, which did not ease until 1897. Such enrollment increases became commonplace in the twentieth century when jobs were hard to find and improving one's credentials seemed prudent.

A major reason for the rapid growth of the University of Nebraska during the 1890s both in terms of enrollment and academic quality was due to the chancellorship of James Hulme Canfield between 1891 and 1895. This was precisely the time when students were seeking an education in a profession, business, or applied science. Chancellor Canfield was a "man of the people" with a genial manner who was also an effective public speaker. Although he did not ignore scholarship, he was more interested in serving the immediate practical needs of Nebraskans, which happened to be especially dire during the early to mid-1890s. He traveled ten thousand miles his first year in office and eight thousand during each of the following years promoting the university and encouraging faculty to speak to various organizations on subjects related to their expertise. The result was that the university became popular throughout the state for the first time, even in Omaha, whose press had usually been hostile toward the university.[38] He popularized the university still more by encouraging the public to take tours of the campus, which they did at the rate of six hundred visitors a month. Not least Canfield encouraged women to pursue higher education and introduced a course himself called "The Status of Women in America."[39]

By 1890 Omaha was, for the most part, reconciled to the state university being in Lincoln. Elsewhere an increasing number of Nebraskans were ready to concede that there was a genuine need for a state university. There was also a growing acceptance within the university and the public that at least some of the courses offered at the school should be of immediate, practical use. This is not to say, however, that no controversies existed or were about to emerge. Should most courses be required, or should students be relatively free to choose whatever courses they wanted? What role should fraternities play? Should physical education be required of male or even female students? To what extent should the university be influenced by East Coast universities or the more progressive German universities? To what extent should university authorities attempt to control the social lives of its students?

Thanks to Chancellor Canfield's leadership, enrollment at the

University of Nebraska nearly doubled from 883 in 1891–92 to 1,550 four years later. This increase is all the more impressive because Nebraska was experiencing the worst depression it had ever faced. The decade began ominously with rainfall in 1890 averaging only seventeen inches across the state, the lowest since 1864.[40] To make matters even worse, far below normal rainfall led to almost total crop failures in 1893 and 1894.[41] Nevertheless in 1896 the university became the first institution west of the Mississippi to establish a graduate school.[42] The next year enrollment at the university had reached 1,915, making it the fourteenth largest university in the United States out of the country's three hundred universities and colleges.[43]

By 1900 there were nineteen buildings on the four-square-block campus, which included a museum and a library holding forty thousand books.[44] Robert Knoll, the university's most recent historian, claims that by the turn of the century the university had taken "its place along with Michigan, Wisconsin, and California."[45] Indeed in 1909, when the university had the fifth largest enrollment of any public university in the country, it became the eighteenth member of the Association of American Universities, which was founded in 1900 by Harvard; Columbia; the University of California, Berkeley; Johns Hopkins; and the University of Chicago.[46] By 1914 the university's enrollment had reached 4,133 of which there were 803 more women than men.[47]

With the issue settled by 1890 of whether Nebraska should have a university, a new controversy emerged around 1900 as to whether the university should remain in its original four-square-block location just north of the downtown business district. Some people argued that it should be relocated well to the northeast near the College of Agriculture, which had been established in 1872. By the turn of the twentieth century, the original plot of land that had been assigned to the university was becoming increasingly overcrowded. Reasonable arguments could be made for relocating the campus and for keeping it in place. Ultimately two or perhaps three considerations settled the issue, at least for the time being. Benjamin Andrews, chancellor of the university from 1901 to 1906, urged in the *Lincoln Star* "not [to] let them [the legislature] move the university. It will set the institution back twenty years." He added that the university "would never regain its present standing among the universities in the nation." Moving the main campus would have involved abandoning recently built expensive buildings and replacing them with costly new ones.[48]

A second less obvious reason for keeping the main campus in its original location was that many poor students, including players on the fledgling football team, would have found it difficult if not impossible to get jobs in the business district if the campus were moved to the relatively isolated area near the College of Agriculture.[49] Although there had been no tuition fee charged by the university from the beginning—aside from a one-time $5 entrance fee—annual expenses for room and board, books, and incidentals averaged $150 in 1891. When multiplied by twenty-eight to account for inflation, total expenses would not have been insignificant, especially for the 45 percent of the student body in 1891 who were the sons and daughters of farmers.[50] When compared to other nearby college towns like Lawrence, Kansas, Columbia, Missouri, or Ames, Iowa, Lincoln's population of around forty thousand was relatively large and provided many job opportunities for poor students. It should be kept in mind that scholarships of any kind did not exist for undergraduates until after the Second World War.

A third and probably less serious consideration was a vestige of Victorian morality. Moving the university to the sprawling ag campus, it was alleged, would afford too many secluded "spooning grounds" for amorous young students. Nor could a ban on smoking be easily enforced compared to the old campus, which had been surrounded by a fence since 1892. Finally, and probably most decisively, voters would oppose anything that would require additional taxes. A referendum ended the debate, at least for the time being, when 148,110 voters rejected the move with only 66,883 supporting it.[51] The issue was raised again shortly after World War II with no changes made. The removal of the Nebraska State Fair to Grand Island in 2010 solved the space problem and no doubt ended for good any discussion about relocating the main campus.

By 1910 young people, or at least their parents, had discovered that college education meant the increased likelihood of material success and lifelong friendships; consequently 355,000 young people in their late teens and early twenties were now college students, which was 5 percent of their age cohort, or three times the number enrolled in 1880.[52] After 1890 enrollments at all colleges and universities around the country began to explode as young men realized that they could become something other than a small-town lawyer, physician, or minister.

Much of the increase was also due to young women, who made up 59 percent of all high school students in 1900.[53] For example of the ninety graduates of Harvard High School in Nebraska between 1871 and 1901, only twenty-nine were boys. During the same period only 21 percent of all college students were women, but they comprised 47 percent of all college students in 1920, a figure not attained again until the 1970s.[54] The percentage of bachelor degrees awarded to women doubled from 17 percent in 1890 to 34 percent in 1929; doctorates increased from 1 percent to 15 percent during the same period.[55] (In 2021 women earned 60 percent of bachelor degrees in the United States, 58 percent of MAS, and 54.7 percent of PhDs.)[56] Women were especially well represented in the liberal arts where they often constituted more than half the students.[57] An increasing number of women were no longer satisfied with the prospect of being a decorative housewife. This trend aroused some alarm, and not just among American and European conservatives and theologians, that too much education for women would ruin their health or cause a decline in the birthrate.[58] These fears about the birthrate were not without some justification in the United States and western Europe.

After 1890 school and class "spirit" spread across the Alleghenies to Nebraska and far beyond with athletics, particularly football, along with fraternities being excellent means by which this spirit could be encouraged. Having fun and not studying too hard were major objectives by 1900. Class loads for professors, however, were much heavier than today. During the 1890s the faculty at the University of Nebraska spent no fewer than twenty-five hours a week in the classroom, more than four times the average weekly class load today because of research expectations.[59] Pay was mostly the same in purchasing power as it was until the 1950s but well below today's average compensation.[60]

Another academic trend that set in after the Civil War was the influence of German universities. Prussia, the heartland of what became the German Empire in 1871, was the first country in the world—followed soon thereafter by the United States—to establish a free, common public school system.[61] However, the German example extended far beyond elementary or secondary education. Inaugurated by Johns Hopkins University in Baltimore, the United States also followed the German emphasis on the discovery of new knowledge through sustained experimentation in laboratories for the natural sciences, research in libraries and archives for historians, and research seminars for advanced students. The latter was promoted by Woodrow Wilson, at the time president of Princeton University.[62] No longer were universities to be mere repositories and conveyers of well-known facts, assumptions, or dogmas. It was during the 1880s that history was first regarded as an academic discipline as seen in the founding of the American Historical Association in 1884.

The peak of German influence was in the 1880s, although it was not until after 1896 that the number of Americans studying in Germany began to decline.[63] However, the term *Lehrfreiheit*, or "academic freedom," which American students brought back with them from Germany, proved to be enduring even though it has been tested during times of hysteria and never more so than during the First World War. In Germany and Austria, the term meant that a university was free to govern and police itself without outside interference. The term's definition was extended in the United States to mean that professors could pursue their research even if the results were politically unpopular or contradicted long-held assumptions and points of view.[64]

The impact of German education, not to mention German science, technology, and music, prior to the First World War, is demonstrated by the fact that especially between 1890 and the First World War, the German language was studied by more than a quarter of all high school students, which was more than *all* modern foreign languages put together at the college level.[65] At many colleges and schools, it was the *only* modern foreign language taught. As we will see later, this trend came to a screeching halt soon after the American declaration of war against Germany in 1917. American professors who had studied in Germany were viewed with suspicion if not considered potential or actual traitors.[66]

By the eve of the First World War, there was less of a need for American students to travel abroad to get a good post-secondary education. By 1914 American professors in most fields at elite universities were expected to have a PhD. Continued research and publications were also beginning to become mandatory by 1910 at the more prestigious American schools.[67] The best of the American universities, such as Stanford, Harvard, Yale, Johns Hopkins, and Princeton as well as Wisconsin, Michigan, and Nebraska, now compared favorably with the best universities in Europe, such as Oxford and Cambridge in England, the University of Paris, and the universities in Berlin, Heidelberg, and Vienna.

While the University of Nebraska was rapidly growing, enrolling just short of seven thousand students in 1919–20, the academic and social lives of students were evolving with the times.[68] In 1882 a history department was added with two members. In January 1908 Lincoln became the headquarters of the new Mississippi Valley Historical Association, whose purpose was to "co-operate in the work of collecting material and preserving records . . . [of the] middle western states." The founders of the new organization saw it as being a "declaration of independence . . . [from the] American Historical Association . . . controlled mainly by eastern men."[69]

In 1896 Nebraska became the first university west of the Mississippi to organize a graduate school.[70] By this time graduate education began to be a prerequisite for professions such as law, medicine, dentistry, theology, college teaching, and even journalism, fields, which as previously noted, in many cases had formerly been filled though an apprenticeship demanding no tests or licenses.[71] The emphasis on professionalism was especially strong in the field of medicine. In 1902 the University of Nebraska invited the Medical College in Omaha to join in the endeavor and established a four-year degree program for students in 1905 after they had earned an MS degree. In other words it would take six years of study after graduating from high school.[72] However, as late as the first decade of the new century, these new requirements for prospective physicians did not prevent men in Lincoln, and no doubt elsewhere in Nebraska, from simply calling themselves doctors and practicing medicine.[73] For those who did graduate with a degree in one of the professions, however, entry into the burgeoning middle class was assured.[74]

Despite the modesty of their high school backgrounds, which in most cases before the turn of the century were rural and agricultural, students at the university worked hard, even to the point of exhaustion often worsened by their need to pay their own expenses. The possibility of students being distracted was considerably limited by a list of rules drawn up by the first Board of Regents in 1871 that forbade them from gambling or drinking in any of Lincoln's numerous saloons. They were also expected to attend chapel daily and church on Sunday.[75] In the late 1880s some rebellious coeds decided that they no longer needed male escorts to attend evening lectures and other public functions.[76] By the 1890s daily chapel was no longer required, and other rigid rules began to be replaced or at least supplemented by literary societies, eating clubs, a debating club, a scientific club, a cycling club, three political clubs, two German clubs, and a camera club. In 1911 the Kosmet Club was organized, which put on an annual all-male musical show.[77] There was no place to dance on the campus, but big hotels were not far away and were reachable, as we have seen, by horse-drawn trams (after 1886) and electric streetcars (starting in 1891). For special occasions horse-drawn cabs were readily available. After the turn of the century, fraternities and sororities were able to host their own dances.[78] The ultimate source of entertainment and school spirit was probably the Nebraska football team, whose first game was played in October 1890, a subject to be covered in chapter 7.

The Denominational Schools: Nebraska Wesleyan, Union College, and Cotner College

Lincoln's claim to be the "Athens of the West" would have been dubious to say the least if it only had one or two colleges. But Lincoln was surely unusual for having four such institutions from the early 1890s to the early 1930s.

It is a bit mystifying that so many people could go from wondering how Nebraska could afford even one university to a belief at the end of the 1880s that Lincoln could support four institutions of higher learning. The controversial census of 1890, which claimed that Lincoln's population had grown from 13,000 in 1880 to a wildly inflated 55,000 ten years later, produced euphoric expectations about future growth; two early historians of Lincoln predicted the city would reach 125,000 by 1900.[79] They all ignored the erratic nature of Nebraska's all-important rainfall and the fact that the state was rapidly running out of uncultivated land, let alone land that was suitable for irrigation. The Panic of 1893, which was the country's worst economic disaster to date, and several years of drought, resulted in Lincoln's new colleges barely surviving economically the first decade of their existence.

Cotner College—originally named Nebraska Christian University, then renamed Cotner University in honor of a generous donor, and finally Cotner College after 1900—had a precarious existence almost from its establishment in 1888 because all its income was derived from the sale of lots surrounding the college. No effort was even made to secure cash donations or to establish an endowment.[80] By contrast the state's twenty-five thousand Methodists in the 1890s served as Wesleyan's benefactors.[81]

All three denominational colleges benefited from being near Lincoln's commercial and entertainment area and the nearby railroad stations connecting the city to all forty-eight states. Having only tiny libraries of their own, especially in their early years, they also benefited from their nearness to the University of Nebraska library, Lincoln's new Carnegie library, and the holdings of the Nebraska Historical Society. Like the University of Nebraska, they also profited from the rapidly growing number of fully accredited high schools throughout the state, which reached approximately three hundred by 1917.[82]

Lincoln's new academies in one sense were traditional in being small and affiliated with a religious denomination. Nebraska Wesleyan was associated with the Methodist Church, Union College with the Seventh Day Adventists, and Cotner College when it opened its doors in 1889 with the Disciples of Christ. However, they were modern in other respects. Unlike other nineteenth-century colleges, nearly all of which were only for men when they were founded, all three of Lincoln's new schools were coeducational from the outset, although they limited the mingling of the sexes to varying degrees.[83] Moreover they not only provided education in the classics but also included courses that would be immediately practical. The *Lincoln Star* noted as early as 1891 that when "a student graduates from [Cotner] college he has the skill of a workman as well as the education of a graduate. . . . One very remarkable feature about it is that girls as well as boys are to receive these benefits."[84]

None of these denominational schools were within the boundaries of Lincoln when they were founded, although they were all eventually incorporated into the city. In fact they viewed Lincoln proper with great suspicion for its relative secularism, especially regarding alcohol and dancing. This attitude paralleled the feeling of many Lincolnites, who regarded Omaha with its many breweries as "sin city."

Both Union College and Cotner College were founded on what now seems a curious mixture of hopes for financial gain and religious zealotry. In the words of Cotner's only historian, who was more farsighted than he realized, "The founders of [the college] were all well-meaning Christian men. Perhaps in some instances they were not as wise and farsighted from a business standpoint as they should have been."[85] Cotner's future rested on the assumption that the founder could build a new town called Bethany and would be able to sell thirteen lots. The same could be said of the other two denominational colleges in Lincoln. All of them were based on the hope of the capital city's continued growth and prosperity. They all managed to outlast the Panic of 1893, and Union College and Nebraska Wesleyan barely survived the Great Depression of the 1930s; only Cotner was forced to close its doors in June 1933.

Cotner's mission was laid out during the cornerstone ceremony of the school's one and only building. B. J. Radford of Eureka, Illinois, said that a "nonsectarian college diploma is, after all, a very unsatisfactory indication that the possessor has a good moral character; it does not indicate what his religion is; it tells nothing except that the young man has gone through a little intellectual gymnastics. . . . Secular education has had its day. . . . The Bible [is] the cornerstone of this university. . . . The Bible (is) the greatest of textbooks."[86] Cotner did graduate a high number of missionaries, but it also produced many teachers and was the first college in Lincoln to teach medicine and dentistry.

Nebraska Wesleyan differed from Lincoln's other two private schools in not being a "theological school." It did claim, however, that 98 percent of its graduates were "active Christians." Clark A.

Fulmer, who served as Wesleyan's chancellor from 1910 to 1917, stressed the importance of lifelong learning as well as the "Social Gospel," which included protecting the family, stopping child labor, ending sweatshops, improving care of the old and sick, and abolishing liquor traffic and corruption in public affairs.[87] Union College and Cotner College, on the other hand, stressed the importance of missionary work both at home and abroad.

Not all of Chancellor Fulmer's predecessors had consistently followed Christian principles. In 1897 acting chancellor and professor of chemistry Charles Ellinwood had exhorted students in chapel services "to live more devoted Christian lives." It turned out that Ellinwood, who as treasurer handled all of Wesleyan's funds, had invested them in "properties not being as sound as Mr. Ellinwood thought they were."[88] For years he had been carrying out a series of frauds. On April 21 it was revealed that Ellinwood had embezzled more than $31,000, today worth around $1 million, an enormous figure for a financially struggling school.[89] In September 1898 the Nebraska Conference of the Methodist Church officially announced that "the charges against C. H. Ellinwood of misappropriating university funds are sustained, and the defendant is deposed from the ministry and expelled from the Methodist Episcopal church."[90]

All four of Lincoln's colleges started with a single, relatively huge building in which the administration and all the classes met. Today only Wesleyan's first building, now called "Old Main," still stands albeit minus some of its Victorian embellishments. When opened, it had seventeen office rooms plus science and art classrooms on the main floor. The second floor had a library, museum, and classes for language, English, and philosophy. The third floor had an assembly room, which could also be used as a chapel.[91]

The fate of the University of Nebraska's first building was the saddest. Being built with sandstone that led to the demise of Nebraska's first two capitols, University Hall was rumored to be unsafe before its doors were even opened to students. In 1871 three professional architects recommended it be repaired. Six years later four architects advised that it be torn down and replaced.[92] Instead the building lost its cupola and top three floors in 1925. The surviving first floor and basement were used for classes until they too had to be razed in 1948.[93]

Ironically Cotner College's first and, as it turned out, *only* strictly academic building was quite possibly the most impressive of the four Lincoln colleges' original buildings.[94] The four-story building had a first-class stone foundation and basement as well as walls faced with pressed brick. Its roof was made of slate and included a seventy-five-foot tower.[95] It had thirty-two rooms plus seven offices, a chapel with a seating capacity of four hundred, a reference library, and a large study room.[96] The building was demolished in 1948 along with adjacent bleachers and football goal posts, having survived the demise of the college itself by fifteen years. It is a shame that the building was not put to good use.

One feature that all four of Lincoln's colleges had in common for many years is that students were on their own as far as housing was concerned. Cotner was apparently the first school to acquire a dorm and that was not until 1920. Such housing arrangements varied substantially in quality with many of them being late in acquiring electric lights or central heating. In fact electricity did not reach Wesleyan and the suburb of University Place until 1902, a full decade after it reached the state university.[97] Telephones came in 1904. The temperament of landlords could also vary from kindly and helpful to disagreeable and profane. Poor housing conditions probably contributed to the shockingly high death rate among Wesleyan students, much of it attributed to tuberculosis.[98] Wesleyan would not have its own dormitory until 1949.[99]

Wesleyan was modern in eliminating the required graduation oration in 1898—almost certainly to the relief of the twenty families that would have been expected to sit through an equal number of orations. (The much larger University of Nebraska had given up the practice in 1890.)[100] Nevertheless oratory remained a popular subject if it was a single speech or debate. History, which had been an entertaining form of literature since ancient times, became an academic field that would qualify as a major for the BA around 1901. On the other hand, Wesleyan remained very much in the tradition of religiously affiliated colleges in requiring daily worship services not only for students but for faculty as well. Janitors, and even students and professors, patrolled halls to enforce total attendance for each twenty- to twenty-five-minute assembly.[101]

College life at Wesleyan was far more than classes, chapel, and clubs. A 5-cent, thirty-minute streetcar ride (equal to about $1.25 today) took students to downtown Lincoln and its many theaters, where everything from grand operas to concerts by John Philip Sousa's band could be heard at the Oliver Theater. For those whose tastes were more lowbrow, there were frequent vaudeville shows and dance halls; some Wesleyan students could not resist the temptations of the "cursed saloon" even though the school's newspaper urged students to join the Anti-Saloon League, and the Women's Temperance Christian Union was active on the Wesleyan campus. A speech by President Theodore Roosevelt in Lincoln caused classes to be canceled so that Wesleyan students could attend. Among the popular new forms of entertainment that prevailed before the First World War, only dancing was forbidden, a proscription that was not lifted by the trustees and faculty until 1937.

The kind of social life that students had at Nebraska Wesleyan, not to mention the University of Nebraska, would have been unthinkable at Union College during the decades under review. Much time was taken up by religious services in their residences: an hour in the morning and another hour in the evening. Young men and women came close to living in separate worlds. They were not allowed to go to dances or pool halls, play cards, attend the theater, or compete in sports with students from other schools. Intramural football and later basketball were permitted, and by 1920 the college had a swimming pool. Attending concerts and music recitals was also acceptable.[102]

Out of the classroom, male and female Union College students might just as well have been living in different towns or states. Male and female students had to take separate staircases to their dormitory rooms, which were on different floors. Men were not allowed to accompany female classmates from one building to another or to stroll anywhere with them, nor were couples allowed to sit together for any occasion. A young man could visit a female classmate in her residence just once a week. The visit was to last no more than half an hour, with twenty minutes being considered more appropriate by the school's authorities. "Sentimentalism, flirtation, and courtship were also named as out of place. Sentimentalism was defined as 'softness and foolishness in one's association with the opposite sex.'"[103] Young men and women could take the thirty-minute streetcar ride to downtown Lincoln only on separate days: Mondays and Wednesdays for women and Tuesdays and Thursdays for men. They could engage in "entertainments," which included off-campus lectures, just six times a year and then only if chaperoned by a member of the faculty.

It need hardly be mentioned that Union College students were not allowed to use tobacco or to consume anything that was intoxicating. Profanity and vulgar language were also verboten and subject to discipline if not expulsion. Skating parties, hikes, and picnics were allowed if properly chaperoned. Males and females wishing to return home during academic breaks had to make sure that they went on different trains.[104]

The founding of Union College in 1891 was much like the establishment of Nebraska Wesleyan, which took place in 1888. In each case Lincoln businessmen were eager to see new colleges come to the state capital because it meant a growth in population and hence an increase in the value of building sites. A committee considering both Lincoln and Des Moines for Union College's site ultimately chose Lincoln by a vote of 6 to 2. As in the case of Wesleyan and Cotner, Union's advocates were influenced by the school's location thirty minutes away from Lincoln's downtown area by a promised streetcar link, which was in fact completed by the time the school opened in September 1891. The relatively high elevation and vistas provided by the village of College View were also attractive features of the proposed site. The committee thought that the new school would be far enough away from the city to avoid smoke, noise, and "unfavorable associations" but near enough to enjoy the advantages of contact with a growing city.[105]

The site indeed appears to have been well chosen. As mentioned earlier, Lincolnites soon discovered that the new streetcar line connecting College View with the city proper provided easy access to the Union campus. Some people thought there was "not a prettier spot in all the state of Nebraska than College View with . . . its well-kept homes . . . [and] spacious lawns."[106] Making the excursion even more enjoyable was College View's band, which performed on Sundays and holidays. Beginning in September 1894, musicians would sing hymns under cottonwood trees near the administration building.[107]

Union's curriculum was highly unusual, if not unique, in offering programs in which all the courses were taught in either Danish-Norwegian, German, or Swedish in addition to English. Students were also expected to attend worship service in one of those languages. The idea was to send missionaries to countries where they could proselytize to people in their own language. After just four years the program was discontinued because of a lack of interest even among students whose native language was not English.[108]

The rest of the curriculum, which was unusual although not unique, involved in part housekeeping duties like what was expected of students at the University of Nebraska and Wesleyan regarding their off-campus housing. Such duties could involve collecting ice from ice houses, doing laundry, mopping, sweeping, and tailoring. Young men also learned practical farming. Girls learned how to cook, sew, and mend. These activities for girls were given the grandiose term of "domestic science." Many years later it was called "home economics." Teachers of these subjects, who were kept busy with their academic courses, were no more enthusiastic about these tasks than the students, and the whole program was discontinued after just a few years, although the college's farm continued.[109]

A spontaneous snowball fight by a mixed group of students resulted in a severe reprimand by school authorities who thought that the "unladylike" behavior of the girls was particularly offensive. The girls were forced to write an official apology in which they repented their "disgraceful conduct . . . and humbly ask[ed] their] fellow students to forgive and to overlook [their] failure to meet the high standards of Christian behavior that should characterize the students of Union College."[110]

Although the school regarded a spontaneous and friendly snowball fight disgraceful behavior, the authorities thought it was perfectly proper to have fire escapes from each upper story dormitory room to consist of a rope tied to the foot of a steam radiator. Sleeping arrangements were equally unusual with two students sleeping in one double bed whether they were complete strangers or not.

All four of Lincoln's institutions of higher learning appeared to be in good shape at the beginning of the 1920s. Enrollment at the University of Nebraska, one of the largest universities in the country, was just shy of 7,000. Wesleyan's total enrollment in 1920 was 1,440, by far the largest of any Protestant denominational school in Nebraska.[111] Union's enrollment of 518 in 1921 was the highest the school would achieve until after the Second World War.[112] Lincolnites could be understandably proud that the city and suburbs had twenty-five thousand students from kindergarten to graduate school out of a total population of around seventy-five thousand. And none of its public-school students had to pay even one cent for tuition.[113] Nationally 47 percent of all college students were women, a figure not surpassed until the 1970s.[114]

The relatively good times of the 1920s came to a screeching halt at the end of the decade. Enrollments declined in all of Lincoln's schools of higher education, and indebtedness grew at the private colleges. For Cotner College the Great Depression was fatal; its doors closed in June 1933.[115]

4

The New Woman

As we have seen, by the 1890s girls made up the majority of high school graduates and up to 47 percent of all college students in 1920. Nevertheless until the latter part of the twentieth century, men made all the big decisions about state and national politics, including peace and war, in addition to those involving big and small businesses and the administration of secondary and higher education. Male dominance was so great that when making sweeping generalizations about American history at the turn of the twentieth century, it would be easy to ignore women altogether. Reinforcing that dominance was the belief, held by most women as well as men, that the husband should be a "good provider" and the wife should be the "homemaker" and "child-rearer."[1]

Nevertheless below the level of high politics and big business, well-educated women were making a remarkable impact on American society between 1890 and 1920. They not only won the right to vote in *all* elections, local, state, and national, but also insisted on better working conditions not only for themselves but also for children working in factories and mines. They fought for free kindergartens and for nurses and hot lunches in schools. They were decades ahead of their time in pointing out the medical dangers of smoking and fought for the banning of sales of alcohol. However, they did not yet attain equality in matters of credit or high-level employment opportunities.

New Jobs for the New Woman: "An Unwomanly Desire"?

Below the banner headlines, women were making real progress between 1890 and 1920. In 1910 80 percent of teachers, 79 percent of librarians, and 93 percent of nurses were women, not to mention office secretaries, telephone operators, and those working in consumer sales.[2] In a way they succeeded all too well because these jobs were ultimately stigmatized as "woman's work" and consequently in practice paid less than men would get for the same job. Nebraska was an extreme example of where some work became stereotyped as women's work. Whereas women had made up 48 percent of the state's teaching force in 1871, they comprised 91 percent in 1918.[3] However, this is not how women viewed themselves at the time. These jobs were considered "white collar" and gave women an entry into, at the very least, the lower middle class. The jobs were far better paid than factory or farm work and were much less dangerous. Their working hours were still long but were steadily declining. Their pay gave them a sense of self-worth and enough free time to enjoy dance halls, concerts, vaudeville shows, and after 1900, motion pictures. Working women with their own income were also less likely to remain in a marriage with an abusive husband, and indeed the divorce rate did increase especially after the First World War.[4]

What was still virtually closed to women were positions in management, law, and academe.[5] There were some female doctors after 1900, but they were either looked at with suspicion or ridiculed.[6] There were exceptions, but they usually meant that a woman acquiring an advanced degree was very often giving up marriage and facing an uncertain financial future. If they did marry they would often have no more than one or two children, which led to broad fears of a substantially reduced birthrate, a fear that was widespread not only in the United States but also in France and other parts of Europe.[7] The stigma of never marrying and becoming an "old maid" was not easily ignored and was usually interpreted as a woman having failed in her foremost responsibilities.[8] The consequence was that most young women worked for only a few years after high school or college before marrying and raising a family. However, even girls with no more than a high school diploma married significantly later than those who did not.[9] In Lincoln girls who quit school before graduating from high school still had the option of attending night school. This was a particularly good option for recent immigrants, who were thereby given a chance to learn English and find a job preferable to housework.

A fascinating way of gaining insights into social customs and attitudes of early twentieth-century Lincoln is to read letters to "Minerva's Mail," an advice column written by a Lincolnite that lasted from 1910 to 1946. "Minerva," the Roman goddess of wisdom, was probably a pen name of a Lincolnite who responded to the questions submitted by readers in or near the capital city. More than half the questions were similar to what people ask advice columnists today. Probably the most frequently asked questions were about romance and marriage. "When is the proper time to allow a young man to kiss me?" Minerva: "After he has proposed marriage."[10] "What traits make a good husband?" Minerva: "Choose a man who has already proven his ability to make his own way in the world."[11] "I am eighteen and in love. Would it be right if I should ask him if he loves me?" Minerva: "That is the very last thing you should do."[12] "How can I attract the attention of men, and finally get a husband?" Minerva: "In the first place, a mere husband is no great acquisition. Many a woman who has one is just as anxious to get rid of him as you are to get one. . . . Fill your life with sweetness, contentment, usefulness, and higher aspirations."[13] An example of a relatively modern way of thinking was a letter asking whether "differing religions should be an obstacle to marriage." Minerva: "To me the guiding and most potent force of all religion must be love. . . . And so it is indeed a peculiar religion that casts out love."[14] A nineteen-year-old young woman asked if it was alright to go to a dance hall. Minerva: "A girl may attend public dances if she is properly escorted without any harm resulting, providing she chooses a dance hall of good reputation."[15] An older lady complained that a female "high school graduate used the word 'darn' at least a dozen times." Minerva thought that such language was "lamentable."[16]

Some questions were more practical. "I just moved to Lincoln. What is the proper way to get to know my neighbors?" Minerva: "Make the acquaintance of your pastor's wife. From her you can find out about the women's organizations in the church. She will see to it that the women of the church call on you."[17] One reader wanted to know what to do about an oily face. Minerva: "Try washing your face in oatmeal water. Make a paste of oatmeal and use it as a cream on your skin."[18] Sometimes Minerva made a broad appeal to her readers, as when she asked them "to think up what your favorite economy is . . . so that I may pass it on to my readers."[19] Still other responses by Minerva were both blunt and hilarious, as when one twenty-nine-year-old reader wrote that she had just proposed to a man she had "been keeping company with for four years. . . . I proposed to him three weeks earlier . . . but had not heard from him since. What can I do?" Minerva's answer: "My dear, you can do nothing. You have frightened him away forever, and I am not sure it doesn't serve you right."[20]

By no means was everyone enthusiastic about the rapidly changing role of women. The traditional view, published in 1890 in the conservative *Lincoln Evening Call*, maintained that

> the home is the paradise of life . . . its influence being supreme in molding character and disposition. The head and front of home is her bower [shelter] of which she makes a paradise or a hell for its master. . . . Many young women go out into the world to work simply because they are reproached by friends for not doing so, hence the derisive appellation of "home girl" so commonly used. . . . The true home girl is a queen in the kingdom of womanhood, and a jewel that you men strive for when ready to settle in life. . . . The home girl, though she may not know it, is fulfilling a grander and nobler mission by her devotion to home than a dozen of her girlfriends out in the world. She has planted herself in woman's natural sphere, doing woman's true labor, and endearing herself to those around the hearthstone which she graces.[21]

Another article appearing in the *Lincoln Evening Call* eight years later mourned the "passing of the old maid,"

> who had more friends than she could count. . . . She was loved and respected. . . . This gentle creature, the friend of the entire family, had disappeared and in her place is the energetic, long time, independent bachelor woman. This woman is very much alone. . . . Now it is all right if a woman must earn her living in some congenial, original, and feminine way, but when it is not necessary, when it is only an unwomanly desire to get out into the busy world, I do not think anyone who knows what a woman ought to do, what side of her nature it is best to cultivate, should encourage her.[22]

The invention that had most to do with the employment of women at the turn of the century was the typewriter. Secretaries had been employed since the Roman republic. They were used by the nobility in early modern times and in the United States by men as late as the Civil War and its aftermath. Throughout the centuries, however, most secretaries were men in both public and private offices.[23] Although a commercially successful typewriter was invented in 1870, it was not until the mid-1880s that they began to replace handwritten documents and letters. In some ways this change is regrettable. Would the Declaration of Independence or the Constitution have been more impressive and beautifully written if they had been typed? As a PhD candidate at the University of Rochester (New York), I had the opportunity to read hundreds of handwritten letters to William Henry Seward, Abraham Lincoln's secretary of state and later the purchaser of Alaska. I was deeply impressed by both the penmanship and the composition of these letters. Penmanship and even longhand appear to be lost arts nowadays, as is oratory.

There is no doubt, however, that typing was faster than writing by hand. Whether women are more dexterous at handwriting and typing is debatable, although some people believe that women's relatively slender wrists and dainty fingers give them an advantage with small, closely arranged keys. In any event, by 1900 there were more women in clerical positions in business offices than there were in teaching.[24] By 1920 clerical jobs had become stereotypically feminine. Contributing to the female domination of these fields is the fact that far more young women were graduating from high schools than men. On the other hand, until at least 1900 men far outnumbered college coeds. Many young women were also available because of the rapid decline of the family farm after 1890. Not surprisingly high school graduates also regarded clerical work as being more enjoyable than working in a factory or farm, not to mention it being better paid. Clerical workers also enjoyed shorter hours, vacations, sick leaves, and in general a higher status.[25] Some critics thought that women would not survive in an office setting or at best it would hurt their femininity; proponents thought clerical work would be useful in managing a household.[26]

The impact of the typewriter on the employment of women and the atmosphere of a business office came with startling suddenness. As early as 1885 an article in the *Nebraska State Journal* noted that "type writing has opened a new field for young women. They are almost universally employed for this work. Lawyers and merchants and all businessmen like to have a pleasant young lady in the office. Her presence improves the moral tone of the sanctum and gives the place an air of culture and refinement. 'Typewriters' average about $12 per week," or $300 in today's valuation.[27]

"Some of the prettiest girls in Washington are typewriters," declared the opening line in the *Nebraska State Journal* on July 7, 1890. "They are numbered by the thousands, and they are the most expert of their kind in the United States."[28] This was not a hilarious typographical error but an emphatic observation. Typists, as we call them today, were then known as "typewriters," literally people who type. Typists in Washington DC were even better paid than typists working in New York, Philadelphia, or Chicago.

A job as a secretary must have seemed especially attractive at a time when want ads in Lincoln papers, which were always gender specific, listed jobs for women such as housekeeper, dishwasher, chambermaid, shirt ironer, and general houseworker.[29] The number of young women who became household servants was still significant as late as 1920, but whereas half of all female wage earners had been servants in 1870, only one woman in six accepted such work in 1920.[30] By the latter date being a full-time maid was seen as demeaning. However, one of Minerva's correspondents noted that being paid $6 a week, which included room and board, could easily be superior to a job that paid $13 a week with no such benefits.[31] However, the letter writer did not point out that whether such work was desirable or hellish was determined by how she was treated by her mistress and by the number and behavior of the children in the household. Nor did she mention that live-in maids could be dismissed for any reason, including old age.

A new type of work that attracted young women was being a salesclerk in a department store. Department stores had existed in Britain since the eighteenth century and in France and bigger American cities since the middle of the nineteenth century. They were outgrowths of general stores, which had existed in every American town virtually from the year of its founding. What set them apart was their size and division into separate departments. The most important of these departments was the one devoted to ready-made clothes for women and children as well as the department for cosmetics and jewelry. Cosmetics, previously known as "paint," became respectable around the turn of the century, having previously been associated with actresses and prostitutes. There was a uniform dress code for clerks and a bargain basement. Many department stores also had lunch counters or tea rooms for weary shoppers. A spacious ladies lounge with an attendant was also commonplace. Department stores benefited from the invention of the elevator, patented by Black inventor Alexander Miles in 1884, and the escalator, first commercially produced in 1889. Electric lights were also enormously helpful for illuminating the interiors of department stores and their elaborate display windows. Department stores as well as business districts in general also benefited from electric streetcars, which invariably had a stop near their main entrance.

Women, or more precisely middle-class and wealthy women, quickly became the most numerous customers of department stores. (Less fortunate women shopped at F. W. Woolworth and A&P stores.)[32] By 1915, 80 to 85 percent of consumer purchases were made by women, but women were also most of the stores' employees, although not the managers.[33] In 1870 there were so few "saleswomen" that they were not even designated as such in the census of that year. Nationally there were about 142,000 female salesclerks in 1900. By 1920 that number had doubled.[34] Retail sales, in fact, became another stereotypical female profession. Attractive young women were, like secretaries, the most frequently hired. As in the other "female" professions, saleswomen were most likely to remain in their job for only a few years, although a few made it a lifetime profession. Thanks in part to having at least some income of their own, by 1915 women were responsible for close to 90 percent of all consumer spending in the United States.[35]

Lincoln's first department store was Miller & Paine. Established in 1880 as a small general store on P Street, it evolved into a department store after it moved to the corner of Thirteenth and O Streets in 1890. The store was greatly enlarged on the same site to eight stories in 1916 and remained there until it was taken over by Dillard's department store chain in 1988.[36] As a child in the late 1940s, I was a frequent visitor of the store when I tagged along with

17. Looking east on O Street circa 1926. (Miller & Paine Department Store in foreground.) Courtesy of History Nebraska.

my mother whenever she went shopping. I was impressed by the store's escalator, the first in Nebraska, and by the elevators. Like all elevators at the time, those at Miller & Paine had their own white-gloved operators, now an extinct breed. Their job was to get the elevator to stop at precisely the right spot so that customers did not have to step down or up to get off. It usually took more than one attempt to get the job done. In 1935 Miller & Paine was also the first department store in Nebraska to have air conditioning. Before that, on hotter days, the store might open at 7:30 a.m. to give customers a chance to shop at a relatively cool time of day.[37] It was also the first store in the country to have an automated system that could read price tags and send change and receipts to and from an office by pneumatic tubes.

Turn-of-the-Century Fashions and Sports for Women

It may seem a bit odd to lump the evolution of fashions and sports together as closely related topics. However, a brief glance at this book's illustrations will quickly reveal how closely related they were, especially between 1890 and 1920. To old-timers like myself, who grew up in the 1940s and '50s, it is easy to assume that men's and women's fashions have been radically different throughout recorded history. In fact the opposite is true. Going back only as far as ancient Rome we can see from statues and mosaics that their clothing was remarkably similar, differing mainly in color, although hair styles were quite different. In the eighteenth century, upper-class men and women in both Europe and America wore expensive laces, striking colors like pink and light blue, silk, and satins. Both sexes wore powdered wigs and high heels as seen in any painting of a European monarch or, for that matter, the founding fathers of the United Sates. The most vigorous activities men and women were prepared to undertake with this clothing were genteel dancing and playing cards. Running or jumping would have been next to impossible. Women were supposed to avoid anything that might cause them to sweat.

These similarities began to change at the beginning of the nineteenth century with Napoleon and his courtiers, who wore tailored woolen business suits with dark trousers, light-colored vests, and white shirts. By the middle of the nineteenth century and far beyond, gentlemen were still wearing their somber clothing, which could be used either for relatively formal occasions or business; freedom of movement was paramount.[38] Women, on the other hand, were wearing clothes that strictly confined to their gender and femininity.[39] Men lost their high heels, which inhibited walking, whereas women wore clothes that made vigorous exercise impossible. Men's suits remained essentially unchanged between 1890 and 1920 and even beyond. Stiff collars attached to shirts were popular for decades. The width of lapels and the number of buttons on jackets decreased from four to two or three, and the shape of their stiff collars also changed slightly between 1890 and 1920. In the 1890s their informal wear included knickerbockers that reached just below the knees (like the uniforms of baseball players) and tweed jackets, both of which were suitable for golf. (Like other school children in Lincoln, I wore knickerbockers to grade school in the late 1940s and thought I was quite grown up when I started to wear long pants.) For more formal evening clothes, men wore a long frock coat with silk lapels and a silk hat.

For an informal dinner, men wore special jackets with stiff shirts, not exactly comfortable by our standards, but such clothing still enabled men to move about easily.

Women's fashion grew ever more cumbersome and restraining during the nineteenth century. The empire style of the early part of the century featured incredibly high waistlines just below the bust. But the long skirts were not bulky or heavy and did not prevent walking or engaging in vigorous dancing. Their hair was covered by small bonnets, which also did not inhibit their activities. All this had changed by the middle of the century, when women were burdened by layer after layer of fabric and huge, cumbersome hats that only partially covered their hair, which could fall as low as their waists.

By the 1870s and even more so after 1890, men's and women's fashions, if anything, were more different than ever. Two historians of fashion, Phyllis Tortora and Keith Eubank, maintain that fashions for women "went through a more rapid series of changes than did styles of any preceding period of comparable length. None of the distinct phases of costume can be said to have lasted even ten years."[40] The ideal woman was expected to be voluptuous and plump with a full, nearly round face and long hair either pulled back or piled on top of her head.[41] After the turn of the century, corsets began to disappear, and dresses had much less material. However, the dresses of upper-class women were covered with huge quantities of expensive decoration.

There was one early attempt to bring some rationality into women's fashions. In 1851 a New England temperance activist named Elizabeth Smith Miller adopted what she believed to be a more rational costume for women: loose trousers gathered at the ankles. Like outfits worn in the Middle East and Central Asia, it was topped by a short dress or skirt and vest. It was ultimately popularized by another women's activist and temperance advocate, Amelia Bloomer, who argued in her newspaper, the Lily, that it would not only be comfortable and useful but would also contribute to women's health. The costume soon came to be known as "bloomers" but was subjected to merciless ridicule in the press, denunciations from pulpits, and harassment on the street. For many men trousers were a symbol of male domination, and trousers, even if mostly covered by an overskirt, "were seen as a threat to the whole structure of society."[42] By 1859 even Bloomer gave up her campaign.

Three decades later, thanks to the popularity of the bicycle with women as well as men, bloomers underwent a revival even before Amelia Bloomer's death in Council Bluffs in 1894. The new version of the bloomers, however, was quite different from the original design. Gone was the overskirt, which reached halfway down between the knees and the ankles. Moreover some of the trousers were a little less voluminous, making the whole costume more practical. The narrower version of bloomers made it possible for women to ride bicycles alongside men and often on bicycles built for two. The impact of bloomers and the popularity of bicycles in the 1890s and 1900s were revolutionary, giving women a new freedom while leaving chaperons far behind, both literally and figuratively.

Crinolines only marginally improved the comfort of women's clothing. The steel-hooped cage crinoline, first patented in 1856 in Paris, was mass-produced and quickly became popular with women of every social and economic class on both sides of the Atlantic. They were so flexible that women could sit down and stand up without their skirts losing their shape. They could be either circular, as they were in the 1850s, or flat in front and elongated in back as was the case in the 1860s. They had at least two big disadvantages, however. The hooped skirts could easily catch on fire at a time when candles and open fireplaces were common. They could also easily be caught in machinery or by carriage wheels. Gusts of wind could cause them to flare up, exposing ladies' ankles and legs, much to the horror of genteel Victorian women. By the time Lincoln was founded in 1867, crinolines were passing out of fashion, although there were revivals in the twentieth century.

Probably nothing is more strongly associated with women's fashions in the late nineteenth century than the corset. Together with the bustle, they were intended to exaggerate women's hourglass shape by narrowing the waist, pushing up the breasts to make them appear larger, and flaring out the hips. The better ones were usually made by a corset maker and fitted to the individual wearer. They were tightened by lacings, which were done by lady's maids

WE OFFER FOR THIS WEEK

This Line of Best Fitting Corsets

At 47 Cents,   At 75 Cents.

Worth 75c.   Try Them.   Worth $1.00.

New Dress Trimmings, New Neckwear Just

Received.

HERPOLSHEIMER & CO

18. "This Line of Best Fitting Corsets." *Nebraska State Journal*, November 2, 1891, 6.

in well-to-do families. By wearing them for extended periods of time, women could permanently reduce the size of their waist to eighteen inches or even less.[43]

Dress reformists considered corsets a dangerous moral evil by promoting promiscuous views of female bodies. Other critics pointed out the obvious health risks involved in rearranging internal organs. The clergy and physicians both joined in denouncing the fashion. At the beginning of the twentieth century, corsets were being elongated to reach from the bust to the upper thigh. In Lincoln school girls were still wearing them in the 1910s albeit

19. "New Spring Suitings" for 1907. The cost per square yard of fabric for tailors. *Lincoln Star*, February 17, 1907, 12.

in diminishing numbers.[44] When they finally fell out of fashion, they were usually replaced by girdles and elastic brassieres. The decisive turning point came in 1917, when the U.S. government asked women to stop buying corsets to free up metal for war production. The saving of twenty-eight thousand tons of metal was enough to build two battleships![45]

Aside from bloomers, the only relief for women after the turn of the century was that their clothing was much less voluminous and heavy. However, just when their fashions were becoming more comfortable and better for their overall health, a new fashion came along to severely hinder their activities. The "hobble skirt" may have been inspired by Mrs. Edith Hart O. Berg, who in 1908 asked for a ride in one of the Wright brothers' planes. To prevent the wind from blowing up her skirt, she tied a rope around her ankles. Whatever the cause, the hobble skirt became popular in the last few years preceding the First World War. Although narrower skirts saved fabric, they necessitated a hobble garter, which prevented the wearer from splitting her skirt. Unfortunately they also meant that women were shackled to the point that normal

GOOD GOODS
208-210 So. 12th St.

Get Your Fall Suit NOW
When Stocks Are Complete—Then Take

6 MONTHS TIME TO PAY

It's the Gately way—and it has won over a million friends for our chain of 99 stores. In fact, we should say, with the opening of our store in Topeka, Kan., tomorrow, 919 Kansas Ave., it completes the strong link of 100 Gately stores and this chain of 100 Gately stores makes possible values that are unmatchable anywhere. With this knowledge, that you will get the best merchandise obtainable at the right sort of price, combined with the easy credit plan of 6 months' time to pay, you had better come in and make your selection tomorrow.

No money down. Simply say, charge it.

Women's and Misses'

$25 Suits
$14.95

Once you familiarize yourself with the completeness of the Gately stock you will then know that the one store upon which you can depend for the very style you want is this store. Each suit is tailored to our exact specifications; better linings, better fabrics, with the result we can offer suits that are actually worth $25, at an unmatchable low price, $14.95.

They are shown in all this season's newest fabrics, serges, whipcords, etc., etc., plain tailored, cutaway or straight lines or the more fancy effects, silk braided and elaborately trimmed; all sizes for women and misses. See these tomorrow. Special, $14.95.

Seal Plush Coats, $17.50

Do not confuse these coats with the ordinary plush coats. They are made of genuine Sealette plush, a lustrous silk-finish, seal appearing plush. Tailored on full graceful lines; elaborately lined with satin of contrasting shades; the most elegant garments imaginable; coats that would cost you $35 elsewhere, here and here only _____ **$17.50**

20. "Get Your Fall Suit Now." *Nebraska State Journal*, October 20, 1912, 7.

walking was impossible. Richard Ford, a recent historian of fashions, has concluded that "despite the support of physicians, philosophers, playwrights, moralists, and feminists, rational dress reform [for women prior to the First World War] was a failure."[46] Nor was cross-dressing a solution for women, because it was prohibited in forty-five states at the beginning of the twentieth century. The flapper style, which got started before the war and became much more popular after 1920, had the practical advantage of allowing women to dress without assistance. However, critics worried that it was also too easy to undress.[47]

In discussing the history of fashion in the late nineteenth and early twentieth centuries, it is tempting to focus on newspaper advertisements for the clothing of women and children in well-to-do families looking for outfits to wear at the next banquet or ballroom dance, orchestral concert, play, or opera. Meanwhile servants and women in lower middle-class professions had to make their own clothes and were buying outfits that were much more suitable for their jobs. They had neither the money to buy the latest fashions inspired in Paris or New York nor the time to make them. Fortunately women's clothing was now mass-produced and relatively affordable. Such costumes were likely to be shorter, considerably lighter, and relatively free of ornamentation. They can best be seen in contemporary photographs, not in advertisements.[48]

Perhaps the strangest aspect in the evolution in women's fashions between 1890 and 1920 is that high fashions often contradicted a new emphasis on the importance of women exercising for the benefit of their health. Cultural leaders in the late nineteenth century emphasized the importance of strenuous activities and the value of sport for developing character and self-discipline.[49] Simultaneously, as previously mentioned, the increasing number of college women around the turn of the twentieth century produced an outcry among men and some women that a college education would ruin a woman's health and make her unfit for motherhood.[50] Fortunately neither the University of Nebraska nor Nebraska Wesleyan subscribed to these beliefs about women's health. The University of Nebraska, in fact, had one of the earliest programs of physical education for women in the country. It was, however, hampered by limited facilities and personnel as well as opposition by some women to the program.[51]

Chancellor Canfield at the University of Nebraska did much to promote "the establishment of one of the earliest state university professional physical educations programs. In his first report to the regents, he suggested all women be required to take physical training and that an instructor in physical training be hired."[52] The next year the regents backed the chancellor and "ruled that all women take physical training two hours a week for two years. This new requirement remained in effect, virtually unchanged for over sixty years."[53] Canfield saw the need for a female instructor to give examinations and lectures on physiology and hygiene to young women. In 1896 tennis courts, usable for both genders, were built on the campus. In the academic year 1898–99 a course was established for prospective instructors of physical education, and shortly thereafter a department of physical education was established, the first of its kind in the United States.[54] Its faculty consisted primarily of its own graduates. In 1899 the legislature appropriated $20,000 to provide large locker rooms, bathrooms, and dressing rooms for women on the ground floor of Grant Hall. On their own both women and men "organized, developed, and participated in extracurricular activities that involved exercise: a Tennis association, a Walking Club, a Co-Ed Skating Club, and a bicycling organization."[55]

But Nebraska coeds were not satisfied with gymnastic classes and intramural activities. In 1901 the first intercollegiate contest was a "basket ball" game between Nebraska and the University of Missouri, a contest won by Nebraska, 31–4. The game had been invented only in 1891, when a soccer ball was used and peach baskets were goals. It was modified for women by a Smith College instructor, Senda Berenson, who divided the court into three sections with players being confined to just one section. What was especially odd about the Missouri game is that the two teams could not agree on the rules. So one half was played using the whole court, a rule preferred by Nebraska, while the other half was played according to the Berenson rules favored by Missouri.

Nebraska coeds continued to play intercollegiate basketball for the next seven years against teams from Omaha, Council Bluffs,

21. The 1905 University of Nebraska women's varsity basketball team.
Courtesy of History Nebraska.

and the University of Missouri. Their only loss was to the University of Minnesota, a game played in Minneapolis.[56] All such intercollegiate competition abruptly ended on April 24, 1908, when the regents denied coeds the right to participate in any further interstate athletic contests.[57] The dean of women, Mrs. Edna M. Barkley, was a strong opponent of interscholastic contests, believing that they had a negative effect on the girls. After 1908 basketball could be played only if it was part of a physical education class.[58] Incredibly it was not until the 1970s that the federal government passed Title IX that stipulated that women's sports could no longer be ignored by any high school or college.

Women's athletics at Nebraska Wesleyan suffered a similar fate. Despite the women's basketball team's series of victories against their opponents, the faculty voted, on November 2, 1910, "that the women not be permitted to engage in intercollegiate games of basket ball."[59] However, coeds enjoyed playing in a school tennis club and were required to take four semesters of physical education while wearing their serge or flannel blouses and bloomers and gymnasium shoes. Their classes included Swedish calisthenics, German marches, games, folk dancing, dumbbells, gymnastics with "horse and bar work," and basketball.[60] The aim of the classes was to "enable the students to sustain and improve their health during their university careers, and to aid them in the formation of habits and hygienic living."[61] Union College did not allow any of its students to compete in sports with other colleges: "It [was] felt that this would bring in influences and associations that would not be good for the religious atmosphere of the school."[62]

An outstanding female athlete from the turn of the twentieth century and for many years thereafter was Louise Pound, who lived from 1872 to 1958. However, she was much more than an incredible athlete. Born in Lincoln in 1872, she was part of a remarkable family. Her parents moved to Lincoln in 1869 where she was educated at home by her mother, who taught her to read by age three. Her brother, Roscoe, became dean of the University of Nebraska's Law School and later held the same position at Harvard. Her sister, Olivia, was for many years the principal for girls at Lincoln High School.

At fourteen Louise was admitted by examination to the preparatory school at the University of Nebraska. She earned her bachelor's degree as a Phi Beta Kappa at age nineteen in 1892. In 1899 she studied at the University of Heidelberg, graduating from a seven-semester program in two semesters. After her return to the United States, she became an adjunct professor at the University of Nebraska and taught numerous courses in English and English literature until her retirement in 1955.

Pound excelled in every sport she attempted—croquet, tennis, golf, skiing, and cycling—winning one sports championship after another, and not just against female competition either. She won the Lincoln City Tennis Championship in 1890 at the age of eighteen even though she had never taken lessons. The following two years she defeated men to win the tennis championship at the University of Nebraska. She was one of the first women in Lincoln to play golf and won the state golf championship in 1916. Somehow she also managed to coach the university's women's basketball team for a time.[63] In 1955, when she was eighty-two, she was elected the fourteenth member of the *Lincoln Journal*'s Nebraska

Sports Hall of Fame, the first woman to win this honor.[64] She died three years later, two days before her eighty-sixth birthday.

Downsizing and Modernizing: New Houses, Kitchens, and Bathrooms

The lives of women around the turn of the twentieth century were changed not just by new educational and employment opportunities but also by their domestic surroundings. We have already seen how Thomas Edison's incandescent lightbulb enormously affected the lives of both men and women wherever electricity was available. Important as they were, however, lightbulbs were by no means the only major invention of the period under review. Newer, middle-class houses had modern, labor-saving devices in the kitchens, and for the first time, separate bathrooms including a toilet inside the house.

The houses of my paternal ancestors provide excellent examples in the changes in domestic housing starting with the home of my great-great-grandfather, Heinrich, near Harvard, Nebraska, which was built in the 1880s. With the help of a computer search, my wife and I were able to find what was left of Heinrich's house in 2009. He, his wife, Elizabeth Ross, and their eight children lived in a medium-sized house, which had two bedrooms for children on the second floor. Somehow all five boys (Ludwig, Conrad, Ray, Harold, and Reon) were packed into one bedroom, while the three girls (Pearl, Selma, and Ada) could spread out in the neighboring bedroom. Downstairs was a bedroom for the parents and a living room but not a dining room. It came as no surprise that there was no evidence that the house had ever been electrified. The absence of closets was also not shocking because people made do in those days with wardrobes. Nor was I taken aback by the absence of a bathroom because they did not appear in most American homes until the twentieth century. We did find a large bathtub several feet away from the house, but we had no idea how it got there. Almost certainly it was not included when the house was built. Even more surprising was the absence of a kitchen, although there obviously had to have been one. Kitchens, in fact, were the most important room in the late nineteenth century and the one most frequently used. I can only surmise that the kitchen in Heinrich's house must have been carted away by someone who could find some use for its component parts.

The house belonging to my great-grandfather Conrad was built about thirty years after his childhood home and reflected the many changes in housing that had taken place in the meantime. The exterior of the house in 2009 was unchanged from a picture taken in 1910. Most obvious was the large front yard, which would have been ideal for the popular game of croquet. The house included a wraparound porch. Porches were at the height of their popularity between about 1870 and 1930. They could be used as a play area for children, especially when it was raining, or for young couples who wanted some privacy while still remaining under the watchful eyes and ears of their parents. Often equipped with a swing and wicker furniture, they were a semipublic outdoor space associated with the community and neighborliness.[65] Prior to air conditioning they were among the best ways of surviving the heat. They were also favored by presidential candidates like William McKinley, who could speak to reporters and the public without having to leave their homes. Porches were always included in the bungalow style where they often reached from one side of the house to the other. Alas porches were largely eclipsed after 1930 by street noise, air conditioning, and television and survive today, if at all, as a mostly useless ornament like immovable shutters.

My father's memoirs give excellent details about my great-grandfather's backyard, which must have been typical for a prosperous retired farmer who moved to a nearby town. "There was a barn together with a sizeable henhouse, a combination cob and coal shed, and a rather extensive apple and cherry orchard. Of course, there was the then-ubiquitous 'outhouse' which impressed me as a boy because it was a 'three-holer' rather than the usual 'two holer' and because it was approached by an extensive and colorful arbor." There was also Conrad's favorite cow, Bess, whom my father milked after his grandfather moved to Lincoln in 1915, bringing Bess with him. The barn would have housed Conrad's "surrey with the fringe on top" of *Oklahoma!* fame, which my father loved to ride in as a child.[66]

Just inside Conrad's house was the parlor. In the early twentieth century it would have always been clean and ready for guests.

Its furniture would have been formal and gender specific, with large chairs with arms for men and smaller ones without arms to accommodate women with their full skirts.[67] Late Victorian homes were cluttered, especially the parlors, where people displayed valuable family heirlooms and possibly a small organ, a Victrola, or an upright piano, the latter being almost indispensable in a middle-class home.[68] Typical for the time, the parlor in my great-grandfather's house was separated from the clutter of a large kitchen by sliding wooden pocket doors, which could be closed when guests were present. In Conrad's time the kitchen would have included a sink, a cast iron stove, and an icebox, the latter having become commonplace in American homes since the 1880s.[69] The bedrooms were upstairs. Conrad's central steam heating would not have been strong enough to reach them, which was typical for that period.[70] I remember as a child in the 1940s waking up in my frigid bedroom and hurrying downstairs to get dressed where it was warm, thanks to our coal burning furnace.

Conrad's eldest child was my grandfather, Ludwig Heinrich Pauley. Known simply as L. H. or Lou Pauley, he sought a new and challenging environment for his lumberyard profession, moving to Lincoln in 1915 along with my grandmother, Albertina, and my father, Carroll. In 1919 or 1920 he built a California-style house at 2601 B Street in Lincoln. It had all the conveniences that houses have today including a stove, cabinets, and a refrigerator in the kitchen. However, by the 1920s kitchens were no longer the largest, warmest, and most important room in the house, which had often been used for Saturday baths and even childbirth. Next to my grandparents' kitchen was a breakfast room that overlooked the backyard. I well remember that room as I was sometimes forced to stay there for hours because my grandmother did not allow me to leave until I had cleaned my plate. The house also had a basement filled with fascinating antiques that had outlived their usefulness like a cast iron stove and an old Victrola. The biggest room in the basement was used as a voting precinct on election days.

My grandparents' house had an entirely separate bathroom when bathrooms were still considered a luxury even though huge bathing spas had been common in Rome in the second century BC.[71] Located between two bedrooms, it could be entered from either side. It had a big bathtub, sink, and, most importantly, a flush toilet. Toilets, both public and private, had existed in the Roman Empire but disappeared along with the aqueducts that fed them when the empire fell around 500 AD. Indoor toilets were displayed at the Crystal Palace Exhibition in London in 1851 and were mass-produced and sold commercially in the 1880s. Shaving could now also be done almost anywhere thanks to the invention of the safety razor by a Wisconsin man named King Gillette. (First marketed in 1903, it was issued to all American soldiers during the First World War.)[72]

My grandparents' house had no front porch or parlor. However, it did have a good-sized living room with a fireplace at one end and a generous-sized dining room at the opposite end. Products of the Victorian era, dining rooms were popular throughout the twentieth century until television began to encroach on their use in the second half of the century.[73] Until then it was common for all evening and Sunday noon meals to be eaten in a formal dining room. I well remember Sunday meals because as a child my family always ate at my grandmother's house, my grandfather having died in 1946. I did not mind, however, because while waiting for the food, I happily entertained myself by reading my grandmother's subscriptions to the *Saturday Evening Post*, with its Norman Rockwell covers, *Colliers*, and *Life*, all of which were inexpensive in the 1940s and '50s and enjoyed wide circulation.

Like many other Lincolnites at the time, my grandparents had a big garden in the backyard where they grew sweetcorn, potatoes, and tomatoes of which my family were lucky beneficiaries. The backyard also had a horseshoe pit, a sport popular in Nebraska and elsewhere since pioneer times. In one way my grandparents' house was like the big houses of the late Victorian period: it was large enough to house my great-grandmother, Lena Righter, in a second-floor apartment with its own entrance. Missing from the property was a now superfluous hitching post and mounting block next to the curb. However, such remnants of the by then rapidly disappearing age of carriages could still occasionally be found a few blocks to the west of my grandparents' house as late as the 1940s.

The house I grew up in at 1861 Dakota Street was built in 1929. The house's 1,500 square feet was far bigger than the national average of 1,129 in 1930 or 983 in 1950 (today's standard is nearly 2,700 square feet).[74] But like houses built in the early part of the century, as well as during the interwar period, it reflected the declining birthrate of the late nineteenth and early twentieth centuries, when most families had only two or, at most, three children. Unlike Victorian houses it was not nearly large enough to hold an elderly grandparent let alone a boarder or a maid. By the mid-twentieth century, maids, particularly live-in maids, were rapidly disappearing. So our family was typical in having only two children and three bedrooms and a bathroom, all on the second floor. My parents' bedroom was fairly good-sized, but mine was diminutive. It was big enough, however, for a bookcase holding my Hardy Boy detective books and my Tom Swift science fiction novels published early in the twentieth century and reflective of the new interest in science and technology. Our bathroom, also characteristic of the period, was diminutive, having only a bathtub (but no shower), a toilet, and a sink with a medicine cabinet, but no vanity until later. Its size was supposed to make it a model of efficiency; it was more like a model for claustrophobia.[75]

On the ground floor we had a tiny kitchen. Its size was supposed to save steps to make cooking more efficient; its linoleum floor was touted as being easy to clean and easy on the feet because of its relative softness. Kitchens of the interwar period, like ours, were also better equipped than those of the nineteenth century having a stove, refrigerator, and a pantry, the latter filled with canned goods, cereals, and cleaning items. Many houses had a kitchen with an outside entrance so that service people could enter the house directly into the kitchen.[76] Our backyard was also small, just big enough for a clothesline, driveway, tiny patio, and small patch of grass.

All my female ancestors, starting with Conrad's wife, Alice, benefited from a myriad of new household appliances. Carpet sweepers, sewing machines, washing machines, apple peelers, food choppers and slicers, iceboxes (oddly enough known as "refrigerators" early in the twentieth century), coffee grinders, indoor running water, telephones (for the wealthy), and countless other innovations could be ordered through the more than thousand-page Sears, Roebuck catalog. Such items could be delivered to your house a few days later either by regular mail or by Rural Free Delivery, which began service in 1896. Ice for iceboxes as well as milk could be delivered directly to your house on a regular basis by a horse-drawn wagon. If the back of the icebox faced an outside wall the ice man could put the block of ice directly into it. I can vaguely remember such deliveries being brought to kitchens by horse-drawn wagons in Lincoln as late as the end of the Second World War. Iceboxes did not disappear altogether in American homes until the 1950s.

These inventions and discoveries undoubtedly freed up a good deal of time for women who could not afford a servant at a time when they were becoming increasingly scarce. The savings in time, however, must be qualified. Monday was still wash day, and ironing still took up much of Tuesday. Whatever time was saved often resulted in higher standards of cleanliness. For example changing and washing clothes and bed linens once a week might easily be changed to twice a week.

Nevertheless after 1900 most middle-class women, and even those barely within that category, did have more time for entertainment like dancing, concerts, vaudeville, movies, and sports. They also had more time to fight for causes in which they deeply believed: reducing or eliminating smoking, prohibiting the sale of alcoholic beverages, and gaining the vote.

5

Feminine Reformers

The Revolt against the "Two Spheres" Ideal

As American women were graduating from high schools and colleges in large numbers, entering new professions, becoming more physically fit, and beginning to wear clothes a little less cumbersome, they sought ways to improve society and enhance their own political influence. Their results were mixed. Engaging in great causes was nothing new for women. They had been circulating and presenting petitions since the Revolution. Until the late nineteenth century, however, most of their reform activities had been devoted to self-improvement and cultural activities such as attending lectures, reading books, and hosting musical events. During the Progressive Era they turned to reform efforts involving schools, libraries, playgrounds, and public health.

One of the most deeply held beliefs of the Victorian era was that men and women had rigidly different spheres of activities. Men being physically stronger should oversee chopping wood, plowing fields, building houses and barns, and protecting home and country. They were also supposedly intellectually superior to women, more decisive, and more emotionally stable, therefore better equipped mentally to serve on juries and to hold political offices. Women, on the other hand, being smaller and physically weaker were ill-suited for most heavy work outside the home such as being a blacksmith, plowing a field, or engaging in construction. Even if some women were stronger, they were too busy dealing with menstruation, pregnancies, raising children, cooking, and cleaning to engage in political activities. They were also supposedly timid, self-indulgent, and attracted to luxury.[1] On the other hand, both genders thought that although women were undoubtedly the "weaker sex," they were "morally superior" to men and therefore worthy of respect.

These beliefs and assumptions were almost universally accepted if not regarded as God-given. The division of labor and moral worth seemed perfectly obvious during the first half of the nineteenth century when pregnancies were frequent. Queen Victoria of Britain, who reigned from 1837 to 1901 and became an international symbol of morals and motherhood, was not unusual for having nine children. For that matter twelve children, or at least twelve pregnancies, were also not uncommon in the nineteenth century and even into the early twentieth. Although older children were expected to help raise their younger siblings when there was no servant to help, it still meant that most women spent nearly all their time rearing children and taking care of the household. Beyond going to church, little time was left for other activities, however worthy they might be. My great-grandfather Conrad Pauley, with his nine children born between 1886 and 1907, was a good example of someone who needed all the field help he could get. On the other hand, my grandfathers Ludwig Pauley and Fred Hulsebus, both of whom avoided farming to become small-town businessmen, each sired only two children.

One should not equate the average size of families in the nineteenth century with the number of pregnancies. A visit to any even moderately old burial site, including Wyuka in Lincoln, will reveal a startling number of tiny, sometimes nameless, gravestones often accompanied by sculptured lambs for infants who never even reached their first birthday. It is also common to see the graves of three wives, the first two having died in childbirth.

Despite the prevalence of large families, the birthrate was declining in nineteenth-century America, especially in its second half. Toward the end of the century, there was a steady decline in infant mortality, which accelerated after 1900. The advertising of contraceptives and methods to terminate pregnancies published in women's magazines must have also played a role in the decline.[2] The diminution of family size, together with labor-saving devices and shorter working hours, finally gave women some time for social activities.

Almost from its founding, Lincoln was filled with clubs.[3] Some were just for women, but many included both genders. Others were part of national organizations such as the Women's Christian Temperance Union (WCTU), which was founded in 1874. It became one of the country's leading temperance organizations in the 1880s and 1890s when it had 150,000 dues-paying members.[4] One of its favorite tactics for several years was to hold prayer meetings in saloons. Another was to open a reading room, for example, on South Eleventh Street in Lincoln where they offered coffee and meals to compete with the free meals offered by saloons.[5] Older temperance organizations had espoused the abolitionist cause on the slavery issue, thereby impairing the anti-alcohol crusade in the South. The word "temperance," which was used by the WCTU and other like-minded organizations, was a misnomer; in practice the organization was opposed to the consumption of *any* form of alcoholic beverage and in *any* quantity. The word "Christian" clearly identified the organization with Christianity, but it was composed primarily of denominations then considered evangelical: Methodists, Congregationalists, Presbyterians, and Baptists. They did not reach out to Roman Catholics, Lutherans, or Episcopalians. In retrospect it appears possible that the WCTU and other alcohol reform groups might have had greater success if they had promoted good judgment in drinking and tried harder to clean up the sometimes-sleazy reputation of saloons, which often tolerated prostitution and drunkenness.

Reformist movements, whether they were fighting the consumption of cigarettes or alcohol, or were seeking enfranchisement for women, were marked by other common characteristics besides religion. Those in Lincoln and throughout the Midwest and East were supported by families of well-above-average wealth, enabling them to have at least one servant and considerable free time. In fact married, middle-class women were expected *not* to work. Most important of all, these movements' members were high school or college graduates and therefore highly literate. They also tended to be from families who could trace their heritage back several generations to Britain or other parts of western Europe. Most of them were high-minded, being devoted to music, science, literature, and philanthropy. They were *not* likely to include Black people, Catholics, Jews, or first- or second-generation immigrants from southern or eastern Europe whose English skills were usually poor to nonexistent. We have already seen how Chancellor Canfield at the University of Nebraska encouraged faculty to give presentations related to their expertise to interested organizations in Lincoln and throughout the state.

It follows that reformers were among the hundreds of thousands of readers of newspapers and magazines whose circulations were multiplying in the late nineteenth century. In 1885 there were only four magazines in the United States that had a circulation of at least 350,000. By 1905 there were twenty such magazines. By 1905 the *Saturday Evening Post* alone had a circulation of more than two million.[6] Meanwhile the circulation of newspapers was growing equally fast. In the early twentieth century, the average American family purchased more than three different newspapers, not including magazines, whose growth was also exploding.[7] During the 1880s Lincoln daily newspapers were just four pages long, eight on Sunday. By 1900 average weekday newspapers had grown to eight pages, sixteen on Sunday. Fifteen years later weekday papers were sixteen pages long, forty-four on Sunday.

After 1900 the papers typically had columns about travel and leisure, personal advice, fashions, comics, and sports in addition to a good deal of local, national, and international news. Not surprisingly they were also far longer than their predecessors, which in 1885 were only half as long. Cheaper newsprint and a rapidly growing number of advertisements of fashions and patent medicines enabled both newspapers and magazines to sell for less. The *New York Times* cost one cent, and magazines like the *Saturday Evening Post* sold for a nickel, which even if multiplied by twenty-five made such publications a bargain.[8]

Female reformers could rely heavily on the latest scientific discoveries on the dangers of smoking and heavy alcohol consumption and find inspiration from nationally renowned people such as Henry Ford and his friend Thomas Edison. Other men contributed money to the women's reform efforts, which were often short of cash. Reformers in Lincoln could also count on the backing of the administrations of the University of Nebraska, Nebraska Wesleyan, Union College, and Cotner College.

Cigarettes: "A Plain Case of Self-Destruction"

Coinciding with the growth of clubs, especially women's clubs, along with the rapid increase in the circulation of periodical literature, was the explosive growth in cigarette smoking after 1885. The common denominators in such growth were mass production and cheaper paper used for magazines, newspapers, and even cigarettes that drastically reduced their cost. Meanwhile the rapid expansion of high school and college graduates multiplied the audience for scientific discoveries.

Cigarette smoking was particularly alarming to well-educated Lincolnites. The smoking of cigars in English-speaking North America is nearly as old as the founding of the British colonies. However, cigar smoking was expensive, and the smoking of cigarettes, which had to be individually hand rolled, was almost equally costly. In 1880 a cigarette manufacturing machine was invented that fed a continuous strip of paper into a tube that formed cylinders; a rotary knife cut the cylinders into identical lengths. Each machine could do the work of fifty hand rollers. Still other machines could automatically package and label twenty cigarettes per pack. The machines drastically cut the cost of cigarettes and enormously increased the number sold. It was not long before cigarette companies, the advertising industry, and magazines and newspapers discovered each other. The sale of cigarettes could be multiplied through advertising in newspapers and magazines, which in turn could increase their profits by publishing the advertisements. By 1920 the number of cigarette smokers in the United States was sixteen times greater than it had been in 1900.[9] To their credit, prior to the First World War, Lincoln's newspapers and the University of Nebraska student paper, the *Daily Nebraskan*, resisted the temptation to advertise cigarettes even though the latter desperately needed the revenue.[10]

The administration of the University of Nebraska was adamantly opposed to smoking in the early twentieth century. Acting chancellor Charles E. Bessey said that "for a young man to indulge in the practice until it becomes a habit is a plain case of self-destruction." He frequently walked out of meetings that took place in smoke-filled rooms. (Such smoke-filled rooms, with ashtrays on every other chair, still existed when I was attending historical conventions in the 1960s.) However, even a ban against smoking on campus did not prevent students, particularly in the College of Law, from wanting a smoking room in the college's basement. Nor did the ban prevent students from rushing to the gates of the university to sneak in a quick smoke between classes.[11]

The sudden increase in cigarette smoking was noticed immediately in Lincoln's newspapers. The Lincoln chapter of the wctu, best known for its campaign against alcohol consumption, was equally alarmed by the increasing use of narcotics, patent medicines containing alcohol, and especially cigarettes by all classes in Lincoln, including children.[12] At a meeting held in August 1885 it was noted that discarded cigar butts were being used to make cigarettes. The inhalation of the smoke from these cigarettes, according to the minutes of the meeting, "was injurious to the sensitive organ issues of children. . . . Nicotine was one of the deadliest poisons known to the pharmacologists."[13] The *Lincoln Evening Call* noted five years later that "despite . . . the thundering of the medical press the cigarette business has grown steadily, and the entire output of the factories today is fully one-third greater than that of two years ago."[14]

State superintendent W. K. Fowler maintained that the most common cigarette smokers were eleven- and twelve-year-old boys.[15] A more collective and direct action against cigarette smoking, especially by young boys, occurred in 1910, when Lincoln's principals condemned what were commonly called "coffin nails." The situation was obviously serious because one school reported that 70 out of 250 boys aged fifteen to seventeen were addicted to smoking. The boys made various excuses for smoking, including the claim that smoking was a remedy for colds. Superintendent W. L. Stephens closed a meeting of educators by suggesting that "no boy be allowed to represent his school on any team who used tobacco in any form."[16]

For many years the campaign against smoking was directed primarily against cigarettes, although chewing tobacco was hardly less reputable, probably because it involved spitting. Because of the cheap cost, cigarettes appealed primarily to working-class people, vagrants, and boys. The more expensive habit of smoking pipes or cigars was confined mostly to relatively wealthy men and never acquired the stigma associated with cigarettes. Consequently a law passed by the Nebraska State Legislature in 1905 was directed exclusively against the "sale, manufacturing, or distribution of cigarettes." Ultimately, however, the law failed because it did not actually forbid smoking and could not prevent cigarettes from being shipped into the state or from being made at home.[17] In 1919 the law was repealed not just because it had been ineffective, as one Nebraska historian assumed, but because cigarettes had been given to soldiers by the army and by the YMCA![18] The *Lincoln Star* also thought that the law "was conducive to disrespect for all laws."[19]

The increase in cigarette smoking was not confined to boys. The *Lincoln Star* published an article in 1910 lamenting that smoking cigarettes had become quite fashionable among women. In the same year, fashionable jewelers in Washington DC were carrying a large supply of women's cigarette cases, which men quite often gave as presents to women.[20] The old-fashioned idea of women leaving so men could smoke their cigarettes at the table had almost entirely disappeared. A Catholic priest in Washington DC was quoted as saying that "the habit of smoking is to be more strongly condemned for women than for men because of their greater standing in the social scale." Another priest said that "society demands a different ethical code for women for its own protection."[21]

The campaign against smoking diminished after the First World War, perhaps in part because of the war itself. Compared to the more than 120,000 Americans who died in the war and the tens of thousands more who were maimed, the negative effects of smoking were less obvious, or even seemed trivial. Although many Americans (including my parents) still believed that smoking was harmful to one's health, no convincing scientific proof had been presented that it caused lung cancer. By 1920 cigarettes were more socially accepted than ever. In February the *Lincoln Star* quoted movie actress Constance Binney saying, "[Smoking is] charming and stunning. . . . Five or six cigarettes a day will do no harm."[22] The possible effects of secondhand smoke inhalation had not yet even been suggested. A New York judge announced in January 1920 that smoking was not immoral: "Some of the best women in the country and in the world smoke cigarettes. . . . This isn't Hickville."[23]

22. "Leave It to Camels!" *Nebraska State Journal*, July 8, 1920, 2.

In Lincoln the sale of cigarettes increased rapidly after 1900 and then exponentially after the end of the First World War in 1918.[24] This can be seen in the number of times "cigarette" was used in Lincoln newspapers—1880, 16 times; 1890, 186 times; 1900, 187 times; 1914, 487 times; 1920, 885 times; 1930, 1,852 times. The number of references to cigarettes actually declined in Lincoln during the Great Depression—1,825 in 1940—but this was likely due to advertisements appearing in magazines and on the radio instead of in newspapers.

What never changed after about 1918 was that the word cigarette usually appeared in ads touting the virtues of brand-name cigarettes such as Camel and Lucky Strike, which cost 20 cents and came in beautifully wrapped packages of twenty. Ultimately it was during America's involvement in the First World War that our soldiers became addicted to smoking. As is clear from the aforementioned statistics, the habit carried over to their civilian lives and effectively ended the campaign against smoking. Cigarette companies may have convinced "society women" that smoking was modern and fashionable.[25]

Although the effects of smoking on the individual were well known in the nineteenth century, smoking bans were often considered a violation of personal freedom. Even the announcement by the surgeon general of the United States in 1964 that smoking was dangerous to one's health merely caused only a brief decline in cigarette sales. A dramatic decline in cigarette sales occurred only when extensive research proved that the inhalation of *secondhand* smoke could cause heart disease, cancer, emphysema, and other diseases. This discovery led to laws banning smoking in public places. In 2004, 62 percent of Lincolnites voted to ban smoking in public establishments, which was followed the next year by the Nebraska State Legislature enacting a similar law.[26]

Saloons and Prohibition: "The Vanguard of Progress"?

The most that can be said for the women farsighted enough to condemn smoking between 1890 and 1920 is that they probably convinced a good many people that smoking was bad for their health. However, they certainly did not reduce the total number sold. The Methodist Church, to which my parents and grandparents belonged, frowned on smoking but did not condemn it unequivocally.

Besides cigarettes there were a good many other practices and concepts that were condemned by (mostly) middle-class moralists, including card playing and gambling, horse racing, dance halls, Sabbath breaking, pornography, prostitution, divorce, and contraception. One issue, however, stood above all the others: alcoholic beverages.[27] Alcohol consumption was denounced unequivocally by Methodist ministers despite the Bible's frequent references to wine. Wine could not even be used in Holy Communion; grape juice was used instead. Women's organizations in Lincoln and throughout the United States had far more success in their campaign against alcohol, although here too their achievements were limited and ultimately not long-lasting.

The crusade against alcoholic beverages attracted more women than any other nineteenth- and early twentieth-century cause. It was by no means a new issue in Nebraska. The first session of the territorial legislature in 1855 banned its production and sale, although the law was flagrantly ignored and repealed in 1858.[28] As early as the late 1880s, Lincoln alone had thirteen temperance societies.[29] The cause was not frivolous because many men did spend money on alcohol—money that could have been put to much more productive use at home. Men who came home drunk late at night were prone to abuse their wives and children. The problem, then, was real although at times exaggerated. Lincoln businessmen reasoned that money spent on alcohol could more profitably be spent on clothing and household necessities as well as medicine.[30]

The "all or nothing" attitude of most prohibitionists was a problem. The "wets" regarded prohibition, at a minimum, as an attack on their personal freedom. Many of them regarded saloons as a place of "nutrition, relaxation, and conviviality."[31] Ethnic Germans in particular, whether they were from Germany, Austria-Hungary, or the Volga and Black Sea regions of Russia, regarded prohibition as an attack on their very culture, which they were not about to surrender. Getting drunk, they believed, was the crime, not drinking itself. Families drinking beer together in a biergarten or tavern—while singing and dancing accompanied by a brass band— was simply part of their heritage. This distinction was especially important in Nebraska where more than 20 percent of the population was of first- or second-generation ethnic German origin. Saloons of all types often had the only free toilets in many cities. They all supplied their customers with newspapers, cashed their checks, and even lent money. They would provide newcomers, including recent immigrants, with a temporary mailing address and a place where they could leave messages.[32] Many saloons across the United States served what was called a "free lunch," which, although not quite free, cost only 5 cents between eleven in the morning and three o'clock in the afternoon. Not surprisingly the meal included salty items that encouraged more drinking just as bars today often serve free popcorn to stimulate thirst.

The prohibition movement was closely related to the huge increase in immigration between 1870 and the outbreak of the First World War in 1914. During this period there was a dramatic increase in the number of saloons, which ballooned from one hundred thousand in 1870 to three hundred thousand three decades later. The prohibitionists came mostly from middle-class families that had been in the United States at least three generations and wanted to Americanize the immigrants by eliminating their cultural roots and ancestral languages.[33] They were also most likely to be Methodists, Congregationalists, and Presbyterians whose churches were never stronger in membership, revenues, and attendance than they were at the beginning of the twentieth century.[34]

The campaign against alcohol united women's organizations like no other cause, probably not even the suffrage question. Alcohol abuse was not just a social problem but lay well within the sphere of the family, where women were supposed to be in charge. A nineteenth-century married woman was legally at the mercy of an alcoholic husband.[35] If anything it was more of a local or regional problem than it was a national one. By 1912 two-thirds of the territory of the United States, home to half the country's population, was already "dry."[36] The most ardent proponents of temperance, however, were not yet satisfied. If state legislatures could approve laws outlawing the sale of alcohol, they might later vote to reinstate the legality of alcohol. An amendment to the Constitution would presumably be different since no amendment had ever been reversed.

Prohibitionists were active in Nebraska long before alcohol was prohibited nationwide by the Eighteenth Amendment in 1920. A statewide vote held in 1890—in which women, of course, were not allowed to vote—saw prohibition advocates winning 88,392 votes to 111,728 opposing the measure. The difference was almost certainly due to Omaha, where several breweries were located. Not until November 7, 1916, did the issue come up again for a vote when prohibition was adopted 146,574 in favor and 117,532 opposed, effective May 1, 1917.[37]

Elsewhere state legislatures had voted for full abolition because they had been virtually coerced to do so by the Anti-Saloon League, which had been founded in 1893. Earlier attempts to legislate prohibition had depended on individual politicians who would take up the cause of prohibition or convince a political party to endorse the cause. Several efforts to do so failed. The Anti-Saloon League had a completely different strategy, being the first "one issue" organization in American politics. Its name was misleading; in reality it promised to give its full support to *any* candidate who opposed not just saloons but the sale of *all* alcoholic beverages and to oppose any candidate who did not.[38] Such a tactic was especially effective in an election where a shift of 10 percent of the vote could be decisive. According to one Nebraska historian, "The Anti-Saloon League probably did more than any other group in Nebraska to translate temperance conviction into political action. . . . Nebraska Anti-Saloon Leaguers regarded themselves not as the last defenders of a besieged culture but as the vanguard of progress, leading the way to a more moral, stable, efficient, prosperous, and equitable society."[39]

The temperance movement greatly benefited from the ratification of the Sixteenth Amendment in 1913, which legalized the income tax. The tax was very modest and affected only 1 percent of taxpayers at the time. But nothing could prevent it from being raised later, especially during the two world wars. The most important consequence in the short run was that the functioning of the federal government was no longer highly dependent on the tax on alcoholic beverages.

Lincoln, including all four of its institutions of higher education, was an early and, on the whole, ardent supporter of prohibition.[40] Its thirteen temperance societies helped temporarily outlaw alcohol sales in the city's twenty-five saloons—all concentrated in the downtown area between Eighth and Twelfth Streets—by a close vote in 1909.[41] American saloons varied enormously from very humble and perhaps sleazy to highly reputable and sophisticated. The range was probably not a lot different from our fast-food restaurants to the ones that advertise "fine dining." What the prohibitionists in the Anti-Saloon League did not understand was that the brewing industry could survive quite well without saloons.[42]

Proponents of prohibition were families that had come from the northern or eastern states. Of Lincoln's fifty-one churches, only two were Roman Catholic; among the denominations the Methodists and Presbyterians were most strongly in favor of prohibition. Like other prohibitionists they believed that saloons helped perpetuate drinking, which in turn undermined values of "family, thrift, social order, democracy, and community prosperity."[43] The opponents of prohibition in Lincoln were much the same as they were elsewhere in the United States: first- and second-generation Germans from central Europe. In Omaha there were also recent Irish and Italian immigrants equally opposed to the ban. Omaha wets thought that closing the city's breweries would lead to an overall decline in business activity. An even larger group of opponents were the four thousand ethnic Germans who had recently immigrated to Lincoln from the Volga and Black Sea regions of Russia to be discussed in chapter 8.[44]

The narrow victory of Lincoln's prohibitionists in 1909 to close the city's saloons was only temporary. Wets in the state legislature were alarmed by the passage of a statewide law in the same year forcing saloons to close at 8:00 p.m. They believed the law would threaten Omaha's breweries as well as the city's prosperity. In a bid to win the support of outstate voters, the wets inside and outside the legislature, particularly in such towns as Grand Island and Kearney, proposed relocating the state capital from Lincoln's site near the southeastern corner of the state to a more centralized location.[45] The threat was enough to reverse the 1909 vote by an equally narrow margin in another election in 1911.[46]

The proponents of saloons may have made a fundamental error in maintaining the saloon's all-male customers. In theory at least, accommodating ladies by having a "ladies' day" at least once a week, for example, might have won over some of the less militant opponents of saloons. In practice, however, it took the far more permissive atmosphere of the 1920s and early 1930s to end prohibition and introduce the idea of moderate alcohol consumption.

In the meantime in 1916 Nebraska voters approved a statewide prohibition amendment, with the law going into effect in 1917, by a vote of 146,574 to 117,532.[47] At the national level the coercive efforts of the Anti-Saloon League combined with the wartime hatred of German Americans, breweries owned by German Americans, and the German Empire itself made prohibition seem like a patriotic duty.[48] "On August 1, 1917, the U.S. Senate passed a resolution containing the language of the Eighteenth Amendment to be presented to the states for ratification."[49] The House of Representatives followed suit on December 17, 1917. Then on January 16, 1919, Nebraska, by a vote of 98 to 0 in the lower house, became the decisive thirty-sixth state to ratify the amendment, which went into effect the next year.[50] Ironically there is a question as to whether all Americans realized that they were supporting total abstinence, which included beer and wine along with liquor.

Lincoln newspapers welcomed the ratification of the amendment. The *Nebraska State Journal*'s only regret was that "the corpse, with its smell, will be allowed to remain one year above ground."[51] The *Lincoln Star* noted that prohibitionists regarded ratification as the greatest moral legislation in the history of the world: "Never before had a great nation by popular consent, taken away the rights of all for the purpose of producing better morals." The *Star* added that "the sentiment is growing that the citizens of the United States will never repeal the prohibition amendment." It went on to say that "it remains for those of another century possibly the next, to speak wisely of the virtues and visas of national prohibition. They will be able to look back upon the federal amendment ratified in 1919 and proclaim the legislators fools or salons."[52]

William Jennings Bryan, who considered alcohol a "poison," approved of the amendment but was astute in saying that "we must enforce the law. Laws are not self-enforceable. The believers in prohibition must . . . see to it that the enforcement of this law is not entrusted to those who are in sympathy with its violation."[53] He had good reason for this belief. On the same day the *Lincoln Star* reported that three Nebraskans had just been arrested for possession of whiskey, sour wine, and beer.[54]

The amendment did succeed in shutting down saloons and reduced the consumption of alcohol, at least among poor and middle-class people, and may have improved the health of some Americans. On the other hand, until its repeal in 1933, drunkenness and disorderly conduct increased by 41 percent, arrests for drunk driving jumped by 81 percent, and assaults and batteries were up by 13 percent.[55] The homicide rate alone rose 78 percent. In a broader sense, the amendment encouraged a culture of bribery, blackmail, and official corruption.[56] The prohibitionist assumed that the amendment would be voluntarily obeyed and made no provision for its enforcement. The federal government was loath to spend revenue for compelling obedience. Fortunately the repeal of the amendment in 1933 did not result in a resumption of pre-prohibition levels of alcoholic consumption but led instead to state codes regulating closing hours, age limits, and Sunday blue laws.

About seventeen or eighteen years after the repeal of prohibition in 1933, I became personally aware that the issue of alcohol was by no means dead in the minds of Methodist ministers. While attending a Methodist youth camp near Cozad, Nebraska, our counselors made it clear that alcohol was still an utterly immoral beverage. Two of these counselors, as I recall, were about fifty. Most likely they could remember the campaign against alcohol and the repeal of the Eighteenth Amendment. One of them declared to our group of twelve- and thirteen-year-olds that it was better to commit suicide than it was to be a bartender; the former, he said, takes only one life, whereas the latter ruins the lives of many individuals.

Women For and Against Suffrage: "Masculine Womanhood"?

The campaigns against cigarettes and alcohol were carried out primarily by white, native-born, Protestant, middle-class women. By 1920 there were some women who enjoyed smoking, or at least minimized its dangers, but few claimed that smoking cigarettes was completely harmless. Such near uniformity of opinion did not exist among women concerning the benefits of female suffrage. Not only were there women who did not support the suffrage movement, there were many who actively *opposed* it, a subject that has been relatively unexplored.[57] Certainly no other protest movement at the turn of the century engendered so much public debate. Those for and against female suffrage ironically came mostly from the middle class. Working-class women, not to mention women on farms, were simply too busy—and probably too tired—because of their jobs and families to participate in the issue, one way or the other.[58]

One opponent of suffrage argued that "suffrage is but the first decisive step toward feminism with its attendant train of masculine womanhood and effeminate manhood."[59] Another opponent, John Webster, an Omaha attorney, introduced Mrs. A. J. George, an anti-suffrage lecturer, by saying that "Abraham Lincoln made a mistake in [enfranchising] . . . negroes. The world is now facing a similar calamity in considering the extension of equal suffrage to women. . . . Mrs. George endorsed these views and said that 'if the negro women are given the right to vote a rebellion is sure to follow.'"[60] The *Lincoln Star* reported that the meeting, held in Omaha in October 1914, was "attended by a society gathering. Mr. Webster was attired in full dress as were many of the men in the audience, and the women were elaborately gowned. The theatre was surrounded by limousines and the boxes were filled with parties of Omaha's society women."[61]

Opponents of suffrage were far more likely to be Roman Catholics, who were ethnic Germans, Irish, Polish, French, Dutch, or Bohemian, with the German Catholics being the most conservative. According to the census of 1880, more than a third of eligible voters were foreign born (44,864) compared to 128,082 natives.[62] Altogether Roman Catholics composed 29 percent of Nebraska's pre–World War I population. Opposition also came from turn-of-the-century Democrats, but not from William Jennings Bryan, who favored laissez-faire economics, personal liberty, and social conservatism. Such foes were especially strong in the "Solid South." Even the General Federation of Women's Clubs, by far the most socially active group of women in the nation, refused to endorse women's suffrage for many years. The men's anti-suffrage associations were much smaller and less well-organized than those led by women. They were, however, at times especially useful to women by serving as cover for issues that women did not want to oppose openly. They also provided funding for anti-suffrage campaigns.[63]

Many women in the United States and Europe, probably a large majority, subscribed to long-held Victorian beliefs about their virtues. Their role as mother, caretaker of the family, and upholder of traditional morality was almost universally accepted not only by women but by most men as well. But proponents of female suffrage argued that if women really did possess all the ideals and virtues ascribed to them, it would be a great benefit to society if they brought them into the political arena. Opponents of female suffrage, including some women, argued that political activities and jury duty would do more to degrade women's feminine virtues than they would to improve society. They would be caught up in partisanship and would lose their position as society's moral arbiters and enforcers.[64]

Women opposed to suffrage also argued that by avoiding partisanship they could be more effective in campaigning for causes specifically related to their gender, like pregnancy and childbirth, childcare, public education, and working outside the home. Suffrage would cause a dramatic increase in divorce, which would force many women to enter the labor force, thus overburdening women already busy with childcare.[65] The *Omaha Weekly Tribune and Republican* on June 21, 1871, opined that "women's position has been fixed by those inalienable and divine laws which are higher and more absolute than any legal enactments. The vote would infect the entire social order—religion, morality, and virtue."[66]

The views of women opposed to voting were distinctly expressed by November 1900:

> We stand . . . for the rights and duties of humanity in the home, the right of women to loving maintenance and protection, the right of men to material comforts and affectionate sympathy and co-operation, the birthright of children to a sound physique, affectionate care, in such moral and spiritual instruction as are calculated to make them worthy men and women and good citizens: such instruction as is scarcely to be found elsewhere than at the mother's knee. . . . We believe this social order to be founded upon sound morality, and to be supported by the experience of Christian civilization.[67]

A widely accepted misconception about voting rights for women is that all rights were first enacted by the Nineteenth Amendment in 1920. Women were allowed to vote in school district meetings in 1869, Nebraska being the second state in the country to make that possible.[68] In fact women already had the right to vote in all elections, local or federal, in most states west of the Mississippi. In only nine states were women denied the vote in all instances, whether it be for the local sheriff or for the president of the United States. Seven of those states were among the original thirteen colonies, which were responsible for the Constitution and the Bill of Rights.[69]

In 1856 Amelia Bloomer, the same woman who had advocated for the apparel that came to be called "bloomers," attempted to persuade the Nebraska Territorial Legislature to grant women the vote. If she had succeeded, it would have given Nebraska "the honor of becoming the first American commonwealth to grant full suffrage to women."[70] In 1871 the all-male electorate rejected giving women the vote 12,406 to 3,502.[71] All the western states were interested in attracting women, who were in short supply. In Wyoming, where men outnumbered women six to one, the legislature was the first to enfranchise women in 1869. Utah's legislature followed suit a year later. In 1893 Colorado became the first state to enfranchise women by *popular vote*. Utah gave women the right to vote in 1895 to preserve its Mormon hegemony at a time when it was being threatened by the arrival of "gentiles."[72] By 1914 twelve western states had granted women the right to vote in all elections.

Although the United States was the first country in the world to have a women's suffrage movement dating back at least as far as 1848, New Zealand was the first *country* to give women the right to vote in 1893 followed by Australia in 1902, Norway in 1906, and Finland in 1913. On the other hand, Switzerland, in many respects one of the most democratic countries in the world, did not give women the right to vote in national elections until 1971. Switzerland's tiny neighbor, Liechtenstein, held back until 1984.

Nebraska had its own chapter of the Women's Suffrage Association (NWSA), which held its first true delegate convention in Kearney in 1881. In the same year Nebraska women won the right to vote in school matters.[73] The next year one of the earliest leaders of the women's suffrage movement, Susan B. Anthony, attracted a huge crowd in Grand Island and again in Hastings and Seward. Later that year the NWSA initiated the third and final *attempt* to amend the Nebraska Constitution (the first two being in 1856 and 1871) to make Nebraska the first *state* (Wyoming and Utah had approved female suffrage while still territories) to approve suffrage for women by a *referendum*.

In a speech in Omaha in September, Miss Anthony argued that a similar referendum in Colorado had recently failed to pass even though "native-born white men, temperance men, liberal-minded decent men voted for it. Against it were the rank and file of Mexicans in southern Colorado, miners, foreigners, Germans, and Irish. The Negro also voted against it."[74] She was equally skeptical that the support of three-quarters of the state's newspapers would be decisive in Nebraska's suffrage amendment scheduled for November 1882. She told a supporter that "the difficulty is that the men who will vote will neither go out to lectures nor read tracts or newspapers. They cannot be reached by our educational instrumentalities—they are amenable only to bribes and bitters, neither, nor both of which can we stoop to."[75]

However, the suffrage amendment in Nebraska in 1882 was defeated in a statewide election 50,693 to 25,756. Neither the Republicans nor the Democrats supported the amendment, leaving the suffragists isolated against the well-organized opposition led by opponents who linked women's suffrage with prohibition. The vote was decisive in causing Susan B. Anthony to reject "work at the state level to focus instead on working for a federal constitutional amendment," thus making a dramatic turning point in Anthony's approach to women's suffrage. "Women's rights advocates [who had] hoped to transform national politics by changing their state constitution . . . were to be disappointed. . . . While Nebraska's early suffrage initiatives failed, they were key historical moments shaping the trajectory of the national women's rights movement that ultimately led to a strategy to amend the United States Constitution."[76]

In the meantime in 1890 the two largest suffrage organizations, the American National Women Suffrage Association and the National Women Suffrage Association, completed a merger to become the National American Woman Suffrage Association, or NAWSA.[77] It became the largest and most important advocate of women's right to vote. The era between 1896 and 1910, however, came to be known by the suffragettes as the "doldrums" when no more states gained the right to vote and the death of Susan B. Anthony in 1906 created a vacuum of leadership.[78]

During this period Nebraskan women did their part to keep the movement alive by sending a petition to Congress with the signatures of ten thousand citizens, a third of them men. A major turning point in the suffragette movement was a march on Washington DC on March 3, 1913, the first suffragette parade in Washington.

Organized by Alice Paul and Lucy Burns of the National Women's Suffrage Association, the timing of the parade, one day before Woodrow Wilson's inauguration, was designed to attract maximum publicity and to serve notice to the incoming president that suffrage would be a key issue during his term. Some of the marchers literally walked 250 miles to reach Washington. The *Nebraska State Journal* called the reception of the march "one of the most remarkable street demonstrations ever seen [in Washington]."[79]

The media estimated that upwards of half a million people watched the spectacular parade, which consisted of an estimated five to ten thousand marchers. Among the marchers were twenty-six floats, six golden chariots, ten bands, forty-five captains, and two hundred marshals. Each group of marchers was color coded. The first group represented countries that already had female suffrage: New Zealand, Australia, Norway, and Finland. Thereafter were floats and groups representing traditional roles of motherhood and homemaking, professional women including teachers, librarians, and nurses, and nontraditional professionals such as businesswomen, lawyers, actresses, and artists. There was a float depicting the Bill of Rights followed by a banner showing the nine states already having female suffrage.[80]

The parade was marred by hecklers and small groups of men who lunged at the marchers, spat on them, pulled their hair, and slapped and cursed them. Boy Scouts, who had volunteered to hold the lines, were helpless to stop the mob. "The frightening scenes . . . described for days in the newspapers, probably did more than the pageantry itself to stir support for women's suffrage. . . . A common tendency at the time to see the women's movement as a joke changed if not wholly to unqualified support, then certainly to a measure of sympathy. . . . Many more now took the movement seriously and were thus less detached."[81] The *Nebraska State Journal* echoed these sentiments by saying that "so far as the suffragists were concerned, they have reason to be satisfied with the event. It supports their claim that the chivalry men talk about is a pretense, and that women in their present position have not the respect of men. Such an incident advertises the movement and excites sympathy for it among people with a sense of fairness. It will pay the anti-suffragists to see that no such luck befalls future suffrage parades."[82]

Although the attacks on the marchers were far less brutal than those carried out by Alabama state troopers against six hundred civil rights workers at the Edmund Pettus bridge in Selma in March 1965, both incidents proved to be turning points. Alice Paul, organizer of the suffragist parade, believed that the attacks would have a lasting visual effect, which proved true not only for suffragists, but also for their opponents, including women. Women gaining the right to vote in Kansas in 1912, Illinois in 1913, and Nevada and Montana in 1914 convinced Nebraska's female anti-suffragists that they had to take the movement seriously. Although there had been a women's anti-suffragist organization since 1911, not until 1914 was there such an organization in Nebraska. The female anti-suffragists did not cling to the Victorian concept of womanhood but argued that the ballot would hamper women's unique contributions to society in terms of social reforms and charity. Indeed their contributions in these areas would be hampered because they would no longer be disinterested parties. They also feared a doubling of the divorce rate. Like pro-suffragists, they appealed to racist, nativist, and class-based attitudes that were common in the early twentieth century.[83] Both groups attacked their opponents by claiming that they had connection with German imports.

Nebraska suffragists did not simply disappear following the disappointing referendum of 1882. Annual conventions of the NWSA took place every year except 1893, when they turned their attention to the world's fair in Chicago. In other years they set up information booths at Chautauqua assemblies, Grand Army of the Republic encampments, Old Settlers picnics, Epworth League conferences, and at state and county fairs. They also asked clergymen to preach pro-suffrage sermons and organized debates about the suffrage question in high schools around the state, just to name a few of their activities.[84]

In 1911 Lincoln suffragettes were inspired by a visit from Mrs. Emmeline Pankhurst, the leader of a militant British movement for women's suffrage. In an address to nearly 1,400 people in the city auditorium on Thirteenth and M Streets, she likened the struggle of British women to get the vote to "the American struggle to throw off British rule." According to the *Lincoln Star*, she "was given a rousing applause as she concluded her lecture."[85]

The last referendum on women's suffrage to be held before the American entry into World War I convened in Nebraska in November 1914. This time women were remarkably well organized. A full year before the vote for the amendment to the Nebraska Constitution, the thirty-third annual convention of the NWSA was held in Lincoln. Its purpose was to ensure that the state campaign would employ "every ounce of energy . . . to attain success." Suffrage organizations were also organized at the county level.[86]

Facilitating their efforts was the nearly three-fold increase in available railroad mileage from 1,868 miles in 1880 to 5,144 miles in 1890, making campaigning much easier and more efficient.[87] Moreover automobiles were now available for campaigning, especially in southeastern Nebraska if rains had not turned roads into quagmires. For example groups of twenty prominent women and men from Omaha, enjoying the comradery and convenience provided by automobiles, drove to surrounding towns to speak on the suffrage question.[88] It was now possible for suffragettes to hold meetings in three or four towns in a single day.[89] "Posters advocating woman suffrage were distributed in the appropriate areas in the Czech language, in German and in Danish. The burden of their message was that home life would not be injured . . . and that women were seeking simple justice, not an opportunity to revolutionize society."[90] Other suffragettes were busy with their grassroot activities by hosting picnics. In Lincoln suffragettes went house to house in an attempt to spread their message.[91]

On Saturday, October 3, 1914, three thousand voters were contacted by means of automobile parties in all parts of Lancaster County. Similar efforts were made across the state.[92] To increase the turnout, music was provided, which included soloists, quartets, a children's chorus singing suffrage songs, and even bands.[93] Out-of-state help was provided by Dr. Anna Howard Shaw, the president of the National Equal Suffrage Association, who came to Nebraska in the middle of the month and was the featured speaker in huge meetings in the sixteen towns she visited.[94]

However, suffragettes in Lincoln were not dependent on outside help. A very active campaigner was Dr. Inez Philbrick, who was elected president of the NWSA in March 1911. A physician, she was appointed to the Lincoln Board of Health in 1914.[95] Still active in the cause were two women, Mrs. Ada Bittenbender and Mrs. D. G. King, both of Lincoln, who had been involved in the campaign of 1881.[96] Prominent men in Lincoln also supported female suffrage including Chancellor Samuel Avery, Governor Chester Aldrich, and many other local leaders in business and other professions.[97]

The climax of the suffrage campaign in Lancaster County was an outdoor rally held on the corner of Thirteenth and O Streets in the heart of downtown Lincoln on October 24 at 7:30 in the evening. A large crowd turned out in part because the rally came before a football game the next day between the Cornhuskers and the Michigan (State) Aggies (Nebraska won, 24–0).

Ultimately the suffragettes lost the statewide vote on November 4 with 90,738 *men* voting for the measure and 100,842 against it.[98] Voters in Lincoln and Lancaster County favored the referendum 6,117 to 5,227. The outcome in Omaha and Douglas County, despite many breweries owned by German Americans and patronized by many immigrants, surprisingly conformed to the statewide 10-to-9 ratio, with 10,654 voters opposed to female suffrage while 9,486 men favored the amendment.[99] The referendum, even though disappointing for its supporters, showed that suffragettes had made encouraging progress since 1882. The opposition to female suffrage had gone from a 3.5-to-1 ratio in 1858 to 2-to-1 in 1882 to 10-to-9 in 1914. The suffragettes also gained a good deal of respect for their cause. The *Omaha Bee*, which admitted to not supporting the cause, complimented the ladies handsomely upon the manner in which they carried on their campaign:

> It is only fair to say that they have conducted their contest on a plane higher than the usual level of men's political campaigns and have indulged in few personalities and resorted rarely to pettiness. . . . It is hard to find where the women have made a serious blunder in tactics or management. They pressed their cause persistently but always with fairness and courtesy and without giving offense. . . . Where they were the most active, they scored the most telling results. Their achievement in almost winning Douglas County is the most certain sign we have that the battle can be won when it is next taken up, probably in 1918.[100]

Ultimately it would be the alleged identification of those anti-suffragists and anti-prohibitionists with the German "menace" during World War I—conceived as originating from ethnic Germans in the United States and from the German Empire—that would lead to the downfall of the opponents of suffrage by the end of the war in 1918. But the story of that outcome will have to wait until chapter 9.

6

Amusements for All

The Increase in Leisure Time

A new phenomenon emerged in the last third or so of the nineteenth century: what to do when not working? It had not been
much of an issue for people too poor to employ servants, which
was most of the population in both America and Europe. Farmers
had plenty of time during winter months when they could not cultivate their fields. However, during those months it was usually too
cold in much of the country for many outdoor activities. During
the growing season northern farmers worked an average of eleven
hours a day.[1] Moreover, prior to trains with branch lines, reliable
automobiles, and decent roads, they were unable to take advantage of entertainment in urban centers. Sports such as baseball and
football did not even exist. Women's lives were filled with household chores at least six days a week. For both women and men,
church-related activities consumed most of every Sunday. Slowly
at first, and then more rapidly after 1890, farm machinery and new
household appliances made free time available for the middle and
lower classes. And new modes of transportation could take such
people quickly and conveniently to new forms of entertainment.

More leisure time, essential in enabling women to play a major
role in social reform causes, was equally apparent in the rapidly
increasing popularity of amusements of all kinds. Real income for
nonfarm workers increased by more than 50 percent between 1870
and 1900 at a time when the cost of living, as measured by the consumer price index, dropped by 50 percent. Meanwhile there was a
steady decrease in the average number of work hours per week due
in part to the introduction of Saturday half-holidays.[2] These statistics, however, as startling as they are, ignore the fact that many

jobs filled by women left them with too little time and energy at the end of a workday to enjoy amusements.

My father had far worse hours than the new jobholders just mentioned. He arrived at the Pauley Lumber Company around 7:00 each workday morning, well before the men who unloaded coal and lumber from railroad cars did. After having a quick lunch at home, he did not leave his office until almost six in the evening. He once told me that he felt fortunate to have Saturday afternoons off in July and August during the Great Depression.

Many forms of entertainment reached new heights of popularity between 1890 and 1920. Tennis and golf date back to the fifteenth and sixteenth centuries but were played only in Scotland, England, and France and then just by the very wealthy. Dancing, horse racing, circuses, boxing, wrestling, plays, and musical productions had their origins in ancient Greece and Rome. Sports like baseball and American-style football did not exist until the last third of the nineteenth century.

Coinciding with the growing popularity of these amusements, both for participants and spectators, was the vast improvement in the availability, speed, and comfort of streetcars and trains, which were both at the peak of their popularity between 1890 and 1920. This was not only true for people who lived in big cities like New York and Chicago or midsize cities like Lincoln; it was also true for people residing in nearby small towns like Beatrice, Seward, or York. For the latter, special trains would take spectators to a central station where they could take streetcars that would drop them off in front of their destination, be it a theater, state fair, or football stadium. A railroad timetable published in the *Lincoln Star* in 1908 lists forty-six trains arriving in and departing from Lincoln every day from cities all over Nebraska and the whole nation.[3] Railway mileage in Nebraska increased from 1,868 in 1886 to 7,879 in 1910.[4] For the country as a whole, railroad mileage peaked in 1916 at 254,000 miles, or one-third of all the rail mileage in the world.[5]

Highbrow Entertainment: Opera, Opera Houses, and Theaters

Special trains were especially convenient for people attending strictly urban and secular forms of entertainment in Lincoln and throughout the United States that took place in what were called "opera houses." The term, however, is misleading. Although they were sometimes the site of opera performances, they were by no means limited to such relatively expensive productions. A better term would probably be "auditorium." For example when my grandfather Pauley graduated from Harvard High School in 1902, the ceremony took place in the town's "opera house" that was completed two years earlier. The same building could be used for all sorts of occasions, including club meetings and agricultural displays as well as theatrical and musical performances. The first opera houses in Nebraska often had only one story and a raised stage. They were used by lodges and housed dances as well as plays. Using this definition Lincoln acquired its first opera house in 1869.[6] Many of them were eventually converted into movie theaters before being torn down.

A play titled *Alone in London* had been performed in the capitol building in 1871, when Lincoln was little more than a village. The earliest playhouse in Lincoln, which opened in December 1872, was Mac Lynch and John Barsby's for-men-only Winter Garden variety house near Ninth and P Streets.[7] Beginning in early 1873, the most impressive building in town was a six-hundred-seat theater on the third story of the Academy of Music on Tenth and O Streets. However, it proved to be unsuitable for operatic performances.[8]

In October 1873, when Lincoln had a population of only about five thousand, a three-story, 1,200-seat building called Hallo's Opera was constructed on the corner of Twelfth and O Streets. Built at a cost of $40,000, or around $884,000 adjusted for inflation, the owner had not expected to make a profit immediately but was hoping for better times in the future. As early as the winter and spring of 1874–75, troupes from the East Coast and Midwest were filling the theater's calendar, which was otherwise devoted to lectures, musicales, and political and religious meetings. Dances were the most common form of entertainment in the opera houses of smaller towns.[9] In 1875 gaslights ignited the stage curtain causing Hallo's Opera to burn to the ground during a production of *The Two Orphans*. Fortunately the audience did not panic, and no lives were lost.[10]

Although Lincoln was in the middle of a recession brought on by the Panic of 1873, a drought, and a grasshopper plague, within twenty-four hours a group of businessmen had pledged to help build a new opera house on the same site. A year later, in the centennial year 1876, the new house was completed and named Centennial. In 1885 a third floor was added, and the theater was given the name of its owner, Frederick Funke.[11] The Funke Opera House remained Lincoln's premier theater until 1892, when it was superseded by a new and grander opera house, the Oliver, which flourished until 1918.[12] Although Chautauqua performances (to be described later) provided Lincolnites with more than enough entertainment during the summer months, the lectures and performances ended with the coming of fall. Thereafter the more serious (and expensive) forms of entertainment took place in either one or both of Lincoln's opera houses. When the Funke and the Oliver were both functioning, there were sometimes five or six plays performed each week.[13]

Both the Centennial and Oliver benefited from the advent of touring road shows. By 1886 there were almost three hundred such companies, most of them organized in New York, which toured the country offering both popular and classical plays prepared and performed from September through May.[14] Audiences in Lincoln and Omaha attracted plays featuring stars of national and international reputation.[15] By the end of the century "a list of the names of players who came to Lincoln . . . reads like a Who's Who of the American stage."[16] And by that time no town in the United States was without railroad service, and no medium to large town did not have electric streetcars.[17] Lincoln, being on the main line between New York, Chicago, Denver, and San Francisco, benefited from its rail connections. Moreover touring companies liked to stop in Lincoln because they could usually expect a sold-out and appreciative audience. The increasing popularity of vaudeville as well as silent movies after about 1910 with even lower admission charges gradually put an end to the golden age of these companies and the theaters that supported them.[18]

Late nineteenth-century theater, at least outside New York City, was not divided into a wide range of "highbrow" and "lowbrow" performances. Indeed the popularity of Shakespeare's plays during the nineteenth century among both the working class and members of the social and economic elite is astonishing.[19] The same

OPERA HOUSE.

TWO NIGHTS.

Wednesday and Thursday, April 1 & 2,

Engagement of the Tragedian,

THOS. W.

KEENE

Supported by a powerful dramatic company under the management of Mr. W. R. Hayden. Wednesday evening, April 1, will be presented Colley Cibber's version of Shakespeare's historical tragedy

RICHARD III.

DUKE OF GLOSTER, (afterwards King Richard III).............................THOS. W. KEENE

Thursday evening, April 2, last appearance of Mr. Keene in Shakespeare's sublime tragedy

OTHELLO.

SCALE OF PRICES:

Parquette and Parquette Circle, reserved ...$1 00
Reserved in Balcony............................ 75
General admission in Balcony.................. 50
    Seats on sale at Dennis' Hat Store, Saturday morning. March 28. Sale of seats closes at Dennis' at 5:30 on the evening of the performance.

23. Advertisement for *Richard III* and *Othello* at the Opera House. *Nebraska State Journal*, March 31, 1885, 7.

theater in Lincoln where a cast of more than two hundred from the National Opera Company performed Richard Wagner's *Lohengrin* on December 14, 1887, could put on a children's fairy tale the next day and host a performance by John Philip Sousa's band in April 1891.[20]

The three thousand bands that existed in nineteenth-century America made up the most popular form of music, and Sousa's band was the most popular of them all.[21] It should be noted that Sousa also composed cantatas, operettas, overtures, waltzes, and songs, not to mention three novels.[22] Above all the theater appealed to almost all Lincolnites, including its politicians, at one time or another. Before the Funke had completed its first season, many of the theater world's best-known stars had performed there.[23] Not to be ignored are the performances of the Lincoln Philharmonic Orchestra, which during the second half of the 1890s drew increasing approval by Lincoln audiences at a time when there was only a handful of such orchestras in the country.[24]

The year 1900 was not unique so far as opera in Lincoln was concerned. It began in spectacular fashion with a double feature at the city auditorium with the Kansas City Grau Opera Company performing Charles Gounod's *Faust* in the afternoon and *Lucia di Lammermoor* by Gaetano Donizetti in the evening, the latter performance being sold out.[25] In February 1908 Giuseppe Verdi's *Aida* was performed one night at the Oliver by the Italian Grand Opera Company, which was followed the next evening by *Lucia di Lammermoor*. The following week the Oliver hosted a performance of Giacomo Puccini's *Madam Butterfly* by the English Grand Opera Company and Orchestra. Tickets cost between $1 and $3 for the latter two performances and $1 and $2 for *Lucia*, or $25 to $75 taking inflation into account.[26] By comparison, seats at the Metropolitan Opera in New York City for the season 2020–21 ranged from $250 to $600.

By no means were professional companies the only source of musical entertainment for Lincolnites. As early as 1873 the Lincoln Choral Union was established, which included the best singers in the city and performed in June 1875 in Hallo's Opera House.[27] Just a month later the Lincoln Glee Club was formed. In 1886 the Lincoln Oratorical Society presented the *Messiah* in the Funke

24. ROTC cadet band on library steps circa 1895. Originally published in the 1895 edition of *Sombrero*, the student annual. 33-21-00-000005, Archives and Special Collections, University of Nebraska–Lincoln Libraries.

Opera House with soloists coming from Chicago and Kansas as well as Lincoln.[28] Their annual May concert was "regarded as the crowning musical event of the year, not in Lincoln alone, but in the entire state."[29] The Lincoln Philharmonic Orchestra performed at least five times a season in the 1890s.[30] The University of Nebraska established a school of music in 1876, and three years later an all-male Cadet Band was organized.[31] Members wore rather drab, gray, military-style uniforms until 1936. By the time my father attended the university, the group was called the Reserve Officers Training Corps Band. During his senior year, 1929–30, he was both its captain and drum major while also the president of both his senior class and his Delta Upsilon fraternity.[32] He admitted in his memoirs that he was "somewhat of an 'activities major'" in both high school and college.[33] I checked his transcript a few years ago, including courses he took in the College of Law his senior year, which revealed that his activities had taken a toll on his grades, explaining why he never became a lawyer.

Among the most popular forms of entertainment at the Funke

were minstrel shows.[34] Minstrels were developed in the early nineteenth century and consisted of comic skits, variety music performances, and dancing. At least in the beginning, all the performers wore blackface, including African Americans. By ridiculing Black people as dim-witted, lazy, superstitious, buffoonish, and happy-go-lucky, they helped create stereotypes characteristically found in the comic strip *Little Black Sambo* discussed in chapter 8.

Despite the Funke's successes, it was sold in 1902 so that its auditorium could be converted into more lucrative office space. The loss of its brilliant manager, Frank C. Zehrung, in 1899, a costly fire in the same year, increasing competition from the newer and more glamorous Oliver theater, and competition from movie houses with their far cheaper tickets, all contributed to the Funke's undoing.[35]

In many ways the Oliver picked up where the Funke left off. For a time they even shared the same manager, Frank Zehrung, who was instrumental in making the Oliver one of the nation's leading theaters. With a capacity of around 2,500 including standing room, the Oliver was newer, bigger, and even more glamorous than the Funke. Enhancing its appeal were floors covered with special-made carpets, a grand stairway leading to the balcony, walls adorned with mirrors, numerous potted plants, four enormous and expensive chandeliers suspended from the ceiling seventy feet above the main floor, and more than a thousand dimmable electric lights.[36] In addition to the Oliver's impressive beauty, it was a relatively safe structure for its time, thanks in part to lessons learned from the fire at the Iroquois Theater in Chicago in 1903 that resulted in the death of around six hundred patrons, most of them women and children, which was about twice the number killed in the more famous Great Chicago Fire of 1871.[37] Manager Zehrung closed the Oliver for ten days to add numerous safety features, including more exits.

A four-story building, the Oliver was on the southwest corner of P and Thirteenth Streets. Like the Funke it was easily accessible by streetcar from any part of the city and was close to the university; trains from the main railroad station brought audiences to the Oliver from as far as fifty miles for special performances. Once theatergoers reached downtown Lincoln, they could expect streets well illuminated by electric lights. In later decades many Lincolnites looked back to the two decades of the Oliver's existence with nostalgia. It was the place for important Lincolnites to "be seen, when glamorous evening clothes and even opera cloaks were a prerequisite."[38]

Established in 1897 the Oliver had to compete with cheaper forms of entertainment almost from the beginning. The first performance of a moving picture show took place in Lincoln in December 1896, although it would be another decade before movies became serious competitors for "legitimate" theaters.[39] After 1908 the Temple theater, the first structure built outside the original four square blocks of the University of Nebraska campus, gave legitimate shows but not as often or as professional as those presented at the Oliver.[40] In the same year a motion picture theater called the Wonderland opened in February, and the Joyo theater at 1330 O Street, which presented both movies and vaudeville, opened in March, followed by another vaudeville theater that opened in May.[41] Whereas the Oliver typically charged between $1.50 and $2.50 for admission to its top attractions, prices at movie or vaudeville theaters were between 5 and 10 cents.

The downfall of the Oliver in 1919 had multiple causes: the opening of two movie theaters in the fall of 1917, the scarcity of road shows because of World War I, the Spanish Flu epidemic, which was at its worse in the fall of 1918, and the decision to concentrate on the relatively cheap vaudeville acts in the same year. Legitimate theaters were particularly hard hit during the war because increased rates on the railroads made the cost of touring productions prohibitive.[42]

Respectable Entertainment: The Chautauqua Movement

Among the new forms of entertainment that benefited enormously from improved transit were Chautauqua programs, which often included lectures on reform movements related to cigarettes, alcohol, women's suffrage, and religion. However, Chautauqua programs did not take political stands; they were an interesting blend of the Victorian values of self-restraint and self-improvement. Drinking and smoking were not allowed, and the Sabbath was strictly observed even though the trend toward more secular means of enjoyment continued.[43] The movement had its origins in the southwestern corner of New York State in 1874 on the shores of a lake of the same name. The Chautauqua movement's weeks-long summer programs were regarded by adherents as wholesome entertainment. During the 1890s there were around seventy Chautauqua performances; by 1919 there were about ten thousand.[44] They included a mixture of religious topics, culture, general education, and nonreligious forms of entertainment, and they were especially appealing to well-educated families and religious people.

People wishing to continue their self-improvement during the nine months when Chautauqua was not meeting could apply to join a local chapter of the Chautauqua Literary and Scientific Circle. Led by old stock Protestant professionals such as lawyers, doctors, teachers, bankers, and businessmen, the organization required all members to read the same four books with each year having a different theme on such subjects as history, literature, science, and religion. After four years they could earn a diploma at an annual banquet held in the home of one of the members.[45]

The movement was based on the idea "that moral and spiritual instruction was more important than entertainment. Over time, however, this balance . . . shifted in favor of entertainment, an emphasis that constituted the dynamic of the traveling circuit Chautauquas after 1903."[46] For example one of the first Chautauqua programs was established in Crete, Nebraska, in 1884. Its program of 1891, which drew visitors from Lincoln, included thirty-three lectures, seventeen chorus productions, and three grand concerts as well as seventeen hours devoted to literary study, twenty-seven to Sunday school classes, and thirty to devotional services.[47] However, despite having twenty permanent buildings on its grounds by the mid-1890s, it failed by 1897 because it was superseded by much larger assemblies in Beatrice and Lincoln, and it did not become more secular.[48]

As Chautauqua programs spread throughout the United States, they became particularly popular with middle-class people in the Midwest. Although Chautauqua was founded by Methodists, it was nondenominational and included Roman Catholics. It reached thousands of communities throughout the United States and sold about forty million single or season tickets. In 1920 Iowa ranked first in the nation in the number of tickets sold, with Nebraska ranked fourth.[49]

One of the so-called Chautauqua circuits was located at Epworth Park, now the site of Wilderness Park in southwest Lincoln. I fondly remember it in the early 1950s as a place where Boy Scouts like me camped. From its beginnings in 1888, Epworth Park could be reached by horse-drawn buggies or a streetcar line. Later the Burlington Railroad built a spur that took visitors directly to and from the park on half-priced tickets costing 25 cents. Entrance to the park itself was also 25 cents, which seems cheap to us, but when inflation is taken into account, it would be $6.25, a price big enough to keep out the poor.[50]

Epworth Park was an ideal venue for a Chautauqua. It was a veritable town in itself having numerous permanent houses, a huge assembly hall, lakes, two hundred acres of beautiful shade trees, and a man-made, doughnut-shaped pond fed by Salt Creek. The latter was large enough for boating and fishing. Lincoln Park Restaurant, one of four restaurants, was a favorite place to eat. By 1911 the site had a hotel and a dormitory and a seventy-by-seventy-foot amphitheater capable of seating at least 2,500 people. There were also many cabins and 857 wooden raised tent bases for walk-in tents.

The Epworth Park Chautauqua was able to attract famous speakers, who drew crowds from throughout Nebraska and neighboring states. Speakers included presidents Theodore Roosevelt and William Howard Taft, liberal Wisconsin senator Robert M. LaFollette, civil rights leader Booker T. Washington, opera star Enrico Caruso, and numerous authors, popular singers, humorists, scientists, and artists. The flamboyant evangelist Billy Sunday drew huge crowds as far as his unaided voice could reach in the days before loudspeakers.[51]

However, of all the Chautauqua speakers, William Jennings Bryan was the biggest, most frequent, and best-paid attraction in the weeklong programs. His recent biographer has noted that "his appeal was extraordinary for both its zeal and its longevity" over a period of twenty straight years beginning in 1904, in large part because he managed to transcend partisanship and found "the middle ground between sober worship and commercial hedonism."[52]

Attendance at the park reached its peak in 1908. For the next two decades, it was exceeded in attendance only by the original Chautauqua in Upstate New York.[53] Beginning in 1930 at the latest, the Great Depression, radio, and sound movies all took their toll on attendance. The park was severely damaged in 1935 by a torrential rain and flood followed by an even worse flood in 1942, which led to the park closing the next year.

Risqué Entertainment: Vaudeville and Silent Movies

Vaudeville, originally a French name for a comedy without any moral or psychological content, reached the United States around 1860. It arrived in Lincoln about the same time that plays, operas, and concerts were being performed in Lincoln's theaters. Like actors and opera singers, vaudeville performers toured in traveling companies to cities and towns throughout the United States. Unlike actors and opera singers, however, vaudeville performers were more likely to be recent immigrants, members of the working class, and not highly educated. Their purpose was simply to entertain, not to educate or inspire. As such vaudeville could easily coexist with other forms of entertainment including movies, especially prior to the First World War. Vaudeville could also appeal to all classes. However, in its early days, vaudeville shows were much more likely to attract recent immigrants and working-class audiences with limited educations. Ethnic humor, in fact, was one of the mainstays of vaudeville entertainment.

Vaudeville entrepreneurs loved to boast that their productions had something for everyone. In its early days, vaudeville's bawdy humor appealed almost exclusively to the working class and was, in fact, often performed in saloons. Over time, however, vaudeville cleaned up its productions by eliminating profanity, smoking, and alcohol and managed to win over many clergymen as well as members of "respectable" middle-class families by trying to have something for everyone.[54] A two-hour production of five to nine acts could include magicians, acrobats, comedy routines, jugglers, performing animals, boxers, baseball stars, and even opera singers. Each production included a "star" to attract a large audience. At a time when segregation was intensifying, Black people were often in the program but never more than once or as a featured act. They were also expected to perform in blackface and speak and sing in dialect while wearing funny costumes.[55]

By the 1920s some real stars had emerged like George Burns and Gracie Allen, Milton Berle, the Marx Brothers, Jimmy Durante, Cary Grant, Red Skelton, Will Rogers, and Jack Benny. These actors soon discovered, however, that they could make more money in one silent movie production than in a whole season of vaudeville shows. Nevertheless until 1926 it appeared that vaudeville and silent films could coexist because music and synchronized spoken words were impossible in motion pictures. To call them silent, however, is somewhat misleading as they were often preceded and accompanied by music.[56] (My mother helped pay her way through Grinnell College by playing piano to accompany silent films in Harlan, Iowa.) However, when the first talking picture was produced in 1927, the handwriting was on the wall, even though it was not until 1930 that most movie theaters were wired for sound. In Lincoln vaudeville survived for a time in a limited format when there were two or three acts between movies. The popular *Ed Sullivan Show* on Sunday evenings between 1948 and 1971 featured acts reminiscent of vaudeville. For the most part, however, vaudeville's five decades of popular acclaim was dead by 1932.[57]

The first motion picture was shown in Lincoln in 1896, but for the better part of a decade, movies were little more than a curiosity. Owing to the unstable light sources used for projection, they were hard on the eyes to watch, hence the popular name "flickers," or "flicks." They also had no real plot. Watching a train come down a track or firefighters rushing into a burning building might seem fascinating when seen for the first time or between vaudeville acts, but they soon became boring and incapable of existing on their own. As movies expanded to fifteen or twenty minutes, they became appealing and cheap enough for children to watch on their way home from school, for a housewife to watch in the middle of a shopping trip, or for a clerk to watch on her way home from work.[58] For a few years so-called nickelodeons filled the bill across the country.[59]

Even before the fall of 1907, movies had expanded enough to have real plots, which justified the creation of the Jewel Theatre, the first in Lincoln devoted primarily to motion pictures. It was followed the next February by the Wonderland, which showcased both vaudeville and movies. By 1910 twenty-six million people, or almost one-quarter of the nation's population, were going to the movies every week. That figure doubled by 1920, while the number of movie theaters reached fifteen thousand.[60] By 1929, the peak year for movie attendance per capita, 73 percent of Americans saw at least one movie a week.[61] Prices for vaudeville and motion pictures ranged from 5 cents to 25 cents, whereas the cost of admission at the Oliver, as noted earlier, ranged from $1.50 to $2.50, in each case multiplied by twenty-five to reckon in today's currency.

Prices did not change drastically during the next forty years, at least for an afternoon performance for second-run movies at the cheapest theaters. In the late 1940s, I could take the Arapahoe bus downtown for a nickel and pay 9 cents for a cowboys-and-Indians movie featuring Gene Autry or Roy Rogers at the Husker Theatre on the corner of Fifteenth and O Streets. A sack of unbuttered popcorn would set me back another 10 cents. Of course nicer theaters would charge a quarter for an adult in the afternoon and 50 cents for an evening performance, or about $5.50 when accounting for today's inflation.

As early as 1905, the Oliver itself helped advance the popularity of motion pictures by presenting a movie called *Ben-Hur*. Having been anticipated for five years, it was set in first-century Rome and had a cast of three hundred, with a chariot race being the most exciting part of the movie. Seats cost between 50 cents and $2.[62] It was another eleven years before Lincolnites were offered such a monumental, not to mention controversial, film.

That motion picture was *The Birth of a Nation*, shown at the request of President Woodrow Wilson and the first movie viewed at the White House. It was described as "the first masterpiece in the history of cinema."[63] Before reaching Lincoln in January 1916, it had a record-breaking run of six weeks at the Brandeis Theatre in Omaha. Originally called *The Clansman*, it made more money than any other film of its time.[64] It was advertised as including eighteen thousand actors and three thousand horses, and it was the longest motion picture yet filmed and the first to require an

25. Advertisement for *The Birth of a Nation*. *Lincoln Star*, January 9, 1916, 8.

intermission during its three-hour production. It was also the first picture to have a musical score for a full orchestra.[65]

The Birth of a Nation was controversial even before it was seen by the public. African Americans, often played by whites in black-face, were maliciously depicted as ignorant, degenerate, and sexually aggressive toward white women. The Ku Klux Klan was depicted as heroically coming to the aid of a southern family and preserving American values.[66] The movie was shown to packed audiences at the Oliver for more than a week and returned that same March for more showings.[67] The theater critic for the *Lincoln Star* described the movie as "a new and stupendous art for which no adequate name has yet been found. . . . It epitomizes the life of a nation."[68] The popular advice columnist Dorothy Dix said that the movie "will make a better American of you."[69] The National Association for the Advancement of Colored People denounced the movie as pernicious, but its opposition merely generated a good deal of free publicity for the production and did nothing to stop the revival of the Ku Klux Klan.

Lincoln's ministers were much less enthusiastic about *The Birth of a Nation*. Rev. T. W. Jeffrey, the pastor of the Saint Paul Methodist Episcopal Church, said that "it seems to exalt the Ku Klux Klan . . . an institution founded on a principle that should never be condoned," although he admitted that he had not actually seen the movie. Other Lincoln ministers said that their negative opinions were based on the movie having been inspired by *The Clansman*, a book written by Thomas Dixon, himself a preacher, who had argued that abuses suffered at the hands of the carpetbaggers had led Black people into viciousness the moment they acquired their freedom. This had led the Ku Klux Klan to counteract the misdeeds of African Americans. However, a meeting of the Ministerial Association of Lincoln unanimously passed a resolution presented by O. J. Burckhardt, pastor of the African Methodist Church, protesting the showing of the film on the grounds that it "was an injustice to the peace-loving better class of colored folk."[70]

The day after the *Lincoln Star* carried the story about the Ministerial Association's protest, and at a time when *The Birth of a Nation* was being shown to sold-out audiences throughout the country, six African American men, who were merely *suspects* in the killing of a sheriff in Georgia, were dragged out of jail and lynched.[71] They were among the fifty Black people lynched in 1916.

Rules established by theaters, whether they were being used for vaudeville or movies, helped establish their respectability as far as middle-class patrons were concerned. Movie "palaces," as they were sometimes called, demanded that members of the audience take off their hats when entering and refrain from talking, smoking, drinking, or flirting in any way that might disturb those sitting near them.[72] Uniformed ushers were prepared to expel nonconformists from the theater, although they could not separate the sexes who might take advantage of the darkness, at least in "Middletown," Indiana.[73] To a substantial degree, movie theaters became a partial fulfillment of an interethnic, cross-class, genderless, urban democracy.[74]

Meanwhile attendance at the country's movie theaters climbed enormously from sixteen million in 1912 to forty million in the early 1920s in more than twenty thousand theaters.[75] Thanks in part to favorable year-round weather and cheap real estate in Southern California and to America's huge and rapidly growing population, the United States came to dominate the film industry. The

COOLED BY CHILLED AIR
MON—TUES—WED

KATHARINE MacDONALD

In a romance of Monte Carlo

'Passion's Playground'

"SATURDAY" a Briggs comedy
News and Topical Pictures

Pollyanna Accordionist

SYMPHONY ORCHESTRA
JEAN L. SCHAEFER, Conductor.

Shows start—1, 3, 5, 7, 9—P. M.

26. Advertisement for *Passion's Playground* at the Rialto, "cooled by chilled air." *Lincoln Star*, July 4, 1920, 2.

impoverishment of Europe by the First World War only accelerated prewar trends.[76]

Dancing: "A Moral Graveyard"?

It might be tempting to simply combine dancing with music and
other forms of entertainment when surveying the years between
1890 and 1920, especially for the latter half of that period. But
early twentieth-century dancing is especially important because it
was probably at least as controversial as the other cultural movements mentioned in this book: the changing social and political
status of women, fashions, exercise and physical fitness, and traditional morality, with the latter including Sabbatarian laws, just
to name a few.

Dancing existed not only in ancient civilizations but also in
tribal societies. American Indians had special dances for war, hunting, rain, medicine, and sun to name a few subjects.[77] Adherents of
dancing in early twentieth-century America celebrated it as excellent exercise that improved physical fitness and even beauty. It was
especially beneficial for people who had been standing or sitting
at their job for nine or ten hours a day. Immediately after World
War I, it was viewed as one means of helping the mind recover
from the shock of war. The superintendent of the Nebraska State
Hospital for the Insane claimed that dancing was an effective aid
in restoring sanity. The *Lincoln Star* opined that the dancing hysteria that swept the country was a natural remedy for war hysteria.[78] Opponents of dancing regarded it as, at best, a waste of time
and, at worst, a work of the Devil.

What was radically different about dancing in the early twentieth century was the level of physical fitness it demanded and the
need for closeness of the dancing partners compared with dances
of the past. An odd characteristic of many new dances is that they
were named after movements of animals. The foxtrot turned out
to be the most enduring, but others included the horse trot, tur-
key trot, crab step, kangaroo dip, camel walk, fish walk, chicken
scratch, lame duck, snake, bunny hug, and grizzly bear.[79]

To accommodate the craze, numerous dance halls were built
around the country, often in business districts; dance instructors
enjoyed a booming business. The University of Nebraska did not

Opening Announcement of the

Castle School for Dancing

THURSDAY EVENING
SEPTEMBER 21st.

1548 O STREET   **8:15 P..M.**

Mrs. T. E. Williams of the Castle Dancing Academy, is opening her new season at 1548 O street, prepared to teach every late modern dance. After closing the Academy last June, Mrs. Williams went east and there learned the latest steps. She extends a cordial invitation to hr former pupils and those who wish to learn the new dances to attend her classes this year.

Regular classes on Tuesdays, Thursdays and Saturday evenings of each week, classes of instruction will be held from 7:30 to 8:45 P. M., the rest of the evening being given over to an Assembly Dance.

Private lessons may be arranged for at the Academy or at home on any hours not taken by classes.

SPECIAL FOR OPENING NIGHT.
Ha mpton's Six-Piece Orchestra. Refreshments Served.

Mrs. Williams will demonstrate all the new eastern dances: Slow Fox Trot, Waltz Walk, One-Step, Castle House Hesitation, Syncopated Waltz Walk.

Castle Academy May Be Rented For Lodge Purposes and Private Dances Only.

CASTLE SCHOOL FOR DANCING
1548 O Street   HAMPTON'S FULL ORCHESTRA. Phone L9386 or L4221
MRS. T. E. WILLIAMS, Mgr., 818 South 10th Street.

27. "Opening Announcement of the Castle School for Dancing." *Lincoln Star*, September 20, 1915, 17.

permit dancing on the campus until after 1900, but plenty of space for dancing was available for students at nearby hotels.[80] A beautiful dance pavilion was built in Lincoln's Antelope Park in 1917.[81] The Pauley Lumber Company eventually joined the trend by building the Turnpike seven miles south of Lincoln on Highway 77 in 1928, which was managed by my father's uncle, Reon Pauley.[82] Although Americans of all ages, including people in their sixties, were swept up by the popularity of dancing, it was undoubtedly young people who were the most enthusiastic.

Conservatives were none too pleased by a new form of music called ragtime, which they regarded as "vulgar and corrupting."[83] Religious conservatives were adamantly opposed to dancing on Sundays, a particularly vexatious issue at a time when most people had to work jobs six days a week. Evangelical denominations denounced dancing on any day of the week. E. N. Tompkins of Trinity Methodist Church said he considered dancing "the entering wedge for other undesirable amusements."[84] Clergymen in Lincoln were not alone in their opposition to the new dances. The Social Science Service Board in Omaha announced on March 22, 1913, that it had drawn up rules for the city's dance halls so that "physical contact in dancing [be] eliminated as far as possible. Enlarged pictures of the correct pose to assume in dancing [are] to be prominently posted in all halls."[85]

One person—who was unequivocal about dancing as well as alcohol, women's suffrage, card playing (often associated with gambling), and the theater—was Billy Sunday.[86] Born in 1862 he was a professional baseball player for seven years during which time he drank intoxicants, gambled, attended theaters, and swore—all activities regarded as immoral by most Protestant denominations. They were also the very activities he denounced after his conversion to evangelical Christianity in 1886.[87] It was then that he started preaching in tents in small Midwestern towns. By 1907 he was delivering sermons in wooden tabernacles; in 1912 he was speaking to huge crowds in big cities. When he came to Nebraska in 1915 on a fifty-day revival tour, he was nearing the height of his popularity, drawing crowds of 5,000 and 8,000 a day in Omaha and more than 742,000 altogether, including people from far outside Omaha.[88]

Billy Sunday left no doubt as to where he stood on what he considered to be the moral issues of the time:

> I have more respect for a saloon keeper than I have for a dancing master. . . . Dancing is a terrible waste of time and of study and a premature incitement of passion. . . . [It] is one of the great recruiting pieces of the brothel . . . [and] a sort of sex love feat, the moral graveyard of young women of America and it has caused more young girls to go to hell than any other institution this side of perdition. As for the tango, it is the most licentious thing that ever stuck its head out of the portals of hell. . . . [It] is a hugging match set to music.[89]

Card playing and the theater did not fare much better in Sunday's mind. The former was the "fiend of modern society. . . . I do not mean to say that all plays and all actors are rotten. But you will have to hunt pretty hard to find those that are not."[90]

One of Minerva's correspondents was in obvious agreement with Sunday's views on dancing, saying that "if our children learn how to dance [in public schools] it will not stop there but will attend the public dance halls. Once let a young girl or boy acquire the dance fever and it breeds a whole host of other evils, greater extravagance in drugs, less satisfactory work in their studies; and parents need not wonder why so many of their children fail in their exams. . . . Dancing deadens a girl's self-respect."[91] Minerva did not respond.

Billy Sunday seems to have made quite an impression on students at the University of Nebraska, who along with the faculty were excused from classes to hear the evangelist preach at Saint Paul Methodist Church in Lincoln for two days. The *Daily Nebraskan* reported that "the church was filled within a few moments, reminding one of football rallies that swept over the assembly; 1,095 students, 90 percent of whom were from the University of Nebraska, pledged to follow his teachings."[92]

It was not until February 1918, however, that the Lincoln City Council passed a highly controversial ordinance that forbade unescorted women from attending dances and slapped a stiff tax on dance halls. Miss Amanda Heppner, the dean of women at the University of Nebraska, said that the university would conform to the city ordinance.[93] She also stated she was "anxious that simpler music replace the popular 'jazz' variety." These restrictions did not survive the war, and at its conclusion the popularity of dance revived with a vengeance. Nebraska Wesleyan took a much sterner approach to dancing, forbidding it until 1937.[94]

Vacations by Rail, Amusement Parks, and Circuses

Chautauqua and vaudeville performances virtually disappeared in the 1930s, if not earlier, because of the Great Depression, movies, and radios. Many other forms of entertainment have survived to this day but are far less popular than they were between 1890 and 1930. Among the more durable diversions for Lincolnites and other Nebraskans were winter vacations in Florida and Southern California. Such long-distance seasonal travel reflected the conjunction of affluent lifestyles with the development of a nationwide railroad network.

It is hard to believe that Nebraska's population in 1890 was more

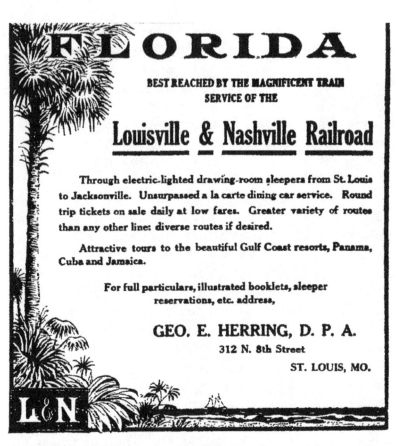

FLORIDA

BEST REACHED BY THE MAGNIFICENT TRAIN
SERVICE OF THE

Louisville & Nashville Railroad

Through electric-lighted drawing-room sleepers from St. Louis
to Jacksonville. Unsurpassed a la carte dining car service. Round
trip tickets on sale daily at low fares. Greater variety of routes
than any other line: diverse routes if desired.

Attractive tours to the beautiful Gulf Coast resorts, Panama,
Cuba and Jamaica.

For full particulars, illustrated booklets, sleeper
reservations, etc. address,

GEO. E. HERRING, D. P. A.

312 N. 8th Street

ST. LOUIS, MO.

L&N

28. "Florida Best Reached by the Magnificent Train Service of the Louisville
& Nashville Railroad." *Nebraska State Journal*, November 25, 1914, 8.

than one million while Florida's was barely three hundred thousand.
Small as the population of Florida was at that time, it was able to
attract winter vacationers from the Midwest, including Nebraska.
By 1888 Henry Morrison Flagler, cofounder of the Standard Oil
Company, built in his retirement years a railroad along Florida's
east coast; by 1912 it terminated at the island of Key West. What
was important for Nebraskans, however, was that by 1888 the railroad reached the city of St. Augustine, where Flagler built one of
his huge and luxurious hotels, the Ponce de Leon Hotel. It was
one of the first buildings to be wired for electricity from the start.
By 1894 Flagler's rail line had reached West Palm Beach where
he built the equally magnificent Breakers Hotel.

By 1897 Nebraskans were beginning to recover from the Panic

of 1893 and a drought; the wealthier among them were looking for a place to spend at least part of the winter. Until the 1920s, and scarcely even then, no reasonably sane person tried to reach Florida from Nebraska by any means other than train. Fortunately railroad companies such as the Burlington, the Rock Island, the Missouri Pacific, and the Louisville and Nashville were all eager to oblige any Lincolnite who cared to escape a Nebraska winter. The Rock Island and the Burlington also stood ready to take vacationers to California.

In case the thought of mild winter weather was not enough to entice potential vacationers, the railroads offered other inducements. The Rock Island advertised that California was particularly advantageous for "elderly people who feared the rigors of a northern clime . . . and those who are distracted by the worries and cares of business."[95] The Burlington made a round trip to Florida especially attractive by having special group excursions accompanied by a guide familiar with points of interest along the route. For example the trip was interrupted for a day in Chattanooga, Tennessee, which could be spent visiting historic points of interest. After reaching Jacksonville, members of a party had the choice of numerous attractive side trips. The group made the whole trip in sleepers without needing to make any transfers. Members of the group could return home "at their leisure."[96]

Travelers on mainline routes after 1890 enjoyed meals on trains that we can only fantasize about today. Railroad cars devoted solely to dining first appeared in 1868 thanks to George Pullman (1831–97), who had created a sleeping car the year before.[97] On the Omaha to Chicago route, a passenger could expect to find on a menu thirty-seven meat entrees including venison and other game. In addition there were fifteen seafood dishes such as blue point oysters from Long Island Sound, frog legs, canvasback wild ducks, English plum pudding, fruits, nuts, and ice cream, to be followed by a liquor.[98] (This menu confirms my father's belief that prior to the Second World War, the best place for a truly superb meal was in the dining car of a train.) Not to be outdone, the Rock Island Railroad promised that passengers on their Golden State Limited to California would have use of "a buffet, library, observation car, a mission-style dining car, Pullmans, a barber, and a valet to press garments, [all at] 'no excess fare.'"[99] After a meal men and women could adjourn to separate club cars with their comfortable chairs and rich upholstery where men could smoke, drink, and gamble; both genders could find well-stocked libraries in their respective lounge cars.[100]

Trains were essential not only in taking Lincolnites escaping to Florida or Southern California in the winter but also for people wishing to visit national parks in the summer. The Northern Pacific Railroad began taking vacationers to Yellowstone National Park in 1883. The Atchison, Topeka, and Santa Fe Railroad took vacationers to the southern rim of the Grand Canyon starting in 1901. Especially popular with Lincolnites because of its proximity was Estes Park and the Colorado Rockies, which could be easily reached by the Union Pacific and the Burlington. They could get to the lakes of Minnesota by the Rock Island rail line, the North Western Railroad, and the Chicago Great Western.[101] The Burlington offered round trips with accommodations to the Black Hills of South Dakota, the Big Horn Mountains of Wyoming, and Yellowstone National Park. The Burlington and Great Northern Express teamed up in 1914 to offer round trips, including tours and accommodations, to Glacier National Park.[102]

"Standard railroad time" was introduced in 1883 in order to avoid the confusion created by each town having its own time, often called "God's time," based on twelve noon, when the sun was at its highest. Both time calculations lasted until 1918, when standard railroad time became the only legal time.[103]

If luxurious trains with their elegant dining cars destined for faraway mild climates were the favorite pastimes of wealthy senior citizens, amusement parks were the inexpensive playgrounds for the young and exuberant. The idea of an amusement park with mechanical rides originated in the Tivoli Gardens established in 1843 in Copenhagen. The Prater, a huge amusement park in Vienna, dated back to the time of co-Emperor Joseph II, who established it as an amusement park in 1766. But it was not until a world exhibition was held in Vienna in 1873 that mechanical rides were added. In the United States, the best-known example of an amusement park was Coney Island, founded in 1897 in New York City. Inspired in part by Chicago's World Fair in 1893, it was the first amusement park to be enclosed and meant to be permanent.[104] Crucial to the success of these parks were streetcars that could quickly transport large numbers of patrons to and from the parks.

At the beginning of the new century, teenagers and young adults looking for summertime activities more daring and less family oriented than what they could find in Epworth Park, went to Burlington Beach, established in 1891 three miles northwest of downtown Lincoln. By the following year, an unsightly salt marsh, fed by the salt-laden Oak Creek, had been replaced by a beautiful, four- to nine-foot-deep, mile-and-a-half-long lake bordered by sandy beaches. Near the lake was a dance pavilion, a dining hall and brewery, and 290 bath houses for changing. Guests were also given the opportunity to ride on three steamboats and seventy-five sailboats. There was a dance hall built on pilings on the lake and boats that could be rented. Burlington Beach could be reached by streetcars that ran every ten minutes from the Union Pacific Depot.[105]

The timing of Burlington Beach turned out to be unfortunate. The year after its opening, Nebraska, along with most of the United States, was hit by the depression of 1893–97 that caused the park to close by the end of the decade. However, an improving economy helped it to reopen in 1905 under a new name, Capital Beach, which called itself "Nebraska's Beautiful Resort on the Lake" and "The Playground of the Middle West." Once again boats and canoes were available, along with a dance pavilion, a movie theater, and later, a roller coaster.[106]

Spectacular events were often held at Capital Beach on the Fourth of July. In 1908 there was a cannonade that could be heard for miles around. Rockets were set off showing the red, white, and blue national colors.[107] An advertisement in 1910 urged families to come to the celebration because there was a shady place to have a picnic and enjoy a Ferris wheel ride, a bowling alley, and a so-called fun factory.[108] Patrons who came on the holiday in 1912 could look forward to a balloon race, parachute jump, moving pictures, band concerts, fireworks, all-day dancing, and even an elaborate public wedding.[109] Two years later they could anticipate seeing highly talented circus acts and band concerts and enjoying a saltwater swimming pool.[110] Capital Beach was far from unique. By 1900 every large American city had its own outdoor amusement park. They were especially popular with single, working women.[111]

29. "Capital Beach, Nebraska's Beautiful Resort on the Lake." *Nebraska State Journal*, June 14, 1914, 20.

Capital Beach closed its gates in 1961, perhaps because of competition from Peony Park in Omaha, which had several roller coasters and by then was easily reachable by automobile.[112] Nowadays the closest thing to an amusement park is Walt Disney World in Orlando, Florida, and similar enormous and expensive entertainment centers featuring rides and displays of all kinds.

Circuses were simply one more of the forms of entertainment that reached the height of their popularity during the same decades that railroads and streetcars reached their maximum usage in the 1920s. The use of wild animals for entertainment goes back at least as far as ancient Rome. Circuses existed in England in the 1770s and made use of wild animals captured in Great Britain's far-flung colonies. Circuses in Europe were in already-built urban theaters. The American contribution came in 1825, when Joshua Purdy Brown from Upstate New York put his circus under a canvas tent. However, it was the completion of the Transcontinental Railroad that truly revolutionized the American circus and made it possible to perform even in small towns.

I can remember my father telling me that the coming of the circus was undoubtedly the most exciting thing that he could remember as a child. As early as 1872, P. T. Barnum could transport his circus on one hundred railroad flatcars. Rival showmen quickly imitated Barnum's success. Very soon these traveling circuses became America's favorite form of family amusement, aided by weeks of colored posters advertising the coming attraction.[113]

Lincoln hosted numerous circuses through the years and by the early twentieth century held two circuses each summer.[114] In August 1880, when Lincoln's population stood at just thirteen thousand, a circus attracted twenty thousand spectators.[115] As early as 1890, the Sells Brothers together with S. H. Barret brought their three-ring circus to the capital city.[116] The much bigger Ringling Brothers Circus came to Lincoln in 1908 and was greeted by a crowd that had waited all night to see the arrival of 85 rail cars, 1,200 employees, 650 horses, 400 elephants, several hundred cages, and 20 tents for the performances. In addition there were Japanese and Turkish musicians and four hundred gymnasts and jugglers. Perhaps the climax of the show was an automobile that did two complete somersaults in the air before landing on a distant runway. Breakfast was ready for the hungry workmen an hour after their arrival in Lincoln, and at 10:00 a.m. the whole circus set off on a parade through downtown Lincoln.[117] Less famous but still impressive was the Hagenbeck-Wallace Circus that visited Lincoln in 1914 with its 8 bands and 387 performers. Special excursion rates for all railroads brought thousands of people to the capital city.

The State Fair and Buffalo Bill's Wild West Show

The state fair was another form of amusement for Nebraskans. The first one was held in Nebraska City in 1859 but was not repeated until 1868, when it again took place in Nebraska City. After 1872 it switched back and forth between Omaha and Lincoln until 1901, when the Nebraska State Legislature made Lincoln its official home. Having its own space in north Lincoln meant that permanent buildings could replace tents and helped make the fair a success.[118] The fair remained in the capital city until 2010, when it was relocated to Grand Island in part to enable the University of Nebraska to expand its campus.

It may seem at first glance absurd to compare the Nebraska State Fair, held annually the first week in September, with the Chautauqua programs that were so popular during the first three decades of the twentieth century. There were obvious differences, of course.

Like state fairs all over the country, Nebraska's was aimed first and foremost at farmers and other non-city-dwellers and was secular and practical. Chautauqua programs, as we have seen, had a significant religious component and were popular with the urban middle class. However, they were both educational to some degree. The state fair was an opportunity for farmers to learn the latest practices in "scientific farming," examine the most up-to-date farm machinery, and learn about the best ways to grow vegetables and care for farm animals.

Entertainment was a major component of both the state fair and Chautauqua events. The Nebraska State Fair had a midway with rides especially appealing to children and young adults. Chautauqua programs had nothing similar. Music played a big part in both venues but was probably more important and more upscale in the Chautauqua programs. However, the fair of 1908 featured "grand opera selections [that] made a decided hit and the singers were repeatedly recalled."[119] The state fairs also featured bands from all over the state that performed all day. Chautauqua events had nothing to compare with horse and motor car races that were always popular at the fair. Nor could Chautauqua programs match the cooking contests that were major features at the fair. (My grandmother Albertina Pauley was somewhat of a celebrity for baking the best cinnamon rolls in the late 1930s and early 1940s, an accomplishment that, unfortunately, she failed to pass on to my wife, Marianne.)[120]

Not ordinarily coupled with state fairs and circuses was Buffalo Bill's Wild West show, organized in 1883 and ten years later renamed Buffalo Bill's Wild West and Congress of Rough Riders of the World. His entourage attracted massive attention at the Chicago World's Fair in 1893, when for six months it was performed 318 times before audiences numbering nearly four million.[121] Like the circuses of the time, it began with a parade featuring numerous groups on horseback including American Indians, members of the military, cowboys, and performers from all over the world in colorful native costumes. The main events included feats of skill, especially marksmanship, sideshows, and races. Some of the performers, like sharpshooters Annie Oakley and her husband, Frank Butler, were famous in their own right. The shows usually ended with an

Indian attack on a settler's cabin, with William "Bill" Cody and a group of cowboys coming to the rescue.[122] Although the show came to Lincoln on at least one occasion—my father had vague memories of having seen one—Buffalo Bill and his show spent much of their time on eight tours in Europe between 1887 and 1906. At the height of his popularity, his show employed nearly seven hundred people. In its best year, 1899, the show put on 341 performances during a two-hundred-day season.[123] Although Buffalo Bill was born in Iowa in 1846, he was instrumental in the founding of Cody, Wyoming, in 1895; he died and was buried in Denver in 1917. Nevertheless he regarded his home as North Platte, Nebraska, where much of his memorabilia regarding his life and career in show business can be seen today.[124]

The number and variety of forms of entertainment available for Lincolnites at the turn of the twentieth century were enormous, perhaps even greater than exist today. No longer is Lincoln the regular host of nationally ranked grand opera or theater companies. Circuses and state fairs no longer come to the capital city, and no amusement park exists in the entire state. Glamorous and comfortable train rides to Florida no longer exist.[125] Jet planes flying from New York or Chicago to the West Coast make Nebraska and the rest of Middle America literally, and unfortunately, a "flyover" region. We do go out to restaurants far more frequently than before the First World War, at least prior to the COVID-19 pandemic. But doing so has involved precious little exercise, and the steadily increasing size of portions has decidedly added to our waistlines.

On the other hand, many forms of entertainment today have little, if anything, to do with religious beliefs. A century ago only Chautauqua performances were acceptable for all but the most religiously conservative Christians, and movies and plays were viewed with deep suspicion by religious conservatives. Dancing and card playing, the latter often associated with gambling, were out of the question, especially if such activities were indulged in on Sundays. Football was just one more controversial activity around the turn of the twentieth century, being suspect not just by religious conservatives but also by some politicians, pastors, college professors, and university presidents.

7

College Football

Birth Pains and Reforms

School Spirit and a Controversial New Sport

Once again the last decades of the nineteenth century marked the beginning of new and sometimes controversial changes in social customs and forms of entertainment. Alcoholic drinks, cigarettes, suffrage for women, women's fashions, academic curricula, plays, movies, dancing, and card playing all had their proponents, or at least defenders, on the one side, and vociferous critics on the other. Added to these controversies was the dispute over what activities should be allowed or proscribed on Sundays. Football joined the list of American institutions that were affected by the reforming spirit of the period.

The year 1890 was of no special importance as far as the history of football in general is concerned. On the other hand, a game played between Princeton and Rutgers in 1869 was celebrated with great fanfare a century later as the official beginning of the sport. However, if we were to see that game replayed today—with twenty-five players on each side, no line of scrimmage, a round ball, no helmets, and no passing—we would probably not even recognize the game as football.

If Lincolnites thought of football in 1890, it was primarily because they were aware that the sport could attract twenty thousand spectators when played by Ivy League schools. In retrospect, however, the year is huge for Nebraskans because of its symbolic importance; 1890 was the first time that the University of Nebraska played a football game even though interest was only minimal beyond the boundaries of the campus itself. On November 27 the university played what has been labeled its very first football game. However, the characterization is doubtful because the game was played according to the rules of rugby, not football, against a team, Omaha YMCA, that did not represent a college. University of Nebraska won 10–0. Nevertheless the *Lincoln Call*, which covered the game on the last page of its November 28 issue, was impressed enough to suggest the creation of a football league that would include Wesleyan, Doane College in nearby Crete, Cotner, and the University of Nebraska.[1]

The Omaha game was not the first played in the state of Nebraska. University of Nebraska students had been pleading with the administration since 1883 to authorize a football team.[2] In 1889 a series of games was played on the campus between classes. On November 23 the senior class defeated the sophomores 10–4 before three hundred spectators. The players hoped there would be an all-university team formed the next year, a challenge for a game having already been received from the University of South Dakota.[3]

Given the university's enrollment in 1890, a league involving only small Nebraska colleges was the only realistic possibility. As noted in chapter 1, enrollment at the university in October 1890 was just five hundred, of whom nearly half were preparatory students. It was only about that time that the state legislature, the regents, and the people of Omaha accepted the university as an established fact. All this was to change in the 1890s, when the university's population began to boom along with that of other colleges and universities across the country.

The 1890s was also the decade when "school spirit" began to flourish, with college football being a big part of that transformation.[4] Whether the university could have fielded a team before 1890, however, is doubtful. As late as 1893, talent on the campus was so sparse that every student trying out for the team was guaranteed a position! A Lincoln sportswriter surmised that the overall quality of the team would improve if two or three players competed for the same position.[5] Moreover a game against Doane the same fall drew a crowd of only five hundred, most of them students.

Meanwhile the rules of the game were rapidly changing. As one commentator noted in 1910, "No American sport has been obliged to undergo so much reconstruction as football. . . . Critics attacked the game not only because of the injuries . . . [but also] because it had resolved itself into a stupidly slow pushing match."[6] In 1875 the shape of the football changed from round to egg shaped and slightly elongated. In 1882 the field was marked with lines every five yards. Five yards had to be gained in three downs for the offensive team to retain possession of the ball.

Touchdowns underwent a remarkable rise in importance over the years. They were worth just two points in 1883, four points the next year, five in 1898, and finally six in 1912. Field goals underwent a steady diminution: five points in 1883, four in 1904, and just three in 1909. To make the attempt more difficult, uprights were moved from the goal line to the back end of the end zone in 1927, although from a safety point of view this change was certainly sensible. In the meantime the poor dropkick has suffered a miserable fate. Once an important and frequently used part of the game, it became the victim of the trend to make the shape of the football ever more spherical, which led to improved accuracy and frequency of passing.[7] Although still legal, the last successful college dropkick was made in 1998.[8] The last time it was even attempted against Nebraska in Lincoln was an unsuccessful effort by Iowa State in 1954.[9]

A Game "Fit for Savages"?

While college (and high school) football was growing in the number of schools fielding teams and the number of spectators watching them, a controversy arose about the increasing number of serious injuries and deaths resulting from the game.[10] The most persistent criticisms came from college presidents, college faculty, and clergymen. In 1897 even the Nebraska State Legislature seriously considered a bill to abolish the game throughout the state in both colleges and high schools, but the bill was ultimately defeated in a close vote. Another effort by the legislature to ban the sport failed the next year.[11]

It is hardly surprising that there were voices denouncing the game as brutal. In the 1880s and '90s, gouged eyes, broken noses and ribs, and injured kidneys were commonplace. Punching an opponent with one's fist was illegal only when done for the third time in a game. An injured player could leave a game only if the captain of the opposing team allowed it. Not until 1906 could he return to the game and then only at the beginning of the next quarter.[12] Overall the action was described as two passenger trains meeting in a head-on collision. The *Nebraska State Journal* opined, with probably more than a little tongue in cheek, that "the game seems a sort of raving idiocy. . . . People who understand football are comparatively few, and to them the game looks like an effort of . . . long-haired young men to put each other to an agonizing death."[13]

A relatively early academic critic was President Jarvis G. Evans of the now-extinct Hedding College in Abington, Illinois, who made national headlines in 1895 when he denounced football because the physical aspects of college football were given precedent over the mental and moral side of education. Football, he said, had "come to be a disgrace, not only in the college life, but to the Christian civilization of the country. . . . College girls have also been greatly injured by the brutalizing effect of this game. . . . They yell with delight upon witnessing the most shocking brutality. . . . Football [belongs] to the same category with the common prize fight and the Mexican bull fight. Those who are killed in the football game are murdered just as certainly as the saloonkeeper murders his victims."[14] H. M. Bushman, the president of the University of Vermont, denounced football as "a game more fit for savages."[15]

A much more influential academic critic of football was Charles William Eliot, the president of Harvard University from 1869 to 1909. In 1906 he described football as a "monstrous evil" and worse than prize fighting. The duty of colleges was to purge themselves of this immorality. He thought the rules of boxing were better enforced than those of football and believed that the public was "kept ignorant concerning the number and gravity of these injuries."[16] He also thought that basketball was too rough. In his opinion only "two college sports were clean and honorable: rowing and lawn tennis."[17] In 1907 President Eliot decried the "excesses of cheering," which characterized intercollegiate contests as "absolutely unnatural." Fortunately for the future history of Nebraska football, Benjamin Andrews, chancellor of the University of Nebraska, had a far more favorable attitude toward the game. At a pregame rally in 1908, he complimented the team for the "clean and manly" way it played the sport. The *Lincoln Star* opined that the chancellor had "a friendly, sympathetic faculty who are responsible for the character of sport that prevails on the campus."[18]

Authorities at Nebraska Wesleyan University were much more critical of football than those at the University of Nebraska, at least for a time. Four years after a team was organized in 1893, the faculty voted to eliminate it. That decision turned out to be temporary, the sport being revived in 1908 at a time when football was enjoying a new wave of popularity and presumably safer games. The school may have regretted that decision as far as games against the University of Nebraska were concerned. Nebraska beat Wesleyan 42–7 in 1913, 100–0 in 1916, and 55–0 in their very last game in 1921.

Criticism from a different academic source came from representatives of the Big Nine (today's Big Ten), founded in 1895 and still the oldest collegiate athletic association in the country. The aim of a two-day conference of professors held in January 1906 was to "curb as far as possible all tendencies toward professionalism. . . . It was recommended that the game . . . be abolished as an intercollegiate and collegiate contest in the conference . . . and that football rules . . . [be modified] to free the game from brutality and unnecessary danger." The professors also wanted to "compel football players to have as many recitations [classes] during the football season as at any other time of the year."[19]

The Ministerial Association of Lincoln directed its ire against special trains that took fans to out-of-town games and then failed to bring them back to the capital city in time for worship services the next day.[20] An even broader attack on college football was made by Rev. J. W. Cowan of Crete at a meeting of the Federation of Nebraska churches in 1910: "Football . . . was a perversion of student life . . . [and was] allowed to seriously interfere with the real purpose of education in its preparation for the sterner duties of existence."[21]

The persistence of football fatalities and serious injuries brought about a furious debate throughout the country, especially around 1905 and 1906. The casualties were often blamed on rules that gave an advantage to teams with many heavy players, or lots of "beef." When a team had three downs to gain just five yards to maintain possession, they needed fewer than two yards per carry. Teams with a big weight advantage could simply smash into the line of the smaller team with little or no need for trick or "scientific" plays as they were called. Superior weight could also be augmented by pushing or pulling the ball carrier after he was on the ground. Enormous pileups were often the outcome with the ball carrier being crushed on the bottom of the stack. Other critics complained that "close play" provided little opportunity to gain "personal glory" and robbed the game of "spectacular features."[22] It was often difficult for spectators to even see the ball, in part because it could be hidden under a jersey and in part because players did not wear numbers until 1913, and even then it was merely made optional.[23]

With football scholarships and out-of-state recruiting being unknown until after the Second World War, universities with high student enrollments like the University of Minnesota were likely to have more "beefy" players than smaller schools like the University of Nebraska.

Changing the Rules: "An Outdoor Game of Basketball"?

Numerous rule changes were made, particularly between 1900 and 1914, to reduce the number of injuries and to lessen the advantage of pure weight. It would be safe to say that no other American sport went through as much reconstruction as did football. By 1906 the debate over injuries had become so heated that the very existence of the sport appeared in doubt.

An influential defender of football was President Theodore Roosevelt, who thought that the rougher forms of athletics were good because they tended to develop courage. He "emphatically" opposed "seeing Harvard [his alma mater] or any other college turn out mollycoddles instead of men."[24] To head off the game being outlawed, Roosevelt invited six coaches and representatives of alumni from mostly Ivy League colleges to meet with him at the White House in 1906 to discuss brutality and lack of sportsmanship in the sport. A second meeting in New York consisting of representatives from twelve eastern colleges decided, by a narrow margin, to reform rather than abolish the sport.[25]

To minimize the importance of weight, in 1906 the down and distance rule was changed to give the offensive team just three

THE "NEW DOWN" ADDED TO FOOTBALL

3ʳᴰ DOWN
6 YDS. TO GO

FOURTH DOWN
4 YDS TO GO.

the ten yards have not been gained. If the side in possession of the ball did not elect to kick, it would be permissible to advance the ball by a running formation. If the distance were not gained the ball would go to the side defending the goal on the spot of the fifth down, which in turn would become their first down as they lined up in scrimmage to advance the ball. Were the old rule in effect, the ball would have gone to the side not in possession of the ball, on or near the spot where the third down is noted.

30. "The 'New Down' Added to Football." Note the shape and size of the football. *Nebraska State Journal*, September 22, 1912, 26.

downs to make ten yards instead of three downs to make five. In 1912 the offense was given four downs to make ten yards.[26] Merely smashing into the opponent's line time after time was less likely to produce a first down. Other rule changes made in 1906 banned hurdling and authorized fifteen-yard penalties for tripping or for hitting with a fist, elbow, or knee. The rules could be more consistently enforced because there would now be one referee, two umpires, and one linesman.[27]

The forward pass, which was also approved in 1906, seemed to be a way to make the game more exciting and safer at the same time. No other innovation was more controversial, involved more changes, or was accompanied by so many efforts to limit its application. For example in 1908 an incomplete pass resulted in a fifteen-yard penalty.[28] In 1910 the quarterback could throw a pass only from at least five yards behind the line of scrimmage and at least five yards to the left or right of the center; the receiver could be no farther down field than twenty yards from where the ball was thrown.[29] Incomplete passes resulted in the possession changing sides with the ball placed where it had been thrown. Lines were drawn parallel to the sidelines, which made the field look more like a checkerboard than a gridiron. It was difficult at best for a referee to know if the five-yard minimum had been achieved. Nevertheless even the possibility of a pass meant that a defending team could not concentrate all their players on or near the line of scrimmage.

The legalization of the forward pass did not go unopposed. To many coaches, including W. C. "King" Cole of the University of Nebraska, the proposed change would lessen the role of the "foot" in "*foot*ball" and make the game much more like basketball. No one questioned, however, that speed, though not all-important, was now much more consequential than it had been. Making the ball more spherical made passing easier. But it also made the bouncing of the ball when it touched the ground after a punt or a kickoff much less predictable; consequently fumbles and upsets became much more likely. Football traditionalists took a long time adjusting to the idea of passing. They continued to call the combination of "straight" football and passing an "outdoor game of basketball."[30] In 1910 another rule made it illegal to interfere with a potential pass receiver.[31] Pushing and pulling a ball carrier was also proscribed by making a play "dead" when any part of a ball carrier's body, other than his hands or feet, touched the ground.[32] This rule, perhaps more than any other, was one of the most effective in reducing injuries.

An important rule change in 1912 increased the effectiveness of passes by not only eliminating the 20-yard passing rule but also reducing the distance between goal lines from 120 yards to 100. However, passes could be completed inside the ten-yard "endzones." In 1914 a rule against "roughing the passer" resulted in a fifteen-yard penalty. Another rule to make the game safer was allowing a punt receiver to call for a "fair catch." An "unnecessary roughness" penalty of fifteen yards was established for hitting a player out of bounds. An "unsportsmanlike" penalty was created for insulting the opponent or any official.[33] The following year running into a punter resulted in a fifteen-yard penalty.[34]

The numerous changes related to passing, including changes in the shape of the ball, undoubtedly made the game more exciting by increasing the number of upsets by smaller and less hefty teams. On the other hand, it did little to decrease the number of shutouts. For example the twenty games of October 26, 1907, listed by the *Sunday State Journal* resulted in nine shutouts. No losing team scored more than twelve points.[35] Nor did the rules governing passing lead to a sudden or dramatic increase in the number thrown. When Nebraska stunned mighty Michigan in a 6–6 tie in 1911, the Huskers threw only three times, completing one, while Michigan passed four times without a single completion. On the same day, among the top twelve teams in the country, the average score was 7.5 for the victors and 2.8 for the losers. Incidentally of the ninety total points scored by the winning teams, twenty-nine of them belonged to the legendary Carlisle Indians of Pennsylvania, who had beaten Nebraska 37–6 in 1908.[36]

The upshot of the rule changes was to make the game much more interesting by decreasing the number of brute-force rushes and increasing the variety of carefully planned plays. What it did *not* do, ironically, was reduce the number of injuries and fatalities.[37] In 1905 there were eighteen football fatalities in the whole country, but of these all but three were high school players.[38] Not included in this count are the number of fatalities resulting from heart conditions or heat stroke that occurred while playing the game. Fatalities and broken bones were not the only casualties in early American football. There were also torn ligaments, severe strains, and internal injuries including blows to kidneys. One football *proponent* approached football fatalities from a completely different point of view by claiming that around 750 football fans died of *pneumonia* because of watching football games for every player who died on the field.[39] The controversy regarding injuries refused to quietly go away. An article in the *Lincoln Star* in 1915 defended the game by maintaining that hunting was the most dangerous sport. During the year only sixteen football players had been killed,

31. "There's a Big Black Cloud a Threatening." *Nebraska State Journal,*
October 8, 1911, 30.

it noted, compared with fifty-nine hunters and an equal number
of baseball players.[40]

One way in which nonfatal injuries could have been seriously
reduced would have been to require helmets. Almost incredibly
helmets were not mandatory until 1939. In 1909 an average of
three to five players, most frequently ball carriers, refused to use
them on the grounds that they inhibited their hearing. Instead of
wearing helmets many players let their hair grow long.[41] Early helmets provided little protection for players because they were simply made of padded leather. A breakthrough came in 1917, when
straps of fabric inside the helmet created a pattern that absorbed
and distributed the impact of a collision while providing better
ventilation.[42]

The Spanish flu pandemic of 1918–20, in which 675,000 American died, and the First World War, which resulted in another

122,500 American military fatalities, made the ten or twelve annual football fatalities seem, at most, petty by comparison and severely dampened the controversy over injuries. It has only been in recent times that the discovery of the effects of multiple concussions on football players has caused a renewed debate about the dangers of football.

Football, of course, had its defenders from the start, who obviously succeeded in preventing its elimination. They countered moral arguments with moral arguments of their own. Football promoted "manliness" and helped check vices such as sex and drinking. It developed self-reliance and coolness in difficult situations. Of necessity players had to be in good physical condition and know how to control their temper. President of Yale Arthur Hadley argued that football was simply "a major sport like hunting and deep-sea fishing which like them involved much physical hardship and some physical danger."[43]

Acting chancellor Charles E. Bessey of the University of Nebraska was also supportive of the new sport for moral reasons. In a chapel talk following a 12–6 win over Drake University, which turned out to be the team's only victory of the 1899 season, he said that "we honor you [the team] for your grit and your courage and your endurance."[44] Chancellor Bessey was not the only administrator to support the team. The *Lincoln Star* maintained that it was E. Benjamin Andrews, chancellor from 1900 to 1908, and "a friendly, sympathetic faculty who are responsible for the character of sport that prevails on the campus. [He is] one great reason why the team does engage in clean sport . . . [and] is sufficiently interested in the boys and their play to cheer with them, rejoice in their victories and urge them on to greater accomplishments."[45]

Lost in the discussion about football injuries, both at the time and later, by some historians is the astonishing fact that most teams consisted of just fifteen players, and substitution was severely limited.[46] Furthermore the game clock did not stop running when a ball carrier went out of bounds. Obviously there were no commercial breaks when players could catch their breaths. Moreover games were not always played a week apart. For example a Nebraska game against Butte College in Montana in 1895 was followed three days later by a game against the Denver Athletic Club. The latter team was Nebraska's opponent again on November 19, 1898, just two days after Nebraska defeated Colorado in Boulder.

One of the rule changes made in 1906 by the Missouri Valley Conference, which was bitterly opposed by the University of Nebraska, was the decree that games had to be played on college grounds and not in big cities like Omaha or Kansas City.[47] This was no minor issue. Starting with Nebraska's very first game in 1890, twenty-one of them were played in Omaha, the last one in 1906. Such a neutral site made perfect sense, especially from a travel point of view, when playing teams like Iowa, Iowa State, Missouri, and Grinnell, not to mention Creighton. It was also important in creating an interest in Nebraska football in the state's biggest city when the university was attempting to build a fan base.

From "Bugeaters" to "Cornhuskers"

Although football enjoyed strong support from a minority of students, its survival depended more on the backing of its chancellors, beginning with James Canfield (1891–95), and the good fortune of having a series of coaches who worked for little or no money. Of the team's first eleven coaches, who served between 1890 and 1906, all but one was a recent graduate of an eastern college where the game was a full generation older than it was west of the Alleghany Mountains. The coaches were all young, former players with no prior experience in coaching.

The dedication to the game on the part of the coaches in the 1890s was sometimes ambivalent. The very first Nebraska coach, Dr. Landon Frothingham, was a professor of bacteriology and received no income for his athletic responsibilities, which was customary for the sport at the time.[48] To call Frothingham a coach is somewhat misleading. He and his cohorts around the country were more like advisors, who were not even required to attend their team's games. Coaches in these early years did not call plays during games, nor would they be officially sanctioned to do so until 1967.[49] That job was carried out by the team's captain. Not too surprisingly Frothingham was easily lured away by a position at a medical institution at Harvard. His departure was barely noticed in the *Nebraska State Journal*.[50] J. S. Williams coached for a grand total of one game in 1892; Lincoln papers did not even note which game it was.

The first Nebraska coach to hold the position for more than one season and gain any kind of notoriety during his tenure was Frank Crawford, a graduate of Yale University, who compiled a record of nine wins, four losses, and one tie during his two seasons in 1893 and 1894. The highlight of his record was defeating Iowa twice, both times in Omaha. What is perhaps most remarkable about Crawford's tenure is that he was not only the team's coach but at times also its quarterback! One journalist claimed that "his presence in a game is worth 25 percent more in the chances for winning."[51]

Coach Crawford's best player by far was George Flippin, who was also Nebraska's first Black athlete and just one of five Black players at predominantly white universities in the United States at the time. At six feet tall and weighing two hundred pounds, he was regarded as a giant. In addition to football, he played basketball, set University of Nebraska records in track and field, and won championships as a wrestler. He was the leading player bar none on the Nebraska football team in 1892 and 1893.

Flippin first gained notoriety when Missouri forfeited a game against Nebraska in Omaha in November 1892. The *Lincoln Star* said that Missouri would not compromise "their southern dignity, by gawd, sah, by playing against a colored man."[52] The forfeiture, however, was not the end of the story. The Paxton Hotel in Omaha at first did not allow Flippin to eat in their dining room. The *Nebraska State Journal* noted that when the team "manfully stood up for their fellow student . . . the management yielded so far as to actually allow Flippin to eat in the hotel . . . but in a private dining room . . . so the other guests might not know the awful fact than a negro was actually a guest at the house."[53]

One person who did not care for Flippin was his coach, Frank Crawford, who said that he had "coached for 'em [the team] for two years . . . and I know their methods. It takes a man with brains to be a captain; all there is to Flippin is brute force. He is slow in getting signals. He can't play a fast game. I don't take exceptions to him because he's colored, but it takes a head to be a football captain."[54] For someone who did not have the "brains to be a captain," it is worth noting that Flippin was later a medical doctor who practiced in Stromsburg.

It was against Iowa that Nebraska changed its nickname from the Old Gold Knights to the Bugeaters. Other off and on nicknames were Rattlesnake Boys, Tree Planters, and Antelopes.[55] However, Bugeaters was the most common nickname until Cornhusker was suggested in 1899 by Charles "Cy" Sherman, a brand-new Lincoln sports editor. A year later the name became official.[56] The 1892 season began more successfully with Nebraska gaining its first victory over a major team—6–0 against the University of Illinois— played at M Street Park in Lincoln and witnessed by eight hundred students. The game also marked the first time the team wore the university's official new colors, scarlet and cream (sometimes also called by the less glamorous term "crimson and white").[57]

Frank Crawford was Nebraska's first coach to be paid ($500, about $12,500 taking inflation into account) for his services. Not paying a football coach was the norm in the late nineteenth century. Harvard, which had one of the best teams in the country, did not pay its coach until 1905.[58] Crawford's successor, Charles Thomas, could not have been too encouraged when just twelve players showed up for their first meeting in the fall. Nor could he have been impressed by the home field being a baseball stadium on M Street. Nevertheless he managed to establish a six-and-three record in his one season at Nebraska. Perhaps the most unusual feature of the season was that it included a game against the Butte Athletic Club in faraway Montana, a game that was completely ignored by the press.

Despite the backing of the university's administration and an unbroken series of winning seasons, it was not until 1895 that the team became popular outside the campus and paid for itself financially. A big game played in Omaha in 1892 against Iowa, ending in a 10–10 tie, was witnessed by just one thousand fans. The game, however, was promising in some respects. The crowd was described as "small, but exceedingly enthusiastic." The reporter went on to say that "football has done as much to arouse outside interest in the university than anything connected with the institution."[59] As late as 1894, the Bugeaters only managed to attract on average about five hundred spectators per game at a time when one thousand were needed to break even financially.[60] A breakthrough came later in the same season when Nebraska beat Iowa, again in

Omaha, 36–0 before nearly four thousand fans. The *Nebraska State Journal* thought that the crowd "gave the managers of the university team a social and financial support that will have a strong influence upon its [football's] future . . . in this state."[61]

Part of Nebraska's problem was not having big-name traditional rivals, Iowa being the lone exception. The Bugeaters' most frequent opponent between 1891 and 1896 by far was Doane College, which in eight games Nebraska outscored 162–30. Having the best football team in the state, however, was not likely to do much for its national reputation. The other likely cause was that Nebraska lacked a real football stadium of its own. Just "650 football cranks" showed up for a game against Grinnell College on October 24, 1894. Even fewer fans—around five hundred—watched Nebraska lose to Doane on a windy day the next week.[62] Until it finally acquired a real stadium, the team usually played on a baseball field on M Street near Lincoln High School.[63] Not until after Yale graduate Walter C. "Bummy" Booth became the coach in 1900 did the team acquire a covered grandstand and start to enjoy large crowds. And it was 1923 before Memorial Stadium was built, which, until the Bob Devaney era began in 1962, could accommodate all but the largest crowds.

The second half of the 1890s saw no fewer than four coaches in five years. Charles Thomas, a graduate of Michigan, won six and lost three in his only season. E. N. Robinson established a 11-4-1 record in his two years as coach, 1896–97. Fielding H. Yost won eight games and lost three in 1898, which included lopsided Nebraska wins over Missouri and Colorado.

However, the decade ended disastrously under the leadership of A. Edwin Branch, who had graduated from Williams College in Massachusetts. Branch had played for two years at Andover College and three at Williams. The *Lincoln Star* wrote enthusiastically that "the new coach was a hard worker, a close student of the game, had the best instructors, and was preparing for a position as coach."[64] None of these qualifications paid off, however, as his team ended the season with a dismal one win, seven losses, and one tie. It is possible that Brunch was confronted with an unusually inept group of players. The *Lincoln Star* reported that at the team's first practice, he "spent most of his time in teaching them how to pass and catch the ball."[65] Looking back five years later, the newspaper noted that "all through the year there was dissension in the team, and although Branch worked hard, he was not able to get the men to work together."[66] It should not be forgotten in those days of no scholarships and no money for recruitment that a coach's fortunes were at the mercy of whomever decided to join the team. Not until the war-affected season of 1918 did the Cornhuskers suffer another losing season, and not until 1957 did they have an even worse win-loss record.

A few statistics about the team's first ten years are fascinating. Despite the decade's last disastrous season, the Bugeaters won a very respectable thirty-five games, lost twenty-two, and tied four. Of these games, thirty-one were on the opponents' fields, only twenty-eight were in Lincoln, and seventeen were in Omaha.

From Obscurity to Fame:
Bummy Booth and the Stiehm Rollers

It would not be much of an exaggeration to claim that the real start of Nebraska football was 1900, not 1890. No dramatic change in football rules occurred in the first year of the new century. The game was still played by the old rules in which straight-ahead running was supreme and passing did not yet exist, at least not legally. Of considerable symbolic importance is the fact that the nickname "Cornhuskers," often shortened to just "Huskers," was made official, mercifully replacing "Bugeaters" once and for all.

Of far more importance than the nickname, however, was the hiring of a new coach, Walter C. Booth, better known as Bummy. In six seasons his teams won forty-six games, lost eight, and tied one for a winning average of 84.5 percent. Booth was twenty-four when he arrived in Lincoln just after graduating from Princeton following four years of factory work to pay his tuition. He came to Nebraska not just to coach football but also to study law. He seems to have made a positive impression almost immediately. The *Lincoln Star* described him as "a Hercules in build, standing six feet and three-quarters of an inch, and playing at 210 pounds. . . . He inspires . . . confidence. He knows the game, and his boys know he knows it. He takes a personal interest in every candidate on the field and no man has been heard to complain of partiality. . . .

Mr. Booth has the good will and the confidence of every candidate. Never was a more popular coach at Nebraska, and through his influence, to a very great extent, the prospects for a winning team were never better."[67] It is easy to see why Booth's players were impressed with their coach's physical appearance. His 210 pounds were 25 pounds more than the heaviest player in 1903 and 44 pounds heavier than the average of his starters (150 pounds). The lightest player weighed all of 139 pounds, the heaviest 185.[68]

In the early twentieth century, football coaches were expected to coach at least one other sport; Nebraska was no exception. At the end of his first football season in 1901, Booth was made assistant physical director by the Board of Regents. In addition he was "given charge of outdoor athletics, which [meant] supervision of all track, baseball, and football teams." He was expected to "have sufficient time to continue his work with the junior law class."[69] The 1903 team went undefeated and outscored its opponents 322–11. Two of the games were blowouts against small Nebraska colleges, but the record also included a 31–0 victory over Colorado, a 17–6 win against Iowa, and a 16–0 shutout of Illinois. The latter game was watched by a crowd brought to Lincoln by special trains from all over Nebraska. One often-overlooked reason for Booth's success was introducing spring football training following the practice of the larger eastern schools.[70]

It is odd but true that an early Nebraska *defeat* by Minnesota marked a huge milestone in the history of the team. On November 29, 1901, no fewer than 3,500 Cornhusker fans helped fill to overflowing the eight-thousand-seat stadium after making the fourteen-hour train ride to Minneapolis. The Huskers, outweighed by more than twenty pounds per man, lost 19–0 to the Gophers, who had been cochampions of the Big Nine Conference the year before. However, the huge contingent proved what loyal fans Nebraskans could be. Just twelve months later, the Cornhuskers returned to the Twin Cities and shut out the Gophers 6–0 in what was certainly their biggest victory to date.

Between 1,000 and 1,500 fans were at Burlington Station to greet the Cornhuskers on their return from Minneapolis. "Among the throng were business and professional men, gushing young women and stately dames jammed into the crush with an abandon that brought delight to the heart of the milliner [maker of hats for women]. The university cadet marching band played everything that was stirring and exhilarating while the multitude waited. Fred Fling, a distinguished professor of history at the university, predicted that 1902 would be 'the date from which all university affairs will be reckoned, and the degrees will be designated as before and after the meeting with Minnesota.'"[71]

Although Husker fans had already become boisterous boosters of the team, the enthusiasm shown by Nebraska fans in both games with the Gophers was just a preview of what was to come. Big banquets including players and coaches from both sides along with leading politicians had been commonplace since the beginning of the century. The victory over the vaunted Gophers came near the beginning of a twenty-four-game winning streak, which was not surpassed until Tom Osborne's team won twenty-six in a row between 1994 and 1996. Booth's winning streak began in 1902 and ended only in 1904 with a 6–0 loss to Colorado.[72]

Booth's unbeaten and unscored-upon season in 1902 had immediate repercussions. For the first time in its history, the University Athletic Board was "troubled with too many applications for the honor of meeting the football team." Its chairman said that "we could have two games for every available date."[73] Not all the pressure to capitalize on the team's newly acquired fame was positive. "Among the players and students . . . there is said to be a strong sentiment in favor of entering the [Big Nine] conference. But among some of the athletic authorities this feeling is not so strong." One prominent football fan made the prescient observation that "Lincoln [was] too far away from the other members of the [Big Nine] conference to arrange regular games." Coach Booth said that he preferred to keep the "institution as a high class second rater, but not up to 'major league' caliber."[74] Nebraska's relatively small population compared to the Big Nine states would often put the Cornhuskers at a competitive disadvantage. The same discrepancy applied to any Big Nine school regarding differences in enrollment. Whereas Nebraska's enrollment in 1902 was about 2,400, the average enrollment for Big Nine powerhouses like Michigan and Wisconsin was 4,000.[75] This apprehension seemed to be born out in Booth's last year, 1905, when Nebraska was soundly beaten by two of the largest Big Nine schools: Michigan shut out the Huskers in Ann Arbor, 31–0, and Minnesota beat the Huskers in Minneapolis, 35–0.

Conference affiliations remained a controversial subject for much of the history of Nebraska football. From 1892 to 1906 it belonged to the Western Independent University Football Association along with the universities of Iowa, Kansas, and Missouri. From 1907 to 1917 it was part of the Missouri Valley Conference (MVC). In 1918 and 1919 it became independent before rejoining the MVC in 1920, where it remained until 1928, when the Big Six was formed, predecessor of the Big Twelve.

Amos Foster became the Nebraska coach in 1906. A 1904 graduate of Dartmouth College, he was one of thirty candidates for the position. Having just completed two years coaching at the University of Cincinnati, he was Nebraska's first coach who came to Lincoln with actual coaching experience. He had been offered a position at Purdue but turned it down because the school had no courses in law, a problem that did not exist at Nebraska. However, his passion was apparently more about legal work than coaching football. After posting a six-win, four-loss record with the Cornhuskers in 1906, he resigned and returned to Cincinnati to practice law.

Foster's tenure was followed by W. C. "King" Cole, a 1902 graduate of Marietta College in Ohio. Although he compiled a very respectable 25-8-3 record in his four years at Nebraska, his team lacked major victories and was shut out by St. Louis University at the end of the 1907 season by the embarrassing score of 34–0.

King Cole left Nebraska because of unfortunate circumstances. In early 1911 the MVC adopted a new rule, which required coaches to be full-time faculty members. Cole had just bought a ranch in Montana, which required his attention in the off season, thus leading to his resignation. His replacement, Ewald O. Stiehm, from the University of Wisconsin, soon came to be known as "Jumbo" because of his six-foot-four-inch stature. Stiehm had been a three-year starter in football at Wisconsin, had played center on its basketball team for four years, and was a shot putter on their track team. Being a three-season athlete at a major university today is simply unthinkable, but it was a huge advantage in 1911, when

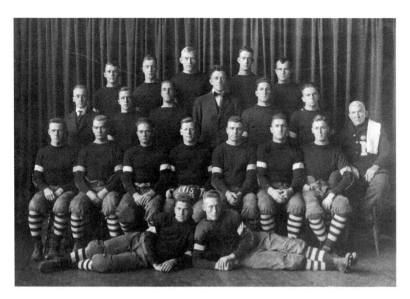

32. The 1915 University of Nebraska football team. Courtesy of History Nebraska.

football coaches were expected to coach at least one other sport, which in Stiehm's case was basketball. Aside from Stiehm's remarkable achievements as a player, the University Athletic Board, which recommended that he be hired by the Board of Regents, was influenced by the fact that undergraduates were impressed with his vigor and energy.

The choice of Jumbo Stiehm to coach both football and basketball for Nebraska proved to be brilliant. His thirty-five wins, two losses, and three ties gave him a 91.3 winning percentage for his five years at Nebraska, which to this day remains unequaled. Each year his teams either won or tied for the MVC championship.

Coach Stiehm's first season ended with a 6–6 tie against Michigan—the oldest and most prestigious team west of the Alleghenies—resulting in one of the most impressive ties in the history of Cornhusker football. In front of a record-breaking crowd of eleven thousand in their new Nebraska Field stadium, the Cornhuskers gained 323 yards to 123 for Michigan and twenty-four first downs to Michigan's five. Indicative of how unimportant passes still were at that time, Nebraska tried two passes and completed one, and Michigan completed one pass out of four.[76]

Two years later in 1913, passing made the difference in the

"Stiehm Rollers'" 7–0 victory over the Gophers. The *Nebraska State Journal* said that Minnesota's line was a "stone wall that Nebraska could not penetrate, and only twice during the entire game were the Cornhuskers able to make their distance [a first down] on *straight* football. . . . It was a spectacular game from start to finish and was largely the old style of football against the new—and the new won. . . . At least a dozen passes were tried by the Gophers of which number not more than one netted them a successful gain."[77] What is perhaps most remarkable to football fans today is that Nebraska played the entire game without making a single substitution and suffered no injuries.[78]

Passing was even more decisive in the previously mentioned Nebraska 24–0 victory over the Michigan Aggies (today's Michigan State Spartans) in 1914. The *Nebraska State Journal* stated the Cornhuskers had "played the best game that they [had] ever played." Nebraska outgained the Aggies 332 yards to 231, but the real difference was in passing: the Cornhuskers passed just nine times but completed five, whereas the Aggies threw twenty-one times, completing only four.[79]

Jumbo Stiehm is probably best remembered for his 20–19 victory over Notre Dame in 1915, almost certainly the most exciting game of the entire series, and one that we would have no trouble understanding or appreciating today. We would be surprised at the near absence of substitutions—just two for each team—and the goal posts being at the goal line. We would have found it odd that extra points had to be kicked wherever the goal line had been crossed for a touchdown, which might have been the "coffin corner." However, we would not have regretted missing frequent TV timeouts—football games in the 1910s typically lasted no more than two and a half hours. The Notre Dame game of 1915 was modern most notably in passing. The *Nebraska State Journal* concluded that "it was the forward flips that won the game for the Cornhuskers," who completed five of eight passes for 105 of their 343 total yards. Meanwhile the "Catholics," as they were often called then—who under their coach, Knute Rockne, would soon become famous for their passing attack—completed two of six passes for just 37 of their 314 yards.[80]

The game was not only fascinating because of its relative modernity but also because of the relatively high number of points scored by the loser. Since 1890 there had been countless close games involving Nebraska, but they had always involved low scoring by both teams. In fact 0–0 ties were commonplace. Nebraska had already been involved in four such dual shutouts before 1915 and would be part of another one against Notre Dame itself in 1918. In fact the Cornhuskers would share such scoreless ties ten times during the next thirty years, the last one against Indiana in 1938. Not until 1943 would Nebraska score more than 19 points and lose as it did in a 54–20 game against Missouri.

The eleven-game series with Notre Dame ended with an even split: both teams won five games and lost five with the 1918 game ending in a no-score tie. That game, played in the mud, probably set two Nebraska records: no first downs and fifteen punts, often on first downs. Also noteworthy is that all games but the 1924 game were played in Lincoln. The reason for this disparity is quite simple. The game could draw bigger crowds in the Nebraska capital, making the payout bigger for both teams. Regrettably the 1924 game ended in a controversy with some Notre Dame officials complaining that they had received anti-Catholic taunts by Husker fans. Coach Rockne insisted that he and his players had always been well treated in Lincoln, but he lost the argument; the teams did not meet again until 1948.[81] The series now stands at eight wins for Nebraska, seven for Notre Dame, and one tie.

Jumbo Stiehm was not just a great football and basketball coach; he was also a staunch advocate for equal treatment of Black athletes. In 1913 the race issue reappeared when Kansas University and the Kansas State Aggies (today's Wildcats) complained about Nebraska's African American player, Clinton Ross, a 220-pound guard. Stiehm's reaction was unequivocal: "If the Aggies pushed their claims much further, [I would be] very much in favor of cutting them out of Nebraska's schedule."[82] Chancellor Samuel Avery (1908–27) was equally unequivocal, announcing that he would "request the board of regents to pass a rule that the right of students to participate in any athletic contest . . . shall not be abridged on account of race or color and that Nebraska will not remain in any athletic association where such right is abridged."[83] Ultimately both the Jayhawks and Aggies not only failed to intimidate Stiehm or Avery but lost to the Huskers 24–6 and 9–0.

Unfortunately Nebraska's principled stand did not change the minds of the southern members of the MVC. Sometime in the 1920s, at the insistence of representatives of the Universities of Missouri and Oklahoma, members of the MVC made a "gentlemen's agreement" that teams having Black players on their rosters would be "unwelcome in both Columbia and Norman." Thereafter, de facto if not de jure, there was a color line in the Missouri Valley Conference and its successor, the Big Six. Following years of protest against the ban by students in the northern states belonging to the Big Six, student senators at the University of Oklahoma "approved by a two-to-one margin a resolution that Negro athletes be permitted to compete against the Sooners." The action of the Oklahoma students was followed the next year by an announcement from the Kansas State football coach, Ralph Graham, that "until the Big Seven makes a definite ruling against it, Kansas State will use colored men providing they are able to make the team."[84]

Coach Stiehm's last game was against the Iowa Hawkeyes, 52–0. What followed that game was possibly the biggest blunder in the history of Cornhusker football. Stiehm's salary for the last two years of his tenure had been $3,500, or $87,500 today. Indiana University offered him $4,500, or $127,500 today, a big jump in salary, but not shocking considering Stiehm's winning percentage (almost surely the best in the country), five straight Missouri Valley football championships, and two championships in basketball. Not quantifiable was the fame that Stiehm had brought the university, the likely increases in enrollment, and the dollars spent by Nebraska fans who came from outside Lincoln as well as the many fans from visiting universities. The *Lincoln Star* noted that "businessmen . . . feel that the team has done wonders in advertising Nebraska and that Lincoln hasn't suffered any through the long string of victories. It is a certainty that they will be ready to make the coach a neat present any time he wants to sign up a three-year contract. . . . About the surest way to get a howl from the gentlemen who have secured degrees from a school is to impair its chances in athletics. . . . Coach Stiehm repeatedly has said that he wants to stay at Nebraska." Chancellor Avery stayed "somewhat aloof . . . but the matter of another increase in salary probably would bother the university executive. There are many instructors . . . who do not receive the salary of the head coach and there would be a general howl if Stiehm's salary were boosted to $4,250."[85]

The failure to retain Jumbo Stiehm was apparent during the next four seasons. Three coaches were able to win just twenty-one games while losing thirteen, with four games ending in ties. Not until 1931 did Nebraska win eight games again and that was in a ten-game season. Nebraska did succeed in winning three of its last four contests with Notre Dame. The last game, under coach Ernest Bearg—a 17–0 shutout in Lincoln in 1925—drew an estimated forty-one thousand to forty-five thousand fans to the Huskers' new Memorial Stadium, the largest crowd to watch a game in Lincoln until the stadium was enlarged in 1964 following the hiring of Bob Devaney as coach.

The "Secrets" of Success

First of all it is by no means a secret that the Cornhuskers' road to success was due to three of its early coaches: Walter "Bummy" Booth, W. C. "King" Cole, and Ewald "Jumbo" Stiehm, who between them won 106 games, lost 18, and tied 7, thus establishing a winning tradition and a die-hard following. Another obvious reason for the Huskers' success is that from the beginning, the team usually enjoyed the support of the administration. The university's chancellors were quick to realize what a successful football team could do in attracting students and balancing budgets. The willingness of Nebraska's athletic authorities to schedule twenty-one games in Omaha between 1890 and 1909 helped build a solid fan base in the state's largest city. The receipts for Nebraska home games not only paid for football expenses but also for the costs of all the other athletic teams, a fact that was true of other schools like Harvard and Yale.[86] In an age of no football scholarships and no budgets for recruiting, coaches were dependent on volunteers from the student body, and the size of a college's enrollment depended to a high degree on the population of the city and region in which it was located. When Nebraska played its nearby traditional rivals, it was highly successful.

A much less obvious reason for the team's success is that it enjoyed a huge advantage in population when playing most of its conference rivals prior to the formation of the Big Six in 1928. Lincoln's population was just under fifty-five thousand in 1920. That year Lawrence, Kansas, had a population of 12,400, and Manhattan, Kansas, had 8,000. Ames, Iowa, had 6,279, and Columbia, Missouri, had 10,390 residents. A further advantage for Nebraska was that there were two major state universities in both Iowa and Kansas, and Missouri had to compete with powerful St. Louis University. Nebraska, on the other hand, did not have to share the spotlight with any other Nebraska team after beating Doane 24–0 in 1895. Against its three traditional rivals in Iowa, Kansas, and Missouri, the Cornhuskers won eight and lost four during the 1890s, won fourteen and lost four in the 1900s, and came out on the winning side twenty times while losing just twice in the 1910s. Against Kansas State, its smallest rival in population, Nebraska won six and lost none during the 1910s while outscoring the Aggies 189–12.

Population was not the only advantage that Nebraska had over its traditional rivals. The campus being adjacent to the downtown business district, with its many stores and big hotels, provided plenty of job opportunities for football players at a time when scholarships were nonexistent. The state capital and the Burlington and Rock Island depots, all easily reachable by foot or streetcar, were also good sources of employment. The *Lincoln Star* noted in 1914 that "out of thirty-one men who have won their football letters upon the Nebraska team during the past three years . . . seventeen have made their own way by working part time."[87]

If we look at the Nebraska-Minnesota rivalry, the tables were decidedly turned. Between 1900 and 1920, Nebraska won two games against the Gophers, lost ten, and tied two, while being outscored 192–51. Meanwhile Lincoln's population was just over 40,000 in 1900 compared to the 650,000 people who lived in Minneapolis–St. Paul. Twenty years later the comparative populations were 55,000 for Lincoln and 921,000 for the Twin Cities. Even if we were to add to the Huskers' possible recruiting base of 153,000 in Omaha, South Omaha, and Council Bluffs, it would still mean that Nebraska was at a huge disadvantage vis-à-vis the Gophers.[88] The Huskers would not succeed in turning the Minnesota series around until 1961. Between that date and 1983, thanks to their ability to recruit nationwide, Nebraska won thirteen straight games, including an 84–13 massacre in 1983 and a 56–0 shutout in 1956.

After the 1983 game, I recall the Gophers' coach famously saying something to the effect of, "We have Nebraska exactly where we want them: off our schedule."

Keeping alumni happy was also important to the Huskers' success. Starting in 1900 the University of Nebraska followed the practice of eastern and midwestern schools in hosting a banquet at the end of the football season.[89] Special trains were chartered for alumni wishing to follow the team at faraway games, beginning, it may be recalled, with the Minnesota Gophers in 1902. However, by far the most outstanding example of maintaining contact with alumni was an eight-day, 4,500-mile, mid-semester round trip that the Huskers took in October 1916 to play the Oregon State Aggies in Portland, a game that Nebraska won 16–7. The team, accompanied by the cadet band, stopped to practice and perform wherever alumni were located.

Nebraska coeds became supporters of the football team starting with the very first game against Omaha YMCA in Omaha in November 1890. The *Lincoln Star* took note that "the bleachers were packed [with] . . . more or less beautiful maidens" in a game Nebraska played against Kansas in November 1895.[90] By 1897 a special section of bleachers was reserved for girls and their escorts.[91] In 1904 a Girls' Rooters Club was formed, which enjoyed the support of university authorities from the beginning.[92] Nor were Lincoln's stores slow in jumping on the football bandwagon. At least as early as 1903, they not only used scarlet and cream on their mannequins in show windows, but also the colors of the visiting team.[93] Women and even men in the pre-Devaney days saw football games as an opportunity to wear the latest outdoor fashions, including fur coats.[94]

Finally, as is true in all aspects of life, success breeds success. At the height of the controversy about injuries, people affiliated with schools having losing records made the loudest complaints, whereas schools having winning records were the least likely to raise objections about the roughness of the game.[95]

8

Minorities and Immigrants

Lincoln's Black People:
"Ambitious Improvement, Not Yet Realized"

The status of African Americans on Cornhusker athletic teams was reflected in the legal, social, and even economic conditions of Lincoln's Black population in the early twentieth century. Much more, however, still needs to be said so far as Lincoln's Black population is concerned. Fortunately a master's thesis written in 1904 by two University of Nebraska graduate students, Mary E. Davies and Genevieve Marsh, provides a detailed and fascinating description of everyday lives in this small community in the early twentieth century. Davies and Marsh spent the summer of 1903 interviewing members of all 149 African American families then living in the Nebraska capital.[1]

Only about a quarter of those interviewed had been born in Nebraska, with the majority coming from border states such as Missouri and Kentucky. Nearly all of them had been slaves or were children of slaves. Their memories of their former masters were mixed. Some of them showed Davies and Marsh scars from whippings they had received when working in cotton fields. However, "a good many of them received help from their old masters in land or houses or work. In some cases, they were retained in the same family, and stayed very happily with them for years. . . . Most of them seem to have much affection for their old master's family."[2]

What was already well known at the time was that the Black population in the state was small, just 7,680 people, or 0.6 percent of the whole population, according to the census of 1910. This figure was down from the 8,913 Nebraskans listed as Black in the census of 1890. Of Lancaster County's 870 Black people in 1910, just 1.3 percent lived in rural areas. By contrast Douglas County, home to metropolitan Omaha, had by far the largest Black population in the state: 3.1 percent compared to 10.7 percent of the Black population in the whole country. Thanks to Nebraska's equal educational opportunities (at least in theory), in 1900 only 6.7 percent of African Americans were illiterate in Nebraska compared to 44 percent among Black people nationwide and 20 percent for all adults nationwide.[3] Another marked difference between Nebraska's Black population and that of the country was that all but 1,068 of the state's Black residents lived in or near cities and not on farms or in small towns as they did in southern states like Mississippi.[4]

There were widespread differences between the living and working conditions of Black people residing in Omaha and Lincoln. The Black population in the state capital was so scattered around the city that no area was predominantly African American. By contrast rigid segregation existed in Omaha: one Black neighborhood was next to the stockyards, and a more numerous area was on the north side near the Union Pacific shops.[5]

The size of African American homes in Lincoln at the beginning of the twentieth century was generally indistinguishable from homes owned by whites. The average number of rooms was four, the same as that for white families, which was more than adequate since the average family size was just under 3.5 persons. There were only four homes with bathrooms, but that was hardly surprising at a time when this convenience was not the norm in Lincoln. Davies and Marsh gave the following general description of African American homes:

> The rooms are generally small, although almost always tidy and thrifty in appearance, sometimes even artistic. Though the poorest houses contrast sadly with the scrupulous cleanliness of the [German-] Russian homes which surround them, the better houses cannot be distinguished from those of the white people which are about them. . . . It is interesting that houses rent back and forth between the two races. . . . The house furnishings are often in excellent taste, although, on the whole, scanty. . . . There are, perhaps, a score of pianos and organs, an occasional mandolin, guitar, violin, music-box or phonograph, but not a single banjo [often presumed to be Black people's favorite musi-

cal instrument].... There are books in fairly good numbers.... The general atmosphere of the homes is that of ambitious improvement, not yet realized to the satisfaction of the owners.[6]

Lincoln's African American population had an average of eight years of schooling thanks to most parents wanting to give their children all the education possible, even if it sometimes meant repeating a grade. Some parents regretted that their children did not take advantage of the University of Nebraska where no tuition was charged.[7] However, 5.5 percent of Lincoln's Black population had received some college education, enabling them to enter a wide variety of occupations, most involving literacy and skills. Davies and Marsh concluded that "the general character of these [Black] students is high and . . . they are respected and liked by the white students."[8]

There was no type of job in which Lincoln's Black people were concentrated. The assumption that Black people were able to get only poorly paid manual labor jobs did not hold true for turn-of-the-century African Americans in Lincoln. While they may have been overrepresented as housekeepers, laundresses, porters, or waiters, not many were common day laborers. Many were cashiers, department heads in department stores, or bartenders. About 30 percent of Lincoln's Black people were entrepreneurs, professionals, tradesmen, or clerks.[9] Barbers, ministers, mail carriers, masons, carpenters, and laundresses enjoyed the longest employment.[10] The one area in which there was real discrimination was skin coloration. Light-skinned Black people found it easier to obtain jobs of their choice and were better paid even when there was no difference in education than dark-skinned African Americans.[11] Even for dark-skinned Black people, however, household income was around $40 a month (about $1,000 in today's evaluation) compared to $32 in expenditures, leaving a surplus of $8 for amusements and property improvements.[12] Davies and Marsh conclude that "Lincoln has a comparatively large average family income; the Negroes are in comfortable circumstances."[13]

According to the authors, one Black proprietor was especially popular. The café he ran "consists of two dining rooms, tastefully arranged with cut flowers upon the tables and good silverware. The restaurant is very popular, being frequented almost entirely by the whites between whom and the proprietor a cordial relationship exists. There is no restaurant in town which serves more satisfactorily the businessmen or the University students of all classes. It is an enterprise in which the city can well take pride."[14]

The social lives of Lincoln's African Americans revolved heavily around the four churches to which they belonged, with Mount Zion Baptist Church the largest with 104 members. The African Methodist Episcopal Church had another large congregation; the smallest was the Newman Methodist Episcopal Church. Five percent of Lincoln's Black population were members of white churches. Davies and Marsh concluded that "the . . . churches bind the people closely together. The whole permanent Negro population seems to be united and welded into a good fellowship for the common betterment and uplifting of the race."[15]

The question about political affiliation was the easiest for the interviewees to answer: "Republicans, of course, we wouldn't dare to be anything else. . . . They need us so we have to be Republicans." Only one person admitted to being a Democrat. Such adherence to the Republican Party might seem preposterous in today's political landscape. However, Lincoln's Black people knew that it had been President Lincoln, a Republican, who had freed the slaves fewer than four decades earlier. More than half of those interviewed, however, claimed a decided indifference concerning politics and no attention to it beyond the vote itself.[16]

In only a few ways did Lincoln's Black people differ significantly from the white population. For example their birthrate was considerably below the average of the whole population, as the average Black family size, as previously mentioned, was just 3.5, with a higher-than-average infant mortality rate being part of the reason.[17] The crime rate was above average. However, nearly all the crimes were petty, and many were thought to be committed by transients; virtually none of them were committed by people under eighteen years of age.[18] Finally, although their eight years of schooling was near the city average, Black people failed to reach the highest marks on examinations.

Davies and Marsh conclude that "there is no active color prejudice [in Lincoln] probably because the Negro population is so small. The two peoples live side by side with little friction, the permanent Negro population attracting but little general attention, because it is wise enough to take care of itself and strong enough to be socially self-sufficient."[19] In short there is no evidence in the Davies and Marsh thesis that Jim Crow laws—which in the 1890s started to segregate schools, restaurants, hotels, theaters, and depots—existed in Lincoln in the early twentieth century.

A more critical view of the status of Lincoln's African American population is described by Jennifer Hildebrand in her article "New Negro Movement in Lincoln, Nebraska," which covers the period from 1890 to 1930.[20] Between 1904, the year that Davies and Marsh completed their research, and 1920, Lincoln's Black population grew 58 percent resulting from the manpower needs of Lincoln's packing houses and railroad companies during and after the World War. Hildebrand's thesis is that "while the new settlers found opportunities not available in the South, they did not so completely escape racism and Jim Crow as they must have hoped."[21]

The territorial legislature had defined a Negro as anyone who was one-quarter Black. In 1913 the state legislature tightened that law to define a person as Black as someone who was one-eighth African American. (The same ratio pertained to Japanese and Chinese people.)[22] The law made marriage between African Americans and Caucasians illegal, a more restrictive definition than Nazi Germany was to employ after 1935 in its infamous Nuremburg Laws, which forbade Jews from marrying "Aryans" only if they had two or more Jewish grandparents and practiced Judaism.[23] Nebraska's anti-miscegenation law also included Asians and made both marriage parties equally guilty. It was not repealed until 1963.[24] The racial law of 1913 was invoked in 1919, when an Omaha man sued for an annulment of his marriage on the grounds that his wife was at least one-eighth Black and that "he was unaware of the fact until so informed by a physician following the birth of a child."[25]

Although the Davies and Marsh thesis paints a surprisingly positive picture of the status of Lincoln's African American population, it is not the whole picture as can be seen in the Hildebrand article. As the illustrations in this book clearly show, Lincolnites were constantly exposed to subtle and not-so-subtle examples of racism in their newspapers and entertainment. We have already

Professor: "When I say 'presto change,' you will disappear and—"
Rastus: "Lod! boss! can't yo' gib me de change befo' yo' commences?"

33. (*above*) "Professor: 'You will disappear.'" *Nebraska State Journal*, March 1, 1896, 16. (*next page, top*) "Sambo's Soliloquy." *Lincoln Star*, March 13, 1909, 4. (*next page, bottom*) "Couldn't Trust Him." *Lincoln Star*, May 17, 1912, 4.

Sambo's Soliloquy.

"I's jes' a littl' niggah;
  But I has the mostest fun
A-eatin' water-million
  An' settin' in the sun.

"I lubs to set a-laffin',
  When dare's nuffin' else ter do,
An' eatin' water-millions
  While I'm visitin' wif you."

Couldn't Trust Him.
Judge.
   Judge—Why didn't you stop beating
him when he cried "Enough"?
   Sambo—W'y, ye see, sah dat niggah
is sich a liah, ye can't nevah bellebe
'im.

---

seen how Black people, no matter how talented, were never the featured act in vaudeville shows. When in a minstrel act, they always
had to appear in blackface. Lincoln's newspapers carried cartoons
called *Little Black Sambo* featuring a little Black boy who spoke in
an exaggerated dialect and was supposed to be funny because his
observations were so absurd. Advertisements for Pullman cars on
long-distance trains depicted porters, all of whom were Black,
with grossly exaggerated lips and noses. In movies Black people
always played the role of a servant or some other demeaning job.
These depictions were by no means limited to the period preceding 1920. Lincoln public schools used *Little Black Sambo* books
until 1964.[26] Lincoln's schools were never segregated. However,
an attempt in 1886 by members of the Black community to persuade the school board to hire Black teachers failed. Omaha did
have two Black teachers in the 1910s, but they were not replaced
by other Black teachers when they moved out of state. No Black
teacher was hired in Lincoln until the 1950s, thus depriving Black
children of models they might have emulated.[27] Lincoln also differed from Omaha in the early twentieth century by not having
any Black physicians, attorneys, or dentists.[28]

In 1909, just five years after Davies and Marsh concluded their
study, a graduation ceremony at the University of Nebraska provided an opportunity for the commencement speaker, Senator John
Sharp Williams of Mississippi, to propose a solution for American
race problems. The southerner, he was convinced,

> knows the north; he had found an amazing ignorance of the south in
> other sections. His mission to Nebraska was to give some facts. . . .
> Assimilation is impossible, amalgamation unthinkable because inter-
> marriage means the destruction of both [races] and the creation of a
> new type. . . . The political phase of the problem has been solved by
> the framing of the new state constitutions which disfranchised the
> Blacks. . . . It is absurd to say that education constitutes a solution of
> the problem. The solution . . . was to redistribute the negroes between
> the various sections and communities so that each might have but a
> small number. . . . The darky is no more a white man with dark skin
> than an ass is a horse with long ears.

34. "The Finest Sleeping Cars in the World." *Nebraska State Journal,*
November 20, 1897, 2.

The *Lincoln Star* noted that the "audience was not wholly in sympathy with the leading thought advanced by Senator Williams
as . . . was shown by the lack of applause during the address and
by the ovation tendered William Wood, a colored student as he
stepped to the platform to receive his sheepskin. Wood was given
more applause than any other senior."[29]

My own memory of Lincoln's African American population is
mostly limited to my experience at Lincoln High School during the
early 1950s, a half century after the research undertaken by Davies
and Marsh. Nevertheless my memory is consistent with the findings of the two young researchers. I recall that African Americans

ate as a group in the cafeteria, and interracial dating was unknown. But Black people did participate in sports and graduated, albeit usually in the industrial arts and not in the college-bound track. But unlike "Middletown," Indiana, there was no blatant discrimination against them in public parks or in motion picture theaters.[30]

A later exception was Lincoln's municipal swimming pool. Black people had been allowed to swim in public pools in the North prior to the First World War, but pools were segregated by gender. After the war *gender* segregation was replaced by *racial* segregation. This discrimination lasted in Lincoln until 1946, when a Japanese American named Jesse Ishikawa took the lead in desegregating the pool even though he was not a victim himself. Born in Los Angeles, he had spent six months in an internment camp before becoming one of more than one hundred Japanese Americans invited to enroll at the University of Nebraska, one of the few universities to issue such an invitation. The desegregation of Lincoln's pool was not accompanied by the violence or court battles that occurred in other northern cities at that time.[31]

Volga Germans: "Thrifty and Independent"

Lincoln's other distinct minority in the early twentieth century consisted of Germans from Russia. They differed from African Americans in almost every possible way. To begin with, they were far more numerous and had large families. Whereas Lincoln's Black people were spread throughout much of the city, the German Russians were concentrated in two compact neighborhoods: the North and South Bottoms, both on the northwest side of Lincoln. Whereas the African Americans were all fluent and usually literate in English, many of the older German Russians could speak only a very archaic form of German. The one similarity is that both groups had homes noted for their cleanliness.

Aside from language, perhaps the biggest difference between the two groups is that the Black population was small and its birthrate low. By contrast in 1915 one in every six Lincolnites had either come from the Volga region of Russia or was a child of such immigrants. *Die Welt-Post* claimed in 1925 that one in three Lincolnites was either born in Russia or was a child of Volga German immigrants.[32] However, the Volgers' high density did not bother them; it merely reminded them of the compact nature of their Russian villages.[33]

So long as the Volga neighborhoods in Lincoln retained their own language and customs, other Lincolnites, including German-speaking immigrants from central Europe, did not know how to classify them. On the one hand, they had immigrated directly from Russia and had Imperial Russian passports. However, they did not speak Russian or feel any loyalty toward the Russian Empire. Unlike many Italian and Greek immigrants who came to Omaha and other American cities after 1890, few Volgers who settled in Lincoln had any desire to return to the Old Country. In fact they were more like mid-nineteenth-century immigrants who came to America for political or religious reasons with the intention of remaining permanently.[34] Finally the Volgers spoke German dialects that clearly distinguished them from Russian-speaking Russians. But their dialect and their customs were so unique that German speakers from the Reich and Austria-Hungary did not accept them as being fellow Germans. Even Lincoln newspapers did not know what to call the Volgers. When the colonies were hit by a flood in 1904, the *Lincoln Star* noted, "Russians Flee from Lowlands."[35] When another big flood hit Lincoln ten years later, the *Lincoln Star* wrote that "German Russians Flee from Flooded Bottoms."[36]

The two colonies established by the Volgers were on inexpensive lots sold to them by the railroads along their rights of way near the Salt Creek floodplain. Unfortunately these districts flooded in June 1871, May 1873, June 1874, and especially in March 1881, when the colonies were left under five feet of water, nine people lost their lives, and hundreds were left homeless. More floods came in 1892, 1902, and 1908, the latter again leaving nine dead and hundreds homeless. I was a witness to the last big flood to hit Lincoln. In May 1950 more than five inches of rain fell southeast of Lincoln affecting not only the Bottoms but also the Pauley Lumber Company. I remember going with my father to witness the disaster. Altogether fourteen people died, and the flood resulted in $53 million in damage. I recall that it took weeks to clean up the mess. The flood led to the establishment of the Salt-Wahoo Watershed Association, which straightened Salt Creek and created levees along its banks.[37]

By 1920 there were an estimated eight thousand people living in the North and South Bottoms. By 1925 as many as twelve thousand lived in these two neighborhoods. These areas were large enough in population and compact enough in size that they became economically and socially self-sufficient. They had their own stores and a post office, thus making it unnecessary for residents to be fluent in English or to shop in Lincoln's nearby commercial district. Even more important, they had their own churches, which were not only places of worship but also centers of social life.

The status of the Germans from Russia cannot be understood without a brief survey of their history. They originated in the Rhineland-Palatinate in what is now southwestern Germany, an area that had been devastated by the invading armies of Louis XIV in the 1680s and again in the Seven Years' War between Prussia and Austria, which ended in 1763. In 1762 a German princess, later known as Catherine the Great, became Empress of Russia. A relatively enlightened ruler, she wished to consolidate Russian rule over a steppe-frontier area bordering the lower Volga River, which was sparsely populated by wild Mongolian tribes. She tried to do this by issuing manifestos in 1762 and 1763 inviting industrious western Europeans to immigrate to Russia. To sweeten the invitation, she promised potential colonists perpetual freedom from conscription into the notorious Russian army, freedom from taxation for up to thirty years, freedom to govern themselves, freedom to have their own religion, and reception of interest-free loans to build homes and purchase farming equipment. Finally she would pay for their migration by sea to St. Petersburg and by boat down the Volga River. My great-great-great-great-great-grandfather Philipp Jacob Paulÿ was one of the people who accepted the invitation.

It seems hard to believe now that anyone would prefer to emigrate from the German Rhineland to Russia rather than to North America. However, in the days of sailing ships, it took several weeks just to reach Rotterdam and several more days for a ship to fill up and for the winds to be favorable before crossing the Atlantic could even begin. After that it would take seven to twelve weeks, or sometimes even longer, to cross the Atlantic, with the mortality rate averaging close to 20 percent and rising to as high as 37 percent.[38] Those people who could not pay for their passage were sold into indentured servitude. Sailing through the Baltic and floating down the Volga, never out of sight of land, seemed like an easier and safer trip. Furthermore immigrants to North America could not expect any help from the colonial government in the 1760s. Between around 1683 and 1750, most German immigrants headed for Pennsylvania, with some help from the British crown. But they usually arrived half-starved, emaciated, and penniless and were forced to become indentured servants until the cost of their passage had been repaid.

After several very rough years, the villages along the Volga River began to prosper, at least by Russian standards. However, in 1871 Czar Alexander II reneged on Catherine's promise of local autonomy. Three years later Alexander made military training compulsory for every male reaching the age of twenty-one, including those living in the German colonies. Service was to be for six years, four for men who had completed primary school, and all draftees were forced to remain in the reserves for five years.

Military conscription was the last straw for my great-great-grandfather Heinrich, who had two sons approaching military age. Consequently the family moved in 1878, this time to the frontier town of Harvard, in south-central Nebraska, where Heinrich and his sons were able to farm. It was a relatively easy transition in some respects because the weather in Nebraska was not terribly different from the Lower Volga area—blizzards and droughts were commonplace in both locations, and the crops that did well in Russia like wheat, rye, barley, oats, and sunflowers did equally well in Nebraska.

Immigration historians often refer to "push and pull" forces that affect the decision to emigrate. The threat that two of my great-great-grandfather's sons might be conscripted was a factor "pushing" Heinrich to move. The threat must have been especially dire in 1877, when Russia was at war with the Ottoman Empire.[39] However, equally important was the rapid growth of the Volga German population, especially after 1860, which reduced the size of the plots allotted each family. As to "pulls," the Homestead Act of 1862 opened vast areas west of the Missouri River to cultivation. The completion of the transcontinental railroad from Omaha to San Francisco in 1869, as well as branch lines built soon thereafter throughout Nebraska by the Burlington and Missouri Railroad, meant that a trip from the Lower Volga all the way to Nebraska was relatively fast and easy. It took Heinrich and his family two days to go thirty-five miles by wagon from their village of Norka to Saratov, a Russian railhead and river port on the Volga, about three or four days by train to reach Hamburg, Germany's main port on the North Sea, two weeks to cross the Atlantic on a hybrid ship (having both sails and steam power), and another four or five days to go from New York to Harvard, Nebraska. It took around twenty-four days in all. It must have been an arduous trip without a private state room on their ship (the *Wieland*) or sleeping bunks on trains in Europe and America. But compared to the fifteen months it took my ancestors and other Volgers to go from the Palatinate to the Volga, the trip in 1878 must have seemed like a summer vacation. The thousands of Volgers who went directly to Lincoln, most notably between 1898 and 1914, must have felt the same way.

Another "pull" factor for my ancestors was provided in part by Christian Pauli, probably a brother or cousin of Heinrich, who arrived in Sutton, Nebraska—sometimes called "Russian town" because of its large German Russian population—along with six other families from Norka.[40] Once settled the families began to write their friends and relatives back home enthusiastically describing the landscape, soil, and climate, all of which were perfect for growing wheat, a grain with which Volga Germans were familiar. Friends and relatives in America did more than write. Sixty-five percent of the Volgers who came to Nebraska came on tickets prepaid by their kinsmen.[41]

The timing of Heinrich and his family was almost certainly not accidental. The years from 1873 through 1877 had begun with banking speculation in Berlin and Vienna and a crash on Wall Street, which in turn was followed by a huge railroad strike, a drought, and grasshopper devastations. All that was in the past when my ancestors arrived in Nebraska in 1878. What did change was the cost of farmland, which had *decreased* by half. Otherwise 1878 marked the beginning of twelve years of ample rain, big harvests, and a doubling of Nebraska's official population to more than one million.

The date of one's arrival in the United States turned out to be a major factor in the economic and social lives of immigrants. Being illiterate, like my great-great-grandfather Heinrich, was not a major handicap for a farmer plowing his fields behind a horse. He and his sons soon became prosperous farmers. My great-grandfather Conrad sold his farm in 1908, when the price of farmland was near a peak, and seven years later moved the family to Lincoln, where he helped my grandfather, Ludwig Heinrich Pauley, establish the Pauley Lumber Company at a time when Lincoln's population was booming and the demand for housing, and thus lumber, was strong. My grandfather, as best I can determine, was the first person of Volga German descent to graduate from high school in the whole state of Nebraska. In deciding to enter the lumber business, where one needs to have a broad geographic and ethnic clientele, he had no choice but to speak and write fluent English. His grandfather Heinrich, a farmer, had no such need and never even learned how to sign his name.

The timing of my ancestors' arrival in Nebraska differed radically from that of the vast majority of 6,500 Volga Germans who eventually settled in Lincoln.[42] In fact the number of Volga Germans who emigrated to Lincoln was in the low single digits until 1887. Even then it was modest until 1898, held down by the Panic of 1893 and several years of drought. Prosperity had returned to Nebraska by 1898 and with it a flood of new German Russian immigrants. After that date fear of a conflict between Russia and Japan caused Volgers to worry that emigration might soon be forbidden.[43] Consequently immigration to Lincoln peaked at 576 in 1913.

The arrival of most Volga Germans starting in 1898 is of great importance for two reasons. By that date all farmland in Nebraska had long since been occupied. Secondly the late arrival of the Volgers coincided with the annual arrival of huge numbers of Greeks, Italians, Jews, and Slavs from eastern Europe and was now far higher than immigrants coming from northern and western Europe. The fact that the Volgers also came from Russia and spoke a dialect that even immigrants from Germany had difficulty understanding caused them to be lumped together with other unpopular recent immigrants.

Not knowing English was a major handicap for finding a well-paying job in a town like Lincoln. A major employer of Volga men was the nearby Burlington Railroad, which hired them as mainte-

35. Volga Germans arriving in Lincoln (undated). Courtesy of History Nebraska.

nance personnel. Women and girls could get jobs as housekeepers or office janitors. Some Volga German men became thriving small businessmen who catered to other Germans from Russia. Their many businesses, along with their vegetable gardens, chickens, and cows, made the Bottoms virtually self-sufficient.[44]

Each spring a large proportion of Lincoln's Volga population, perhaps as much as 40 percent, took special trains to western Nebraska, especially to the area near Scottsbluff, where they planted, cultivated, and harvested sugar beets before returning to Lincoln in the fall. Much like today's largely Hispanic seasonal workers, they apparently lived in tiny cabins, perhaps resembling cabins built for adventuresome motorists in the 1920s. By 1915 their thrift and independence meant that 60.8 percent of them had fully paid off their mortgages, and 75 percent had partially done so in five years.[45] My father owned a farm near Morrill, Nebraska, near the Wyoming border. I have no idea how or when he purchased it, but sugar beets were growing on it the last time he saw it in September 1987, just days before he died.

Hattie Plum Williams, a graduate student at the University of Nebraska and later a distinguished professor of sociology at the university, described the Volgers in a dissertation completed in 1909 as having "large stores of physical energy and an almost unlimited capacity for work. The majority . . . are literate although the

amount of their education is limited. They are thrifty and independent, almost never applying for public aid. They are law abiding . . .
[and] extremely religious; all their social as well as spiritual life
being bound up in the church which they support right royally."[46]
Thanks to this "capacity for work," these annual treks helped the
Volgers not only to survive but to achieve a modest prosperity.[47]

However, this same capacity for work left the Volgers' hands
stained with beet juice, which led to the popular notion that they
had dirty hands, hence the label "dirty Rooshians." As such the
beet harvesters had a "racial" status just slightly higher than Mexicans or Japanese.[48] A probably more serious consequence of the
Volgers being seasonal farmhands was that their children often
missed a month of school in the spring and another month in the
fall. Hence the assumption that they were not only dirty but also
"dumb" or "slow."[49] Most American schools at that time ignored
the cultural background of immigrant children along with their
special needs and abilities. Old World customs, dances, folklore,
and music were denigrated by teachers who were anxious to Americanize their students, and the young immigrants readily complied.[50]
Whatever educational failing the children of German Russians
appeared to display, chances are they were healthier than native-
born Americans, because while as children in the Volga villages,
they had been given vaccines for diphtheria and smallpox. (Soviet
dictator Josef Stalin was not so fortunate, having to spend his life
with his face covered with smallpox scars.)

The rapid growth of Lincoln's German Russian population,
especially between 1898 and 1914, strongly resembled the immigration of other ethnic or religious groups from eastern and central Europe. By 1915 there were around 6,500 Volga Germans in
Lincoln, just a small part of the 750,000 German Russians who
had come to the United States between 1874 and 1914.[51] The
576 Volgers who settled in Lincoln in 1913 alone were nearly as
numerous as all the German Russians who had come to Lincoln
between 1872 and 1897.[52] Prior to the American Civil War, nearly
all immigrants came to North America by sailing ship, which, as
mentioned above, made for a long, expensive, and dangerous trip.
Unless you were wealthy, like Benjamin Franklin or Thomas Jef-
ferson, you had neither the time nor the money to return to the

Old Country. Until 1856 96.4 percent of immigrants came to this country in steerage class, with the voyage on sailing ships taking anywhere from six weeks to six months depending on the wind. By 1873 an even higher percentage of immigrants came on *steamships*.[53] If the ship left from Liverpool, Le Havre, or Hamburg, the voyage to New York would take around ten days to two weeks. Ships coming from Italy or Greece needed around three weeks to reach the United States. The difference in sailing time and consequently the freshness of the food meant that the mortality rate was cut by 90 percent. The other consequence was that it was now possible to live in the United States for anywhere from a few months to a few years and then return to the Old Country.

Omaha had many of these "New Immigrants," mostly Poles, Italians, and Greeks, nearly all of whom were males between the ages of fifteen and thirty-five, which sometimes led to violence. Many of these minorities, especially young Greeks, expected to return to their homeland and therefore made little or no effort to learn English or adapt to American customs. Consequently they gained the status of unwelcome intruders. When some Greeks made lewd comments about passing women, they were attacked by a thousand men in February 1909.[54] Because the Volga Germans came to America in complete families as had the Pennsylvania Dutch in the eighteenth century, there was no shortage of young women for Volga boys to pursue.[55] The patriarchal family made it less likely that their younger members would want to embarrass their fathers or grandfathers by getting in trouble.

Germans from Russia had no such attachment to their former Russian homeland, where they had been viewed as outsiders and with considerable envy by ethnic Russians because of their privileges and relative prosperity. They were increasingly subjected to Russification during the reign of Alexander II (1881–94) and sporadically during the time when the last czar, Nicholas II (1894–1917), was in power. Very few Volgers ever returned to their old villages, and those who did lived to regret it. However, the fact that most of them arrived in Lincoln between 1898 and 1914 during the same period as other eastern Europeans, and that their dress and speech were equally unfamiliar, almost automatically made them suspect in the eyes of Lincolnites whose ancestors had immigrated to the

United States several generations earlier. Having lived in ethnic "islands" among sometimes hostile Russians forced the Volga Germans to be self-sufficient and cling to their language and religion. Friday afternoon German classes in Lincoln helped preserve the ancestral language for children, and a weekly German-language newspaper, *Die Welt-Post*, which was published in Lincoln from 1916 to 1970, helped create a common German American identity and a German Russian identity for as many as 160,000 German-language readers throughout the Midwest.[56] Their churches served both their spiritual and social needs and were "packed to the rafters" as often as three times a week. Wedding celebrations lasting three days, a practice they may have picked up from Russians, were a particularly important time for socializing in addition to dancing and playing cards.[57]

Volga parents were not at all eager to have their children go to public schools because they feared Americanization might lead to an estrangement between the generations.[58] One saving grace was that the public schools in the United States did not try to change their students' religion, in sharp contrast to schools for American Indians. After around 1926 estrangements rarely occurred between second-generation Volgers, who were bilingual, and the nearly fully assimilated, monolingual third generation. As a fourth-generation Volga German on my father's side, I was not even aware of my Volga heritage until I was in college.

Lincoln's Volga Germans could not count on the support of those Germans who had come to the United States from central Europe. In fact such Germans, even though twice as numerous as the Volgers, were not concentrated in any area but were scattered throughout the city and did not wish to be confused with Volgers. Moreover they had an active cultural life of their own including literary, musical, and dramatic groups.[59] The Volga Germans were equally determined to deny that they were Russians. Some of them even denied being born in Russia.[60]

The Volgers were in fact quite different from the Reich Germans both in speech and in customs. Until the First World War, both groups were intent on retaining their knowledge of German and were quick to use it with other German-speaking people. The central European Germans urged their children to study German in school, which helped make German more frequently studied in American high schools than all the other *modern* foreign languages put together.

The Volgers spoke village dialects of German that had remained essentially unchanged since their ancestors had left the Palatinate in the 1760s. Not surprisingly they resembled the language of the Pennsylvania Dutch, who had settled in the colony between 1683 and 1750 because both groups had come from the Palatinate in Germany.[61] By the late nineteenth and early twentieth centuries, many words used by the Volgers were no longer used by other German speakers. Similar differences exist between the French spoken in France and that spoken in Quebec and the Dutch spoken by Afrikaners in South Africa and that spoken in the Netherlands.

The Volgers were also easily distinguishable by their usually dark clothes, sheepskin coats, felt boots, wide-brimmed hats, and black, three-cornered shawls, which were worn even in the heat of Nebraska summers. Volga women walking three paces behind their husbands only intensified the negative stereotypes and made them seem "different," even compared to other native German speakers. Therefore those Lincolnites whose ancestors had come from central Europe were not always eager to accept the Volgers as full-fledged fellow Germans. All ethnic Germans, however, seemed to agree on their opposition to prohibition and suffrage for women.

The North and South Bottoms retained their distinct character through the 1920s, the Great Depression, and the Second World War. It was the thoroughly Americanized third and fourth generations who left the Bottoms between the late 1940s and the 1960s to seek newer and more spacious neighborhoods elsewhere in Lincoln. Symbolic of this change is the fact that Friedens Lutheran Church in the South Bottoms held its last German-language worship service in 1961. Just prior to the change, I had the opportunity to visit one of their services. As a master's candidate in the Department of History at the University of Nebraska, I was anxious to improve my understanding of spoken German. I was pleasantly surprised to discover that I could easily understand the sermon because it was delivered in the "correct" High German, which was standard in Volga German churches everywhere in the United States just as it had often been in Russia. Widowers sat on the right side of the church, married couples in the middle, and widows on the left side. After the service I chatted with some members of the congregation who seemed pleased to meet a young person who took an interest in their culture.

I was far from being the only person of Volga German heritage curious about my ancestral heritage. In 1968 the American Historical Society of Germans from Russia was founded in Greeley, Colorado, a region in northern Colorado filled with descendants of Germans from Russia. Five years later its international headquarters was moved to Lincoln just across the street from Friedens Lutheran Church in the South Bottoms. Its mission was to ensure that the "discovery, collection, preservation, and dissemination of information related to the history, cultural heritage and genealogy of Germanic Settlers in the Russian Empire and their descendants remained constant."[62]

Whatever distinctions there were between Volga Germans and Germans who had immigrated directly from the Reich soon disappeared after the outbreak of the First World War in 1914 and especially after the American entry into the war in April 1917. The fate of the Volga Germans and German-speaking immigrants can be more easily seen as part of the dramatic changes brought about by the First World War.

9

World War, "Aggressive Patriotism," and the Spanish Flu

The "Great War" and "Scientific" Propaganda

The First World War witnessed both the climax of the era of progress and reform and the beginning of a reaction to it, which included a collapse of the social and political order. The war was especially tragic, because at its outset, Europeans were freer and more prosperous than ever before. The war had a direct and dramatic effect on virtually all aspects of everyday affairs in the United States, even though no dynasty was dethroned. Transportation, entertainment, women's suffrage, prohibition, the sale of cigarettes, football, and especially public health were all affected by the war. Lincoln was no exception.

The American response to the war can only be understood in the overall context of the war and its background. Despite numerous war scares in Europe since 1905, the war came as a shock to most Americans, especially to those relatively isolated in the Midwest, where the war seemed especially remote. There had been numerous wars in Europe since the end of the French Revolutionary and Napoleonic Wars in 1815, but they had all been short-lived, were not terribly destructive, and had not involved the United States.

Surprisingly European military planners had not viewed the carnage of troops in the American Civil War as a predictor for the horrors of modern warfare. There were plenty of European military eyewitnesses to the incredible destructiveness of the war, but they attributed it to neither side having a professional army; in other words, in the condescending views of these observers, the Americans simply did not know what they were doing. The impact of the machine gun had already been demonstrated before the Great War, but the more recent wars had ended before the mind-numbing ability of these guns to kill could be fully grasped. The importance of barbed wire, so obvious to American farmers, especially in prairie states like Nebraska, had also not been fully appreciated by most military strategists.[1] Consequently the model of modern warfare was not the American Civil War but the short German wars of unification, especially the Franco-Prussian War. The latter did resemble the American war in so far as both featured incredibly bloody battles. However, there were few such battles in 1870, the Prussian victors did not demand unconditional surrender from the French, and the French government was not willing to continue a hopeless struggle.

Not just the lessons of warfare during the previous half century were ignored; also the lessons spelled out by one of the greatest military thinkers of all time, Carl von Clausewitz (1780–1831), in his famous book, *On War*, published posthumously in 1832, went unheeded. Clausewitz argued that defense is inherently stronger than offense because it can be fought from prepared and fortified lines. Moreover a retreating army retreats to friendly and familiar territory with shorter lines of supply. Meanwhile an invader's lines are lengthened and become vulnerable to counterattack. Unfortunately von Clausewitz's thesis was widely seen as a "dark stain" on his otherwise brilliant observations. However, it was precisely the superior strength of the defense during World War I that led to a bloody, four-year stalemate.

The war was ignited by the assassinations of Franz Ferdinand, the Austrian archduke and heir apparent to the throne of Austria-Hungary, and his wife in Sarajevo, the capital of the Austro-Hungarian territory of Bosnia-Herzegovina on June 28, 1914. The murders were given extensive coverage in American newspapers. The *New York Times* devoted most of its June 29 front page to the assassinations; diplomatic developments related to them were covered on interior pages for another week. After that it dropped the story. Meanwhile the *Lincoln Daily News* and the *Lincoln Star* gave the assassinations one or two columns on their June 29 front pages and additional coverage the next day. After that they too dropped the story. Like newspapers around the whole country, they did not imagine that assassinations in a remote corner of the world would ultimately draw the United States into war.[2] The *Lincoln Star* responded to the rush to war by saying that "Americans, who are felicitating themselves over the fact that Uncle Sam is not involved in war, but is rather in a position to profit in the aggregate from the threatening and frightful situation in Europe, may well, pause to consider how easily it might have been otherwise. Would the United States be in its present highly gratifying position if Mr. [Theodore] Roosevelt had been elected president two years ago?"[3]

Because of the alliance systems involving all the great powers of Europe, assassinations in a relatively obscure part of the Balkan Peninsula could quickly explode into the first continent-wide war in a century. A fear shared by all the great European powers was that doing nothing would make their governments look weak and insipid, not only in the eyes of their people but also in the eyes of their alliance partners and rivals. Therefore doing nothing could result in a country losing its status as a great power. This fear proved to be greater than the fear of war itself.[4] In 1917 this same dread was a major factor in the American declaration of war against Germany. Ironically once the war had started, no continental power had clear-cut objectives beyond simply winning and protecting its status.[5]

The Allied powers—France, Russia, and Britain—assumed that the war was the result of the Germans using the assassinations in Sarajevo as mere pretext for starting a war, which would lead to Germany dominating the whole Continent if not the world. This "conspiracy theory" seemed confirmed by Germany's declaration of war. To counteract the threat posed by Russia's mobilization on Germany's eastern border, the German army should have been prepared to defend it. Unfortunately the Kaiser quickly learned that no such contingency plan existed. The only plan in the event of an impending war was to attack France by way of neutral Belgium. This invasion, more than any issue, reinforced the assumption of German war guilt. There is no doubt about the German offensive policy of invading France and Belgium. What was *not* known at the time was that *all* countries had *only* offensive plans in the event of war. For example France's contingency plan was to attack Germany by way of Belgium. Moreover it was a doctrine that assumed playing defense would be bad for the soldiers' morale. Allied military leaders held this belief to the very end of the war despite mind-boggling failures.[6] The American army, led by John J. Pershing, followed the same ideology when it entered the war in 1917. Meanwhile rigid censorship in *all* the belligerent countries kept civilians ignorant of the devastating failures of this strategy.

German guilt appeared especially glaring after reports of German atrocities in Belgium began to reach American newspapers. These reports—sometimes true, often exaggerated, and sometimes simply invented—were deliberately published by the British, which also prevented news favorable to Germany from reaching American newspapers. The national German-American Alliance immediately asserted that the "English press has been misleading America with information calculated to stigmatize Germany as the aggressor."[7] But the organization convinced few people who were not already pro-German.

It has often been said that "truth is the first casualty of war." The First World War was no exception. Propaganda had been employed in warfare since ancient times, but two things were new in 1914. *All* belligerent governments created propaganda in a thorough and almost "scientific" way.[8] Moreover the Great War was the first conflict in which propaganda was intended not just to demoralize the enemy but also to influence the recently literate, newspaper-reading public.[9] Moreover governments were not the only source of propaganda. Private citizens and clergymen joined in the effort as well. For example the evangelist Billy Sunday published an advertisement in the *Lincoln Star*, and doubtless hundreds of other newspapers across the country, promoting the purchase of war bonds as demonstrating that "you are either a patriot or a traitor. . . . What a mountain of crime God has on his books against that horde of Hellish Huns."[10]

German atrocity stories were not only either invented or exaggerated, but stories about real suffering of troops were censored, and defeats and retreats were presented as straightening out lines to more defensible positions. However, British and American propagandists had more difficulty gaining and retaining the support of the public for their entries into the war. Germany, Austria-Hungary, and France could argue that they had been attacked or were about

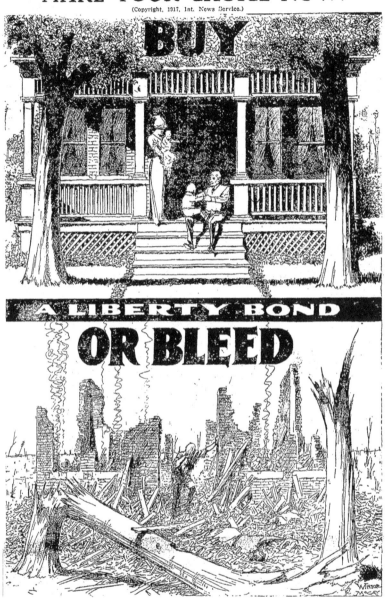

36. "Make Your Choice Now!" *Lincoln Star*, October 17, 1917, 1.

to be attacked, and therefore countermeasures had to be taken. Moreover those three countries, along with Imperial Russia, all had huge standing armies and millions of men in reserves who could be, and were in fact, called up with little to no resistance.[11] On the other hand, neither Britain nor the United States could point to a foreign army about to invade their territory or to a neighbor threatening the integrity of their country. Their volunteer standing armies were tiny compared to those of the continental powers. In 1914 the United States Army had ninety-eight thousand soldiers and twenty-seven thousand men in the National Guard. Preserving morale became an end in itself and a reason for censoring negative news.[12] Popular support in Britain and the United States could only be expected if Germans—whether in Germany or immigrants, along with their culture—could be depicted as evil, threatening, or even subhuman. Making matters even worse for army recruiters was that many immigrants, including the Volga Germans, had come to the United States at least in part to avoid conscription. My own paternal ancestors had the same motivation.

One famous American recruiting poster depicted a German soldier as a gorilla wearing a spiked German helmet and sporting a mustache like the one worn by the Kaiser. In one arm he carried a half-naked girl; his opposite hand grasped a huge club bearing the word *Kultur*. The ruins of a Belgian or French city were in the background; the Atlantic Ocean, which the German monster was about to cross, was in the foreground. The address of a recruiting office was at the bottom of the placard. Mild-mannered farm boys in the American Midwest, or in Yorkshire, Wales, or Scotland, were unlikely to volunteer for service if Germany and Austria-Hungary were depicted as normal, civilized countries, and their people as harmless, law abiding, and cultured.

German military authorities knew their country was not prepared to win a long war against France, Britain, and Russia. Those countries could rely on their combined human and natural resources even before considering the resources of their worldwide empires. Germany seemed to have only one option: it had effectively defeated France in just six weeks during the Franco-Prussian War of 1870. If it could do so again, it would have time to redirect its attention to Russia, whose army would presumably need six weeks to fully mobilize due to the size of its territory and its relatively poor transportation system.

By the end of September 1914, the so-called Schlieffen Plan—originally devised for a quick military knockout of France by Alfred von Schlieffen, the head of the German General Staff from 1894 to 1906—had proven to be a failure.[13] The war had quickly become a stalemate, something that few people, military or civilian, had expected, or if they had, were willing to admit. There appeared to be only two ways of breaking the stalemate: new weapons or persuading neutral countries to enter the war. The Central Powers—Germany and Austria-Hungary—persuaded Bulgaria and the Ottoman Empire to join their side. The entente powers—France, Britain, and Russia—bribed Italy and Romania to join their alliance with promises of Austro-Hungarian territory. The only result was that the war simply expanded. The one remaining neutral power, a state that could tip the balance of power, was the United States.

As previously mentioned most Americans who took an interest in the war accepted the Franco-British conspiracy theory that Germany and Austria-Hungary had used the assassinations at Sarajevo as mere pretext for a war of conquest and territorial expansion. Woodrow Wilson immediately announced the neutrality of the United States but insisted on the right of neutral countries to trade with any country in wartime. Since the British navy controlled the seas, Britain could blockade Germany while it imported weapons, ammunition, and desperately needed food from the United States. Meanwhile it prevented even food from reaching Germany and Austria-Hungary. Wilson objected to British violations of the neutrality laws but did nothing to force its compliance let alone threaten to declare war on the British.[14] In the meantime government-supported propaganda in all belligerent countries succeeded in demonizing enemies and convincing civilians that a compromise peace was unthinkable. German miscalculations, along with British propaganda, resulted in most Americans favoring the Allied side by 1915. Although more than happy to carry out a profitable one-sided trade with the Allies, most Americans did not favor outright military intervention.

This attitude was suddenly threatened in May 1915 with the sinking of the *Lusitania*, a British passenger liner, by a German submarine. The tragedy resulted in the loss of 1,959 lives, including 124 Americans. The British, who were chronically short of munitions at the beginning of the war, claimed that the ship had been carrying no war supplies.[15] However, subsequent investigations by U.S. Customs quickly revealed that the *Lusitania* was carrying a half ton of rifle cartridges, fifty tons of shrapnel shells, and two hundred tons of ammunition. Making the situation even more dangerous for the passengers, the *Lusitania* captain had not ordered lifeboat drills; like the sinking of the *Titanic* in 1912, there were not nearly enough lifeboats for its passengers and crew.[16]

The *Nebraska State Journal* called the sinking a "crowning infamy of a war of infamies" but added that it remained "the supreme duty of the American public to keep its temper. Nothing is to be gained by any other course."[17] Six weeks later the same newspaper maintained that "the American people, if we judge aright their opinions in this crisis, are determined that the result shall be justice without war. America owes it to the world to prove in this way that war is not the only alternative to submission to wrong."[18]

Profiles in Courage: Bryan and Norris

President Wilson announced American neutrality as soon as the war in Europe broke out, even going so far as saying that Americans should be neutral in thought as well as deed. However, by insisting that the United States had the right to sell weapons and ammunition to the Allies, he was hardly neutral in deed. William Jennings Bryan, the secretary of state, however, wanted to prevent the United States from having economic and emotional ties to either side and therefore recommended that Americans be discouraged from even loaning money to the belligerent states. He opposed Americans traveling on British ships carrying armaments, fearing that the loss of American lives would inevitably draw the United States into the war as indeed it eventually did in April 1917. Bryan believed that "Germany ha[d] the right to prevent contraband going to the Allies and a ship carrying contraband should not rely upon passengers to prevent her from attack."[19]

In a public statement explaining his resignation as secretary of state, Bryan asked,

Why should an American citizen be permitted to involve his country in war by traveling upon a belligerent ship when he knows that the ship will pass through a danger zone? The question is not whether an American has a right under international law . . . but whether he ought not, out of consideration for his country, if not for his own safety, avoid danger when avoidance is possible. . . . It is a very one-sided citizenship that compels a government to go to war over a citizen's rights and yet relieves the citizen of all obligations to consider his nation's welfare.[20]

Wilson's refusal to accept Bryan's advice to remain strictly neutral left Bryan isolated in the cabinet. On June 8, 1915, he resigned to protest Wilson's policy of holding Germany "strictly accountable" for any further loss of American lives. In so doing Wilson "surrendered to Berlin the decision on whether or when the United States would enter the war."[21] The *Nebraska State Journal* opined that Bryan's resignation was the "best thing for his country, himself, and the world."[22]

Bryan was not the only prominent Nebraskan to object to President Wilson's anti-German policies. Another was George W. Norris of McCook, already a five-term member of the U.S. House of Representatives, who would go on to serve five terms in the U.S. Senate from 1913 to 1943. Norris first aroused the outrage of the press in Nebraska as well as the state legislature by opposing, in March 1917, the arming of American merchant ships carrying war supplies to Britain fearing that such an action would ultimately lead to war with Germany.[23] His actions were especially risky and courageous because he was running for reelection in November 1918.

Equally outrageous and unpatriotic in the eyes of Norris's critics was his joining five other senators in opposing the declaration of war against Germany in April 1917 in addition to the twelve senators who abstained.[24] Norris's actions caused an outraged response from Nebraska newspapers and prominent citizens. A headline in a political advertisement appearing in the *Lincoln Star* declared that "Nebraska [was on] trial before the nation. . . . If Norris is re-elected, it will be taken as evidence that this is a 'Hun-ridden' state."[25] Another political ad in the same paper denounced Norris for having "voted against a bill that would stop the use of the mails for seditious and treasonable matter."[26] In a front-page edi-torial, the *Lincoln Star* declared that "Senator Norris is the pride of the Nebraska bolsheviki [Communists]. His vaporous arguments and his ranting about the dollar sign being on the American flag appeals strongly to this class. His nefarious opposition to Amer-ica taking her proper place in the war has endeared him to every Hun sympathizer in the state."[27]

Senator Norris's courage in opposing such hostile opposition won over enough Nebraskans for the governor to call off a special recall election and did not prevent Norris from being reelected in November 1918. The *Nebraska State Journal*, in sharp contrast to earlier opinions published by the *Lincoln Star*, remarked just before the end of the war that Norris had "a remarkably consis-tent record for the independence and progressiveness which men long for in their representatives."[28] His willingness to stand by his convictions resulted in then-Senator John F. Kennedy making Norris one of the twelve senators featured in his book, *Profiles in Courage*. Published in 1956, it won the Pulitzer Prize for Biogra-phy the following year.[29]

Ethnically Cleansing German Culture: "America Does Not Want You"

Denunciations of Senator Norris's anti-war views were common-place among most Americans, especially after the entry of the United States into the war. There is only one documented case of a German American being killed because of his heritage: Rob-ert Praeger, who was lynched in Collinsdale, Illinois.[30] However, American newspapers, influenced by British propaganda, depicted Germany and everything associated with Germany as being hell-bent on destroying Western civilization. Such attacks included German music and German food. At a time when British propa-ganda depicted the Germans as "Huns," major orchestras in the United States as well as the Metropolitan Opera in New York stopped performing compositions by German composers. Before the war the Met had presented a disproportionately large number of German operas, especially those composed by Richard Wag-ner. What is particularly ironic and tragic about these attacks on German Americans and German culture is that prior to the war ethnic Germans had been "frequently praised as the most assimilable [minority]."[31]

The censorship of German music was just one example of the attempt to control aspects of American actions, speech, beliefs, and political participation. Mark Sullivan, one of the most prominent journalists of the time, wrote years later that the war years marked "the greatest submission by the individual to the state that had occurred in any country at any time. . . . Government had learned that we could be led to do it, had learned the techniques of bringing the individual to give up his liberty, the cunning of propaganda, the artfulness of slogans, and the other methods for inciting mass solidarity and mass action, for causing majorities to insist on conformance by minorities."[32] When a letter writer said that he (or she) was a German American and "very proud of the German blood in my veins," Minerva, the usually sensible and moderate Lincoln advice columnist mentioned in chapter 4, responded, "If you are proud that your blood is akin to the blood of the Huns who are slaughtering innocent people in Europe today, then you had better leave this country as soon as possible. America does not want you."[33]

Wartime laws against espionage and sedition, passed in June 1917 and amended in May 1918, proscribed penalties for speaking, printing, or in any way expressing contempt for the government, flag, or uniform of the U.S. Army or Navy or saying anything that might inhibit the sale of U.S. bonds.[34] Conscientious objection was against the law, which included a refusal to wear army uniforms. One such case resulted in forty-five violators being sentenced to twenty-five years in prison.[35]

Newspapers did all they could to stir up hatred of the enemy. The use of the word "Huns" to depict modern-day German soldiers was a favorite in American newspapers, including Lincoln's. A check of the computer reveals that it was employed only 3 times in 1914 (before America's entry into the war) but no fewer than 4,356 times in 1918, when the war was reaching its climax.[36] The *Lincoln Star* quoted the *Chicago Daily News* as saying that Prussia, the largest of the German states, was a "robber state from first to last. . . . Prussianism long has meant the worship of force and contempt for morality, justice, law and right. . . . [As] an armed exponent of immoral philosophy [it] must be destroyed."[37]

Motion pictures, which had long been under suspicion for offending middle-class virtues, seized the opportunity to make money and demonstrate their patriotism by producing movies with "hate-the-Hun" themes. Movie theaters also introduced newsreels, which were moving pictures related to the news and in particular the horrors of war. More importantly they "established what we may call the accepted version of the war. . . . However, no filmmaker dared explain why the United States had gone to war."[38] On the other hand, a film called *Battle of the Somme*, produced by the British government to accurately display the horrors of war, was viewed by so many people as peace propaganda that it was quickly withdrawn from public showings.[39]

American movies showed no such ambiguities, as can be seen in such titles as *The Kaiser*, *The Beast of Berlin*, *The Prussian Cur*, and *To Hell with the Kaiser*, which were most common in 1918. It is important to note, however, that such movies and documentaries never dominated the film industry and were not subjected to government censorship. The Liberty Theatre in Lincoln featured a movie in September 1918 titled *The Hun Within*, which promised patrons that they would see "black and damnable schemes as are engineered by The Hun-villain. [They] would see the devil's spawn of Germany actually at work within our gates."[40] The Rialto Theatre in Lincoln showed a movie called *Pershing's Crusaders*, "which every red-blooded American should see [because] it was Uncle Sam's answer to the lies of the Hun."[41] Theaters also allowed their stages to be used by "four-minute men," who would give patriotic speeches between films within that time frame.

The attempt by moviemakers to ingratiate themselves with pro-war civilians as well as people who had long been suspicious of movies sometimes backfired. One movie, *The Spirit of '76*, suffered from bad timing. It depicted British soldiers committing terrible atrocities during the Revolutionary War. Such a movie, if released a few years earlier, might have been a box-office hit. However, its release after America's entry into the war resulted in the producer being tried, convicted, and given a five-year sentence in a federal penitentiary and fined $5,000 ($140,000 today) for besmirching an American ally.[42]

Some wartime laws and practices were sillier and more harmless than politically discriminatory. Such could be said for changing the names of frankfurters to hot dogs, hamburgers to liberty sandwiches, sauerkraut to liberty cabbage, and German measles to liberty measles. There were no ration books during the war, but President Wilson called for Mondays and Wednesdays to be wheatless and Tuesdays and Saturdays to be meatless. A new "victory bread" was to have 20 percent cereals other than wheat.[43] Beside eating less, people were urged to waste nothing. To conserve natural resources, school children collected tin cans, used paper, old toothpaste tubes, and apricot pits.[44] Except for apricot pits, I recall doing the same thing during the Second World War when I was at Prescott School in Lincoln.

Not so harmless were laws passed by the Nebraska State Legislature, which effectively disenfranchised many recent immigrants. The Nebraska Constitution of 1875 had allowed adult alien males to vote and hold office if they had filed appropriate initial papers stating their intent to become U.S. citizens.[45] In the fall of 1918, an amendment to the constitution was adopted that retroactively stiffened voting requirements for residents born outside the United States even if they had previously voted. There seems to be no record of how many men lost their voting rights through this amendment, but it was estimated that there were three thousand such people in Douglas County alone.[46]

> In the spring of 1919 the [State] Legislature passed a series of Americanization laws . . . [that] denied aliens the right to vote in all elections, including school elections and school district meetings; . . . denied aliens the right to hold any office or official position; . . . provided that only citizens might teach in any school; provided for the listing of all aliens in the state . . . and [that] only citizens might teach in any school, public, private, or parochial . . . [and] forbade the use or teaching of any except the English language in any school below the ninth grade.

The last stricture was ultimately declared unconstitutional by the Supreme Court in June 1923.[47]

The Selective Service Act of June 1917 revealed many disturbing aspects of American society, which clearly needed to be addressed. One out of every three men called up by draft boards proved to be physically unfit, with the fittest men coming from rural areas.[48] Of

37. "Lest We Forget." *Lincoln Star*, November 4, 1917, 1

the white recruits, 18 percent were foreign-born. Of these, eight million were German Americans, who often still had warm feelings for their motherland. Many of the foreign-born immigrants were illiterate or could not speak English or both. Twenty-five percent of native-born Americans could not read a newspaper or write a letter. Only 14.5 percent of the native-born people were high school graduates. Many of those who were ultimately drafted discovered the wonders of indoor plumbing, showers, and flush toilets.[49] The draft board revealed that one of three men examined proved to be physically unfit with a disproportionately large number of them coming from cities.

In addition to having an opportunity to learn how to read, write, and speak English, draftees were forced to become physically fit. One way of doing this was to encourage them to join sports teams, which involved not just fitness but also discipline, teamwork, and a willingness and ability to give and follow orders. This policy enabled schools like the University of Nebraska to use membership on the football team to serve as a substitute for the fourteen hours a week each player would have been required to spend on military drill.[50]

The Cornhuskers' football season in 1917 remained unchanged by the war and included Michigan in Ann Arbor, which ended in a 20–0 defeat, and a game against Syracuse in Lincoln, which the Huskers also lost, 10–9. In 1918 the Cornhuskers expected to have the toughest schedule in its history. However, games requiring train trips to Syracuse and West Virginia were canceled to save fuel, and a game against Missouri was called off because the Tigers were quarantined because of the Spanish flu. These contests were replaced by hastily organized training camp games, which often consisted mostly of college football players. On the other hand, after two postponements, Notre Dame once again came to Lincoln for a rain-soaked game that ended in the 0–0 tie described earlier.

The Campaign against Foreign Languages

The demand for conformity and super-patriotism affected all Nebraskans, but none more than ethnic Germans. The intolerance of anything that smacked of being neutral or nonpolitical was especially important in Nebraska with its two hundred thousand citizens who could trace their family roots to a German-speaking country, making ethnic Germans the largest minority not only in Nebraska but in the United States as a whole. Moreover at least forty German-language newspapers were published in Nebraska. By far the largest was Lincoln's weekly *Die Welt-Post*, which had a nationwide circulation of nearly 160,000, the second largest of all the 522 German-language publications in the country on the eve of the war.[51] It had an especially strong impact on the Volga Germans of Lincoln, giving them a strong sense of their unique identity as Germans from Russia.[52] This identity, however, did not prevent Volgers from being harassed by burning crosses, abuse, and vandalism such as dumping garbage on their lawns.[53] Unfortunately nearly half of the country's German-language publications were out of business by the end of the war because of tight censorship and the necessity of providing an expensive English translation before a copy could be issued. However, *Die Welt-Post* was one of the few German-language newspapers to be exempted from printing English translations of war news and survived the war intact. Churches in the Russian Bottoms neighborhood of Lincoln also continued to use German in their worship services.[54]

Lincoln papers were filled with stories about successes in shutting down the use of German.[55] But ardent Germanophobes were not satisfied with mere harassment of German-language newspapers. On April 9, 1919, the Nebraska State Legislature enacted the Siman Act, which related "to the teaching of foreign languages in any school public, private, parochial, or denomination in the state of Nebraska."[56] Based on the U.S. Espionage Act of the previous year, it forbade the use of "disloyal, profane, scurrilous, or abusive language" about the American government and called for transgressors to be imprisoned for up to twenty years. Children could only study a foreign language following the completion of the eighth grade, although it did permit the teaching of foreign languages after school hours.[57] The law was superfluous at Lincoln High School, which had ended the teaching of German in the summer of 1916, about nine months before the American declaration of war.[58] Laws similar to the Espionage Act of varying strictness were enacted in at least fourteen other states.[59] The Nebraska Supreme Court upheld the law in December 1919.

The Pauley family, which was of 100 percent German ethnicity, escaped the anti-German hysteria almost unscathed. My grandfather's birth in 1886 made him one year too old to be drafted. The Pauley name was free of any national identity, and as mentioned earlier, my grandfather was careful never to use his first and middle names, Ludwig and Heinrich. Moreover he avoided speaking German in public even though he could speak it fluently. However, my father noted in his autobiography that his father, like other businessmen, complained "about the number of Liberty

Bonds the Government forced him to buy on behalf of the Pauley Lumber Company." He had reason to object because after the war, the bonds suffered a sharp drop in value.[60]

Willa Cather, who could speak four foreign languages, denounced the language laws in no uncertain terms, "declaring that no child born in Nebraska can hope to gain a fluent speaking knowledge of a foreign language because the languages are barred from the schools under the eighth grade. . . . Will it make a boy or a girl any less an American to know one or two other languages? According to that sort of argument your 100 per cent American would be a deaf mute."[61]

The end of the war did not merely apply to the campaign against the teaching of German or instruction in German. Instead of the German military and language being the threat, it was now "alien doctrines" whose exposure could presumably be best avoided by forbidding the teaching of any foreign language in the lower grades. In 1923 the Siman Act was overturned by the U.S. Supreme Court because it "interfered with the right of a foreign language teacher to teach and of parents to instruct their children."[62]

Nevertheless, as I can personally testify, in the 1950s foreign languages were still not offered in Lincoln public schools prior to the tenth grade, even though the optimum time for learning a foreign language is in the primary grades, if not earlier.[63] Ironically when I was a graduate student at the University of Nebraska, I discovered that a working knowledge of two foreign languages, most commonly German and French, were *prerequisites* for attaining a PhD.

"A Strong Aggressive War Spirit"

The German language was not the only victim of anti-German hysteria. The University of Nebraska, whose reputation and large student enrollment had made it one of the top universities in the country, came under attack in the late spring of 1918 for harboring "a few instructors who have been unable to accept a strong aggressive war spirit and whose actions [have] been entirely lacking in 100 per cent patriotism."[64] The allegation came just as the U.S. Army was beginning to play a major role in slowing down a last-ditch German offensive. War fever in Lincoln and throughout the country was at its peak. The Nebraska State Council of Defense,

LOYALTY

100%

75%

50%

30%

38. "Do You Measure Up to That?" *Lincoln Star*, July 6, 1918, 3.

like similar councils across the country, was created by an act of the legislature shortly after the United States entered the war in April 1917; its role was to coordinate efforts supporting the war. To that end it "vigorously sought out the areas in the state where support of the war appeared to be unsatisfactory."[65] The *Lincoln Star* gave its full-throated support to the investigation of alleged insufficient patriotism. It was joined by the student newspaper, the *Daily Nebraskan*, as well as the university's alumni association.

The University of Nebraska was in a vulnerable situation because like many other institutions of higher learning in the country, some of its best professors and administrators had studied at German universities. As we have seen, scholar-athlete Louise Pound studied at the University of Heidelberg before teaching in the University of Nebraska English department. Fred Fling, a well-published member of the history department, had also studied in Germany, as had Chancellor Samuel Avery, who spoke at many German American functions.

The state university was by no means slow in demonstrating its patriotism. On April 24, 1917, just eighteen days after the U.S. declaration of war against Germany, the university staged a huge patriotic downtown parade and rally. Four thousand students, faculty, and regents, plus the cadet band, took part in the parade. The *Daily Nebraskan* denounced anyone who had not participated as a "dirty yellow coward." By May 3 five hundred students had withdrawn from the university and enlisted.[66] A year later university students along with five thousand school children were among fifteen thousand people who marched in support of the war, the largest such march in the city's history.[67]

The *Lincoln Star*, declaring in May 1918 that the university was a "patriotic institution," demanded that the regents "dismiss all instructors who are not proving themselves fit teachers of American principles. . . . Every trace of weak or stifled patriotism must be swept aside. Instructors whose attitude on the war is unwholesome and wish-washy should not be employed to teach the youth of Nebraska another year."[68] The Nebraska State Council of Defense, as well as other critics of the university, were given a wide latitude in defining "disloyal" or "unpatriotic actions."[69]

On April 18, 1918, the Nebraska State Council of Defense demanded of the university's Board of Regents that "the University of Nebraska be purged of the influence of professors, who are not whole-heartedly supporting the United States in the war." Two departments were singled out by the council for condemnation: the Department of American History (a unified history department came only later) and the Graduate School of Education. "The days when everyone connected with the state university be united by an outspoken fealty to the nation, and that notions of academic freedom which permits no excuses, lack of whole hearted aggressive support of the nation at this time, should be severely frowned upon and dealt with."[70] The *Daily Nebraskan* complained about the continued existence of the two German clubs on campus, the Ger-

39. "Mopping Up." *Lincoln Star*, September 18, 1918, 1.

man Dramatic Club and the Deutsche Geseilige Verein, the latter whose purpose as stated in the university's 1913 yearbook was
to "promote German culture." The student newspaper wanted
to know why these two groups met secretly and conducted their
business in German.[71] The article concluded by asking, "How
long will Nebraska tolerate these questionable Americans?" However, the regents also promised to ignore "anonymous reports and
comments."[72]

The regents responded to the council's demands and those of
the *Daily Nebraskan* by calling for a public hearing, promising that
"anyone who had said, taught or advised anything not proper in
the prosecution of the war or whose behavior is negative, halting

or hesitating in support of the government, shall be summarily dismissed from the service of the university."[73]

Not all Lincoln newspapers were as eager as the *Lincoln Star*, the *Daily Nebraskan*, and the Nebraska State Council of Defense to fire professors for their "faint-hearted and adulterated patriotism."[74] The *Lincoln Herald* called the investigation a "fiasco, or in modern parlance, bunk, from the evidence thus far introduced. It is such charges as these and promiscuous lambasting of citizens who do not kowtow to the powers that be that has given Nebraska such a bad reputation abroad as to its disloyalty. . . . We need peace and harmony at home, but it seems some of the men whose duty it is to promote harmony have done their very best to promote discord."[75]

The issue of disloyalty was finally laid to rest on June 19, 1918, when the Board of Regents issued its findings and stated that the "State Council had failed to prove a single case of disloyalty at the University."[76] Three professors did lose their jobs because "they had involved themselves and the University in public criticism, destroying their usefulness to the university."[77] The *Lincoln Star* charged the regents with a whitewash, but most Nebraska newspapers believed that the hearings had shown the affair had been distorted and exaggerated.[78] The *Nebraska State Journal* concluded by asking, "Was ever an important state matter so bungled or were deadly charges ever brought with so much recklessness as characterized this case involving the honor of men and the reputation of the people's most cherished institution of learning?"[79] Robert Knoll noted in *Prairie University* that "everybody associated with the investigation wished to forget the whole thing."[80] James Olson concluded in his *History of Nebraska* that there were "excesses on the home front of which few would later be proud."[81]

The Spanish Flu: "Not an Unusual Epidemic"?

As I write these lines in 2022 during COVID-19, few subjects covered in this book are likely to be more relevant than the Spanish flu pandemic of 1918–19. The word "Spanish" is misleading. Spain was involved in name only because, as a neutral country in the World War, it was not subjected to wartime censorship and did not hesitate to publicize the virus. In the United States, the flu was mentioned in newspapers but never with bold headlines or anything that might depress wartime morale. As a result the Spanish flu has been virtually omitted from our collective consciousness until recently and is rarely mentioned in American history textbooks.[82] An exception to this widespread amnesia should be made for people who know of ancestors who perished in the epidemic.

We can make only educated guesses as to how many Americans died from the Spanish flu. John Barry, the author of the most comprehensive study of the disease, estimates that 675,000 Americans perished and tens of millions were sickened at a time when the country had a population of fewer than 105 million. Barry estimates that if the population had been as large in 1918–19 as it was in 2006, when the book was written, there would have been well over 1,750,000 victims.[83] A recent estimate is that as many as twenty-five million Americans were infected by the Spanish flu but survived.[84] It is an amazing fact that this epidemic, which killed roughly as many Americans as soldiers who died in the Civil War, was almost entirely blotted from our collective memory. For example historian Paul Johnson does not even mention the Spanish flu in his 1,088-page *A History of the American People*. Nor does Seymour Morris Jr. in his iconoclastic *American History Revised: 200 Startling Facts That Never Made It into the Textbooks*. The same omission occurs in Howard Zinn's best-selling and iconoclastic *A People's History of the United States, 1492–Present* even though he explores many topics previously unexplored by other authors of textbooks. Even the popular *The Growth of the American Republic* by the distinguished historians Samuel Eliot Morison, Henry Steele Commager, and William E. Leuchtenburg does not devote a single sentence to the pandemic.

The pandemic is usually reported as having started in March 1918 in Haskell County, Kansas, in the remote southwestern corner of the state. It is not known why it began there, but a local boy who returned to Camp Funston near Manhattan, Kansas, after a visit home brought the virus with him. The camp housed fifty-six thousand soldiers, who were stacked in bunks without adequate heat or medical facilities. At first one hundred soldiers were affected; a week later the number had grown to five hundred.

However, it was not until the fall of 1918 that the epidemic became serious. On September 28 a parade in Philadelphia—the biggest parade in the city's history—caused the virus to virtually explode. Public health officials had begged the parade organizers to call it off but to no avail. Three days after the parade, every hospital bed in the city was filled, and more than a hundred people were dead in part because many of the city's doctors and nurses were in France.[85] Five days after the parade, all churches, schools, and theaters were closed.[86] The parade marked the beginning of the deadliest two-month period of the epidemic.

What made the Spanish flu especially dangerous was that it occurred during the most violent period of the Great War, a time when a huge number of American physicians and nurses were in France. Of those who remained in the United States, most had graduated from medical schools that would accept any man (but not woman) who applied.[87] Contributing still further to the mortality rate was resistance to the wearing of masks, which became a symbol of government overreach.

The summer of 1918 saw the end of the last German offensive after which Austria-Hungary and Germany began putting out peace feelers. However, President Wilson was determined to impose a punitive peace on the enemy even though in December 1917 he had said that "there must be a peace without victory."[88] To impose a draconian peace, Wilson was determined to keep all factories, with their crowded working conditions, operating at full capacity. Ships, jam-packed with soldiers, continued to set sail for the ten-day crossing of the Atlantic.

President Wilson was also adamant that nothing be said or written about the flu that would lower morale. Although newspapers, including Lincoln's, did publish stories about the flu, they did not reveal its full strength or threat. Some of the stories appeared on the first pages of Lincoln's papers but nothing like the headlines devoted to battles involving Americans in France. Wilson himself never even mentioned the virus, either publicly or privately, even though he was the first president to hold press conferences—in fact two a week.[89] For that matter no other national official spoke publicly about the dangers of the flu. Free speech was perhaps the biggest casualty of the war. Never have freedom of speech, journalism, and the mail been so severely impaired: not during the Civil War, the Second World War, the McCarthy era, or the Vietnam War.[90]

Public health officials for the most part believed that the influenza was airborne and not spread by germs. Otherwise they felt humiliated because they had no idea about the precise cause of the flu or how it should be treated. Many specialists hoped, in vain, that the epidemic would "gradually subside with improved weather."[91] Efforts to cope with the disease were like those employed in 2020 against COVID-19: wearing a face mask, washing one's hands frequently and thoroughly, avoiding wraparound roll towels, and staying away from public places such as theaters and churches. Streetcars were to be ridden only if well ventilated. As for social distancing, authorities recommended just three feet, not today's standard of six. Also, like today, many schools and universities, including the University of Nebraska and Nebraska Wesleyan University, closed their campuses. However, a century ago, as today, many people soon grew tired of the restrictions, especially face masks, which were mandatory in some big western cities, including Denver, San Francisco, and Seattle. Violators could be fined $5 to $10 ($125 to $250 in today's money) or spend forty-eight hours in jail.[92] A surprising difference between now and then is that the Spanish flu did not disproportionally impact different ethnic groups.[93] It also differed from other diseases by attacking the young, strong, and healthy between the ages of twenty and forty, not primarily the old and ill.[94] John Barry concludes that "public officials and the media helped create . . . terror—not by exaggerating the disease but by minimizing it, by trying to reassure. . . . For if there is a single dominant lesson from 1918, it is that governments need to tell the truth in a crisis. Risk communication implies managing the truth. You don't manage the truth. You tell the truth."[95]

Lincolnites were not entirely in the dark as far as flu epidemics were concerned. The *Lincoln Star* reported that the normal, seasonal flu had spread across the country in January 1916.[96] But it was nothing compared to the Spanish flu, which was reported as having broken out in training camps in Massachusetts, New York, and Virginia in September 1918. It was typical that no statistics were cited as to the number of soldiers sick or dead.[97] On October 1, 1918, the health and sanitation committee of the Lincoln Commercial Club passed a resolution that said that "the present epidemic which is in the city is not unusual. It is just an influenza epidemic that sweeps the country at times. It is not an unusual epidemic."[98]

Many newspaper articles in Lincoln and around the country mixed useful advice with advertising, particularly ads related to cure-all products. Advertising regulations were new in 1918, the Federal Trade Commission having been functioning for less than three years. Meanwhile advertising made up close to 66 percent of newspaper revenues.[99] Furthermore it was not always easy to tell the difference because both ads and authentic news were printed with the same type and located in the same general area of a newspaper. A reader did not cognize an ad unless he or she read what was below the article's last line.[100]

On October 4, 1918, the *Lincoln Star* reported in a front-page article the alarming news that 175,000 soldiers and civilians were down with the epidemic but gave no figures as to how many had died. Lincoln's health superintendent was reassuring in an announcement published four days later that "the so-called Spanish influenza exists in a mild form. . . . Few epidemics show such few fatalities considering the large number of cases already reported." The superintendent "wants to allay the unnecessary freight of panic which now exists in the minds of a certain number of people. He saw no necessity for closing the schools, churches, and theaters. . . . People with clean minds and bodies are not likely to contract the disease."[101] More optimistic news came on the same day when the *Lincoln Star* said in a page 5 headline, "Flu Epidemic in Lincoln Reported to Be on Wane. Lincoln Officials Say Disease Is Well under Control. Situation at University in Good Shape—Hearty Response to Appeal." On page 2 of the same issue the *Lincoln Star* printed a long list of forthcoming social and cultural activities. The *Lincoln Star* announced on the front page of its October 8 issue that "Lincoln Officials Say Disease Is Well Under Control." The next day the *Nebraska State Journal* printed an article that upon closer inspection was an ad, stating that the Spanish flu was just like the old grip of 1889–90 and that Vicks VapoRub could prevent infection.[102]

Such reassuring talk suddenly ended in Lincoln with an announcement that after an emergency session, the city council had approved a resolution presented by John Wright, commissioner of public safety. The resolution directly contradicted the policy that the council had adopted at the recommendation of the health superintendent, Chaucer F. Chapman, and the county medical authority that the closing of public places was unnecessary. Wright pointed out that 30 percent of the city's 2,500 school children were out of school. The resolution was that "all public assemblies and churches, all public and private schools, all theaters and moving picture shows, all places where pool and billiards are being played, and all public and private dances were to be closed at once."

The *Daily Nebraskan* had also been optimistic, claiming on October 4 that the Spanish flu was "under control." Just four days later, however, it revealed that the epidemic was "gaining ground." Ten days after that the campus was completely shut down by University of Nebraska chancellor Samuel Avery.[103] It remained so for the next seventeen days until reopening on November 4.[104] Nebraska Wesleyan closed as well. However, department stores and ten-cent stores remained unaffected by the resolution.

By October 16 nineteen deaths caused by the virus had been reported in Lincoln, although it is likely that many others had not been reported. On October 19 the *Lincoln Star* reported that Wyuka Cemetery lacked the workers needed to bury virus victims. By December 4 the *Lincoln Star* claimed that Lincoln had fared better than many cities throughout the country. However, it also admitted that "the best minds in the United States are unable to agree as to the causes of the disease and the best methods for preventing further spread of the epidemic." It was not until December 18 that a conference of the state and local health officials recommended that whole families be quarantined if one member had the virus.[105] A blow to romance was an announcement by Dr. C. F. Chapman, city physician, that couples avoid dancing, converse from a distance of at least three feet, and abstain from kissing anyone who does not observe personal hygiene.[106] However, an Omaha physician, Dr. W. J. McCrann, thought that nothing could be accomplished by quarantining. He came up with the novel idea that "influenza [was] an air-propagating disease caused by violent shell explosions and vibrations in Europe and the subsequent explosion [of] poison gases[!]"[107]

Bess Streeter Aldrich created a vivid if fictional description of the epidemic: "Spanish influenza they called it, and it went through the country like the prairie-fires of the old days. People dropped over at their work—young Mrs. Henry Kratz was frying chicken, fainted, was buried the third day with no one allowed to attend the funeral. A sixteen-year-old boy died, a sixty-year-old woman, a baby—the whole countryside was panicky."[108]

Following a brief lull in early December 1918, the virus returned all over the country toward the end of the month. By that time more than three hundred thousand deaths had been reported nationwide.[109] One prominent health official predicted that the number would reach 750,000 by the end of 1919, an estimate that overshot the best estimate made nearly a century later by only 75,000. Lincoln's final total was 219 deaths out of some 4,000 reported cases, about double the number of fatalities suffered by Lincolnites in the war itself.[110] Probably the most frustrating aspect of the Spanish flu was that even medical authorities admitted that "the medical profession and health authorities frankly admit that ordinary preventive measures such as wearing of masks and closing public places seem of little avail."[111]

It is impossible to say exactly when the Spanish flu epidemic ended. A new wave hit in 1919, and still more deaths occurred in 1920. However, it is safe to say that the worst of the epidemic was over in Lincoln by early 1919. Entering "Spanish flu" on an internet search to see the number of times these two words appeared together gives some idea of its prevalence. Lincoln papers listed "Spanish flu" a total of 229 times, including ads. Of these mentions, sixty-nine occurred in 1918, twenty-five in 1919, a surprising thirty-two times in 1920, and not once after that. Lincoln newspapers were probably correct in believing that Lincoln was not quite as hard hit as other parts of the country, especially big eastern cities like Philadelphia, Boston, New York, and Washington DC, perhaps in part because Lincoln had a relatively low population density, no slums, and no factories with crowded working conditions.[112] Lincoln may have been an usually clean city thanks to its four-member health department responsible for checking alleys, barns, restaurants, wholesale houses, and fruit stands.[113]

The epidemic was at least temporarily forgotten by the end of the war on November 11. Celebrations began in Lincoln soon after the news reached the capital city at 1:49 a.m. on the 12. By morning there were demonstrations all over the city. A monster parade wound its way all through the downtown city streets. The *Lincoln Star* claimed that "never in the history of Lincoln [had] there been a parade which approached that of today in size nor was there ever such a manifestation of enthusiasm . . . of the multitude. . . . The marchers walked from six to ten abreast and stepped along at a lively gait most of the time. It took the parade an hour and a quarter to pass a given point. It is estimated that there were more than 20,000 people in line." Business was particularly brisk at stores selling any kind of noisemaking devises. Horns, rattles, and whistlers were especially popular. Allied flags "smothered every building to its top. The American flag enveloped every automobile on the streets."[114]

The excitement was short lived. The day after the armistice was signed the *Lincoln Star* carried a sobering front-page headline: "Hoover Urges Food Economy to Supply Starving Millions in Stricken Europe." The year ended with mixed feelings in Lincoln and much of the rest of the country. The epidemic lingered, and there was no joyous holiday season. "No Christmas entertainments were held. Many families could not afford to exchange presents or decorate trees."[115] And "local merchants sustained heavy losses from the severe slump in trade during the last six weeks of the year."[116] Many Lincoln families were short of bedding and children's clothing.[117] The hated Huns had been defeated, and Nebraska's huge ethnic German population had emerged despised. No one yet knew for sure whether the Spanish flu had ended or even how many thousands of Americans had died of it. There were hopes that a European league of nations holding tightly to the self-determination of at least some European nationalities (but no African or Asian colonies) would prevent another calamitous disaster. Americans started the postwar era with high expectations and fervent hopes for a return to normalcy. They were soon to be disappointed.

10

Reaction, Prosperity, and Depression

Ending War and Making Peace

For those of us who remember the euphoric ending of the Second World War and its aftermath, the years following the First World War stand out in sharp contrast. In some cities in the late fall of 1918, there were, to be sure, celebrations and patriotic parades featuring returning soldiers. There was also satisfaction that the "Huns" would presumably no longer be a threat to Western civilization. But the celebration lasted at best only a few months and was followed by inflation, unemployment, and a spike in racial animosity. Fear of a Bolshevik revolution created what came to be known as the "Red Summer." The drive for gender equality and the hope that prohibition would lead to domestic tranquility soon gave way to disillusionment and reaction. In international affairs the Wilsonian belief that the creation of nation-states would advance democracy proved disastrously illusory.

Disillusionment was particularly strong in Nebraska where farmers were hard hit by falling prices for their products and rising inflation for their purchases. In the immediate postwar period, returning veterans in Nebraska were confronted by rising racial tensions, a lack of jobs, and a shortage of housing. Many Lincolnites suffered through a cheerless and cold Christmas season because of ongoing sicknesses and lack of bedding and warm clothing.[1]

Much of the postwar disillusionment in Nebraska and elsewhere in the United States was an outcome of the World War and the peace conference held in the Palace of Versailles near Paris. The war, which, in the words of President Wilson, was supposed to "make the world safe for democracy," ended with bitter territorial disputes that lasted throughout the interwar period and had much

40. "Their First Chance at a Real Square Meal." President Wilson spreads the ingredients of democracy to the successor states of Austria-Hungary. *Lincoln Star*, October 22, 1918, 2.

to do with the outbreak of another world war just twenty years after the end of the First World War. The Paris Peace Conference ended with far more people being dissatisfied than happy and with many people presciently predicting another major war. Germany was not only left as the only major power in central Europe but was now bordered on the east not by great power Russia but by the relatively small states of Poland and Czechoslovakia with their numerous minorities including millions of disgruntled German and Magyar speakers. Opportunities for Germany's expansion were now ironically greater than they had been in 1914 and would be exploited within two short decades.[2]

The creation of new states in the eastern part of central Europe, one of the supposed great achievements of the peace conference, was of only fleeting interest to most Nebraskans with the probable exception of the state's considerable Czech and Polish populations. In general, however, Nebraskans quickly lost interest in foreign affairs. What many Americans did not forget was their feeling of having been duped by British propaganda into believing grossly exaggerated atrocity stories and other forms of misinformation about the war. They were determined not to be misled a second time into abandoning their country's traditional policy of resisting entanglements in European quarrels and were, like most Americans, slow to react to the territorial expansion of Nazi Germany in 1938–39.

Black soldiers gained a new perspective on racial segregation during the war by being segregated into separate training camps, provided with inferior facilities, training, and equipment, and, except for the Harlem Hellfighters, denied the opportunity to engage in combat. They were astonished to find that they were much better treated by the French, British, and Germans than they were by their white compatriots.[3] This description of "ill treatment and discrimination" was confirmed by the leading civil rights leader of the time, W. E. B. Du Bois, in a speech "free of bitterness" he gave to a mixed audience at All Souls Church in Lincoln in May 1919. However, he said that his race was "looking for fairer play and more consideration and recognition as Americans. . . . It was not unreasonable for them to expect that they be accorded rights which were guaranteed to them in the constitution."[4]

American taxpayers were surprised to learn that the Great War had cost ten times as much as the Civil War and more than twice as much as the federal government had spent for its operating budget since 1789.[5] After the war American soldiers who remained in occupied parts of western Germany for a short time were surprised to discover that the Germans did not conform to wartime propaganda depicting them as monsters. In fact the American soldiers "found the order and kindliness of the Germans, their '*ordnung* and *gemütlichkeit*,' along with their friendliness and hygienic standards preferable to those of the French."[6]

The League of Nations "Menace" and the Conservative Reaction

The response to the Paris Peace Treaties in the United States was not long in coming. President Wilson's support for a peacekeeping League of Nations was generally well received abroad but with deep skepticism at home. Many Americans, especially those not living on the East Coast, saw the league as a menace to its long tradition of sovereignty and to remaining clear of international commitments.[7] The possibility of joining an international peacekeeping body brought with it an equal chance, in the eyes of some Americans, that the United States might be dragged into disputes, possibly including the use of military support, in faraway quarrels of little or no interest to the United States. To join the league President Wilson needed the support of the Senate, which was controlled by Republicans suspicious of international entanglements. To gain popular support, Wilson embarked on a coast-to-coast speaking campaign much like those of William Jennings Bryan. Among his many stops was an hour-long speech at Omaha's city auditorium in which he declared that he "would feel recreant to my country if this war ended without a guarantee against another. It is not a 100 percent guaranty. But I submit to you whether or not even a 10 percent guaranty is not better than none at all. And I predict that there would be another world war within a generation [if] no pains were taken to prevent it."[8] This declaration seems to have attracted little attention outside of Omaha itself. Unfortunately Wilson lacked Bryan's health and stamina for long-distance whistle-stop campaigning and ultimately suffered a massive stroke on October 2, 1919, which made him an invalid for the rest of his life. Subsequently the United States rejected membership in the league, although it did participate in some of its committees.[9]

Once the debate over the league ended in late 1919, the election of 1920 was around the corner. Theodore Roosevelt had been regarded as a highly likely candidate but died of a blood clot in January 1919 when he was only sixty. Some Republicans considered wartime hero General Pershing as a possible candidate, but he showed no interest in becoming a candidate in part because "he disliked public appearances and was too much of a disciplinarian to succeed in politics." Consequently it is little wonder that his candidacy ended early when he was defeated in a Nebraska primary election.[10]

Herbert Hoover was a possible candidate in early 1920. During World War I he encouraged farmers to grow more so that America's allies would have enough to eat and Americans could avoid food rationing; he showed enormous managerial skills in food relief programs in Belgium, Russia, and even Germany and Austria.[11] Likewise much of what he favored in 1920—like a minimum wage, a forty-eight-hour workweek, the eradication of child labor, improved housing, and equal pay for men and women—was later favored by President Franklin D. Roosevelt. Perhaps above all he was widely admired for his "rags to riches" personal history.[12]

Although his liberal views in 1920 resembled some of those held by the Democrats in 1929, Hoover correctly surmised that the incumbents were likely to lose the next election. He, therefore, half-heartedly decided to run as a Republican but without doing anything to ingratiate himself with the GOP. His later decision to run as a Republican in 1928 was perhaps the most spectacular example of bad timing in the history of American politics. Had he run in 1920, he almost certainly would have won and would have been reelected in 1924, it being next to impossible to defeat an incumbent during times of growing prosperity. His decision to seek the presidency in 1928 resulted in the *biggest* victory of any presidential candidate to that date; his defeat in 1932 was by the largest margin of any candidate in history. However, timing was not Hoover's only problem. A bigger one, particularly as president, was his personality. One historian among many has described him as "frigid." His contemporaries found him "abrasive, abrupt, overbearing, and solitary."[13]

Ultimately the Republicans chose Warren G. Harding as their

presidential candidate in 1920. The *Lincoln Star* claimed that he had been selected by "a small group in a smoke-filled room and later endorsed by a convention worn out and weary. His senatorial record is one of inactivity and negation. . . . He has no definite or steadfast line . . . with exception that he is against the League of Nations."[14] Harding won the election by the largest percentage since the beginning of the two-party system, but with only 49.3 percent of the electorate voting, it was the lowest turnout of eligible voters in American history.[15] His main attributes seemed to be that he looked like a president and promised to return the country to "normalcy." He has frequently been listed as one of the country's worst presidents, but that assessment has more to do with the scandals—which included two extramarital affairs—that came to light only after his death in 1924 than it does with his achievements in office. For example he hosted the Washington Naval Conference from November 1921 to February 1922 that halted a naval race between Britain, France, and Japan, which was not resumed until 1936. Harding also benefited from the return of prosperity in 1922 due in large part to booming car sales and highway construction. He was undoubtedly popular during his presidency, and his sudden death by a heart attack in August 1923, following a long and exhausting trip to Alaska, was deeply mourned by the public.

Harding was succeeded by his vice president, Calvin Coolidge, best known by his nickname, "Silent Cal." He was so reticent that, according to a popular story, a lady attending a White House party bet him that she could get him to say at least three words. His response: "You lose." Coolidge's popularity rested on the unprecedented prosperity that coincided with his years in office thanks in part to his secretary of commerce, Herbert Hoover, and to Coolidge's decision not to run for a second term in 1928. His administration ended on March 4, 1929, just seven months before the Wall Street Crash and the beginning of the Great Depression.

The Roaring Twenties

By no means were all the postwar trends negative. Most of the country witnessed the resumption and growth of overall American prosperity, especially in urban areas, after the interruption of the World War and a brief downturn in 1920 and 1921. When the decade began, much of Europe's economic power lay devastated, even though the damage to housing and factories was far less than what occurred in the Second World War. The United States had become by far the world's greatest power, with an income greater than the combined incomes of the major European states plus Japan.[16] For the decade the U.S. economy grew by an amazing 42 percent.

The most important evidence of this growth was seen in the explosive increase in the sale of new automobiles. Whereas there were seven million cars in the United States in 1919, there were more than twenty-nine million a decade later.[17] Around five out of every six cars in the world were owned by Americans on the eve of the Great Depression. A picture of a traffic jam in 1925 on the corner of Twelfth and R Streets in Lincoln, next to the campus of the University of Nebraska, provides a vivid example of the popularity of cars at that time.[18]

Traffic jams were just one problem caused by the rapid increase in the number of automobiles in Lincoln. Where to park a car was another issue that continued to grow. A dispute arose in 1925 about how long cars could be parked in the downtown area. Many merchants wanted the time limited to one hour to ensure the largest possible number of customers. They were opposed by owners of women's clothing stores, who argued that their patrons needed more time to make decisions.[19] Parking problems were especially acute whenever there was a Husker home game and even more so during the state fair in September and even for county fairs.[20] Meanwhile the number of registered automobiles resumed its steady increase after the First World War, rising every year from 571 in 1905 to 205,000 in 1920. By 1929 it reached a new high of 375,725, a figure not surpassed until 1948.[21] The Great Depression, however, ended the rapid increase in sales even for cheaper cars.

Far more serious than traffic jams and parking problems was the increase in fatalities involving automobiles; 368 people died in 1929 with excessive speed being the main cause. Another twelve people a day were seriously injured.[22] These fatalities occurred even though the speed limit in residential parts of Lincoln was just eighteen miles an hour and thirty-five in the countryside.[23] By contrast only 212 people died in auto accidents in Nebraska in 2019 even though the state's population had grown from 1,202,624 in 1930 to 1,961,504. If deaths per mile driven were considered, the death rate in the much smaller cities of the 1920s would be even more lopsided. The *Nebraska State Journal* said in 1931 that auto accidents were beginning to rival war as a cause of death.[24]

Speeding and auto accidents were not the only concerns of the new era. Traditions harking back to Victorian times were also challenged by young women, or "flappers" as they were often called. Young women with short, bobbed hair and short skirts often smoked, drove cars, and were crazy about dancing. For flappers the first kiss with a suitor was most definitely no longer the equivalent of an engagement to marry. Moreover what had been called "sparking" in the 1890s and "spooning" early in the new century became "petting," "cuddling," or "snugglepupping" in the 1920s. Groups of young people engaged in "petting parties"; they were not orgies, however, because participants remained with one partner. Such activities meant that "young women [were] appropriating as their right the freedom which [had] always been the prerogative of men."[25]

Petting was ill defined but usually involved hugging as well as kissing and perhaps fondling, but not intercourse. It was a means of exploring one's sexuality without losing one's virginity or becoming pregnant. The Women's Christian Temperance Union (WCTU), YMCAS, and YWCAS as well as other organizations carried out campaigns against petting but with mixed results. The *Lincoln Star* cited an Associated Press article that said that "not all social workers considered petting to be an unmitigated evil."[26]

Whatever it was called, traditionalists like the advice columnist Minerva disapproved of the new freedom, especially when it occurred during a petting party.[27] Such occasions, she thought, were "not only saturated with danger of physical and moral decay, but [were] coarsening, depraving, [and] making gross the finer sensibilities of the young people."[28]

Almost as controversial as petting in the 1920s was the increased use of cosmetics. Beautification products were used as early as seven thousand years ago and were especially popular in ancient Egypt. They were frowned upon during the Roman Republic but were more frequently used during the Roman Empire, especially among prostitutes and wealthy women. Cosmetics were used during the European Middle Ages to whiten the face and make rosy the cheeks. Queen Victoria strongly disapproved of them but was not always supported in this respect. Teachers and clergywomen were explicitly forbidden from using them in both Europe and America during the Victorian era.

In the early twentieth century, makeup was mostly worn by prostitutes. Pale skin was preferred by wealthy women because it meant that they had no need to work in the sun. Rouge was considered provocative and was worn mainly by prostitutes. Some department stores did not even sell cosmetics. Disapproval diminished after the First World War, although it did not disappear altogether. The real breakthrough for cosmetics occurred during the 1920s when red lipstick and dark eyeliner became commonplace in the United States and was popularized by Hollywood movie stars. The sale of cosmetics became a big business for special shops even in small towns, prompting legislators in many states to require would-be cosmeticians to take up to 120 hours of coursework to be certified.[29] Cosmetics were now a sign of status and, like cigarettes, were widely advertised in newspapers and magazines. Elevators frequently had mirrors so women could do a last-minute check of their makeup.[30] The desire for beauty was so strong that it prompted a surge in cosmetic surgery as early as 1920.

The cosmetic boom created a backlash in which the WCTU was a leader. This time, however, the organization was joined by physicians who argued that obstructing pores was injurious to skin and that a healthy body promoted by exercise would be the surest and safest way to remain beautiful.[31] Minerva, who was bombarded with letters complaining about the use of cosmetics, thought that

as a campaigner against cosmetics in general I would be a dismal failure. . . . The properly powered nose and even tinted cheeks is a matter of common courtesy. . . . After a hard day's work it is decidedly refreshing to be able to soften the tired lines with cold cream and powder and bring back a sparkle to the eye through applying a bit of becoming pink to the cheeks. . . . There are times when it is a kindness to hide the truth to one's very own self. . . . Nor do I believe that the artful clever use of cosmetics is abhorrent to males.[32]

The prosperity in the mid- to late twenties was accompanied by the growing belief that what had once been luxuries were now necessities that could be purchased on installment plan, which was the expectation that money would be available when the next install- ment was due whether it be for a car, a house, farmland, or any other item that could not be purchased immediately in cash. Such practices had previously been rare before the war, being mostly lim- ited to such expensive items as pianos—which increased across the nation from 32,000 in 1890 to 374,000 in 1904—sewing machines, or expensive furniture, because nonpayment could bring disgrace to a whole family in a small, close-knit community where neigh- bors knew neighbors.[33] However, buying on credit became increas- ingly commonplace after the war, especially in larger cities where social isolation was commonplace.

The reduction in car and home sales after 1929 was partially compensated by the steeply increased sale of electric refrigerators, replacing iceboxes as a major household appliance. It was one of the few major manufactured domestic products, along with elec- tric fans and radios, that did well during the Great Depression.[34] (My maternal grandfather, Fred Hulsebus, a dealer of luxury cars like Hupmobiles and Cadillacs in Harlan, Iowa, was all too famil- iar with this downward trend and managed to survive economi- cally only because of his auto repair shop and his decision to sell electric refrigerators as well as washing machines.)[35]

It should be noted that a major reason for the increased sale of refrigerators and most other new inventions was the rapid spread of access to electricity. Although statistics are not available for Lin- coln, it is likely that most of its homes were wired for electricity by 1920. Nationally the figure was only 35 percent. By 1930, how- ever, that figure had almost doubled, enabling more than twelve million families to purchase a radio.[36] These estimates included the Deep South, remote areas in the North, and many rural parts of Nebraska, which in many cases did not have access to electric- ity until after the Second World War.[37]

The rapidly growing access to electricity after 1920 was seen in the increase of telephones, which grew from 1.3 million in 1900 to 13.3 million in 1920.[38] Another drastic increase came in pur- chases of the recently invented radio. Before 1920 radios had been useful primarily on ships at sea or for sending messages between a few technically adept individuals. Radio broadcasting to the public began with the presidential election returns in 1920 on station KDKA in Pittsburgh but was heard by only the few people who had radio receivers. By the beginning of 1923, broadcasting had reached Omaha and neighboring Council Bluffs, Iowa; it reached Lincoln around 1925.[39] However, it was not until 1926 that the National Broadcasting Company was formed, and not until the next year did it begin broadcasting programs.

What was especially significant about the radio was that it could provide owners, free of charge beyond the cost of the radio itself, the news far faster than newspapers while also offering listeners a variety of daily entertainment including operas, symphony concerts, dramas, comedies, and popular songs. And all this entertainment was available without the need to leave one's home.[40] Radios proved to be the final nail in vaudeville's coffin. One of the questions posed in the census of 1930 was whether a household owned a radio, a mark of membership in the middle class. Radios for a time also threatened the motion picture industry, which responded with sound movies and later with colored ones. What effect the COVID-19 pandemic will have on our willingness to seek outside entertainment is yet to be determined in 2023.

Airplanes, like radios, were another prewar invention, whose use greatly accelerated during the 1920s. However, safety long remained a major concern. In 1912 the *Nebraska State Journal* described aviation as "a deadly sport."[41] Even in the 1930s, flying did not become an integral part of everyday life in the United States in general or Nebraska in particular. Humans had defied gravity near Paris as early as 1783 but only in hot air balloons. As is well known, the two bicycle salesmen and repairmen, Orville and Wilbur Wright, have been credited with building the first heavier-than-air machine that could lift humans off the ground, something few people thought possible at the beginning of the early twentieth century. But until the late 1920s, airplanes were flown by daredevils willing to risk their lives for big audiences and big paychecks, for example at state fairs performing loops or flying with "wing walkers."

Lincoln had a significant role to play in the history of aviation.

Charles Lindbergh, who became an instant international hero after his nonstop flight from New York to Paris in 1927, did much of his early training in Lincoln in 1922–23 at the Nebraska Airplane Flying School. However, he never flew solo while in Lincoln, and his name never appeared in a Lincoln newspaper. Lincoln seemed to be an ideal place to learn to fly because it was near the geographic center of the country and had no natural obstacles to flying.

In the 1920s airplanes mainly profited by carrying mail long distances. For some time pilots did their flying in the daytime with trains carrying bags of mail at night. In 1924 airplanes and trains collaborated to carry mail from New York to San Francisco in thirty-four hours.[42] Forty of the first fifty pilots to enter such service died in crashes. There were some small airlines carrying passengers as early as 1920, but they owned only three or four planes and went out of business after a few weeks or months. Each plane could carry only one or two passengers. Airports and control towers did not yet exist.[43] Commercial air service began regular service in 1926, when 6,000 brave passengers dared to fly. Thereafter the number of passengers grew rapidly from 173,000 in 1929 to around 1 million a decade later. However, the cost of flying remained far out of the reach of all but *very* wealthy Americans.

The Declining Interest in Reforms

With American entry into World War I, the reforming spirit of the three decades preceding the war largely disappeared domestically and was replaced by hyper-nationalism and the war-induced "cult of irrationality."[44] Distinguished historian Richard Hofstadter has argued that it was precisely in the West and the South, in old Bryan country, that the public mood swung most sharply away from the devotion to necessary reforms that had characterized progressivism at its best.[45] Contributing to this cessation was the reaction to the Russian Bolshevik revolution in October 1918 along with the Seattle General Strike, the police strike in Boston, and a bombing campaign by anarchists. The result was the Red Scare in the spring of 1919 in which millions of Americans believed that the country was on the verge of a bloody Communist revolution that would take place on May 1, 1919. When nothing special happened that day, the fear soon melted away.[46]

Far more consequential than the Red Scare was the beginning of a half-century-long hibernation of the drive for women's political, social, and economic equality. The passage of the Eighteenth Amendment, which outlawed the purchase and manufacturing of alcoholic beverages, and the Nineteenth Amendment, which gave all women the right to vote, was both the climax and the beginning of the end to the reformist campaign, at least as far as major successes were concerned. Gaining the right to vote was one of the few goals that most, but by no means all, women had as a goal.[47]

Some laws were passed in the 1920s at the state level protecting women and children in the workplace. American women, joined by many other women around the world who had also recently gained the franchise, helped bring about the Washington Naval Conference of 1921–22 mentioned previously. But by the late 1920s "the American feminist movement was characterized by falling membership, political failure, financial decline, and increasing conservatism."[48] No further goals were powerful enough, or popular enough, to gain even the approval of most women. There was nothing left holding the movement together, a devastating disappointment for some but a big relief for others, both male and female.

Women did not suddenly become masculine. Nor did half of them demand divorces in large numbers because of their more egalitarian status, although there was some increase in the divorce rate. As to virginity, 87 percent of the women born before 1890 claimed that status compared to 32 percent of women born after 1910.[49] Meanwhile premarital pregnancies rose from 10 percent in 1850 to 23 percent for the period between 1880 and 1910. This trend continued into the 1920s, when doctors were forced to pay heavy fines for the distribution of sex education or contraceptives.[50] But these changes did not have much impact on politics, especially at the national level. Gaining the right to vote had become a dead end; it was one of the few things upon which most (but by no means all) women could agree. The election of November 1920 resulted in just 43 percent of all eligible women voting. Poor women, especially those in the South, were the least likely to vote. A bloc of female voters, which suffragettes had hoped for and many men had feared, never materialized.[51] Being elected to high political office had relatively little consequence after the virtually simultaneous victory of prohibition. Those few women elected to high office in the 1920s were nearly all elected to the House of Representatives and were often widows of House members. When not related to an officeholder, they rarely won on their own merit, and when they did, they were seldom reelected. The few who did gain office had little, if any, impact on new legislation.[52]

The campaign against cigarettes came to a screeching halt even before the end of the First World War. Cigarette smoking by females was still frowned upon, but nevertheless it increased. As noted in chapter 5, Lincoln's newspapers began printing the ads of cigarette companies. Even the *Daily Nebraskan* reversed its previous opposition and began accepting cigarette ads in 1925. Smoking, especially of cigarettes, was still recognized as injurious to the user's health and life expectancy, but it was widely regarded as a private affair and nobody's business but the smoker's. The link with cancer, especially lung cancer, was unknown, or at least unproven in the United States, and the dangers of secondhand smoke were not even debated.

The one country where the link between smoking and lung cancer was recognized was Germany. In the late 1920s, about forty years after cigarettes began to be mass produced, scientists in the still-democratic Weimar Republic discovered such a link. Yet it was left to Adolf Hitler to carry out the first nationwide campaign against smoking cigarettes without, however, prohibiting their use. He labeled himself the nation's number one nonsmoker.[53]

About the most that can be said for women's rights in the workplace during this time is that they were *usually* not reversed. Clerical work and sales continued as before to be primary roles for women, as did teaching, especially in elementary schools, along with nursing. Women's pay continued to lag far behind that of men, and they were less likely to be hired and more likely to lose their job if they married. Many businesses refused to employ both a husband and a wife.[54] As previously noted, a woman becoming a physician, lawyer, or professor (except of art and languages, or at a woman's college) was rare. Rising to the status of a business executive was unknown. Serious changes in these limitations on the employment of women lasted until the early 1970s. (In my eight years of college and postgraduate studies at Grinnell College, the

University of Vienna, the University of Nebraska–Lincoln, and the University of Rochester, there was not a single female historian from whom I could have taken a course. There had been a female professor of history at the University of Wyoming, where I taught from 1966 to 1971. Laura Amanda White had been hired as chair and sole member of the history department at Wyoming in 1914, a position she held until 1948. But she would have lost her job had she married.)[55]

Some nineteenth-century inventions like trains and streetcars reached their peak of popularity either during or just after the World War only to begin a decline shortly thereafter, a result of the explosive increase in the sale of automobiles.[56] Trains did become faster, cleaner, and some of them even more luxurious during the interwar period, but service to small towns, including those in Nebraska, began to decline.[57] However, a visit to the beautiful, art nouveau Omaha Union Station, authorized in 1929 and opened in 1931, reveals that optimism about trains still existed at the time. A glance at the schedule for 1937 posted in the station shows that trains still reached many remote parts of the Cornhusker state. The decline in service became truly stark only after the Second World War. Unfortunately Union Station is now largely a museum, albeit a remarkably interesting one.

Prohibition was a huge disappointment. The federal government proved unwilling to pay for the enforcement of the Eighteenth Amendment. Far from leading to a decrease in crime and inebriation, it led to their increase during the prohibition era. The link between patriotism, German breweries, and the campaign against the German language and culture faded along with the disappointment over the cost and outcome of the World War.[58] However, as we have seen, prohibition may have led to a decline in the consumption of alcohol.

When the Eighteenth Amendment was repealed in 1933, Lincoln remained dry, which was almost certainly financially detrimental as far as restaurants were concerned. The city's opposition to alcohol was affirmed in 1946 by a two-to-one vote. The passage of time, however, seems to have cooled passions. In 1966 selling liquor by the drink in restaurants was approved with the support of the Lincoln Chamber of Commerce. Contrary to the fears of prohibitionists, legality did not lead to increased crime. Nor did the Lincoln Council of Churches raise objections to the new permissiveness.[59]

There was one area in which major progress in reform had occurred between 1890 and 1920 that did not experience disillusionment and temptation to backslide: college football. The attempt to greatly reduce serious injuries proved disappointing, but winning through brute strength alone was greatly diminished. The forward pass was well established and was used ever more frequently. Scoring increased, especially for losers, and the game became more unpredictable and hence more interesting and exciting.

Postwar Nebraska

Compared to the three preceding decades, the 1920s were not great for everyday life in Nebraska, and the 1930s were far worse. The state's population grew modestly from 1,296,372 in 1920 to 1,377,963 in 1930, but it fell to 1,315,834 a decade later thanks to the Great Depression, which was made all the worse by a prolonged drought creating the infamous Dust Bowl. The rising cost of living during the World War continued into the early postwar era.[60] A yearlong depression in 1920–21 especially hit people with fixed incomes because of rapidly rising inflation, something that was virtually unknown before the war. Over the whole country the cost of living rose a staggering 66 percent, leading to widespread buyers' strikes and rent strikes.[61] Among those hard hit were clerks and stenographers; many working men were hardly any better off.[62] The cost of food, however, was considerably lower in Nebraska than it was in large metropolitan areas.[63] Nevertheless in December 1918, the Lincoln's Women's Club, with its 1,700 members, decided to boycott certain high-priced foods including eggs and butter. Having succeeded in bringing the price of those items down, they decided to make do with the hats and clothing they had purchased the previous year.[64]

Food was not the only item concerning Nebraskans after the war. There was a shortage of housing all over the state, especially in Lincoln, which needed 1,000 homes, and Omaha, which was short 2,500 houses. Public improvements such as waterworks and sewers as well as schools were needed; moving picture theaters and churches were also needed. The brief postwar depression caused work stoppage on these projects, sometimes for years. Adding to the misery was a national coal strike in December 1919, which closed Lincoln schools and reduced business hours.[65]

The most infamous act in early postwar Nebraska was the lynching of an African American in Omaha on September 28, 1919. Publicized throughout the whole country, it followed more than twenty race riots that occurred in major industrial cities during the summer of 1920. The lynching of William Brown was just one of eighty-three such atrocities to occur nationally that year, the highest number since 1908 and fortunately a figure never to be equaled let alone surpassed again. By 1929 the number had declined to ten.[66] The lynching occurred after the African American population of Omaha had increased from around five thousand in 1910 to double that figure by 1920, giving Omaha a Black population second only to Los Angeles among cities west of the Missouri River. The increase was an outgrowth of hiring in the meatpacking industry, which led to animosity in 1917, when the industry used African Americans as strike breakers.[67]

Inflammatory articles in the *Omaha Bee* helped increase racial tensions and were at least partially responsible for a riot that resulted in the lynching of William Brown, who was accused of raping a white woman, an accusation he denied. A mob, which grew from several hundred to an estimated five to twenty thousand looking on, wrecked the supposedly "mob proof" and "fireproof" million-dollar Douglas County courthouse, destroying valuable public records.[68] Brown was given a physical examination shortly after his arrest and was judged too crippled from either a childhood injury or rheumatism to assault anyone. Yet the mob hanged him from a telephone pole, and his corpse was riddled with hundreds of bullets. The lust for blood not yet satisfied, the mob dragged the corpse through the streets of Omaha and then burned it with oil. Meanwhile two policemen who tried to stop the rioters were killed. The reformist mayor of Omaha, Edward Smith, who had tried to stop the lynching, was also strung up and cut down; he barely survived after several days in a hospital. Meanwhile Black people were dragged from streetcars and beaten.[69] Following the riot a grand jury issued 149 indictments, but no one was convicted.

In the words of one historian of the episode, "Collective guilt prevented individuals from identifying or denouncing fellow rioters. . . . The violence did not evoke any initiatives to assuage racism or to improve conditions for Omaha's African American community."[70]

The mob violence and lynching in Omaha clearly frightened Lincoln's small African American community. Within a week the *Nebraska State Journal* reported that a "committee of Lincoln negroes met with the mayor to ask city authorities to protect them by seeing that the criminal negroes be kept out of town or under restraint." The article noted that "the public does not always stop to think that the lawless negro in the community is a greater menace to negroes . . . than he is to whites. . . . When a negro commits a fiendish crime, thoughtless whites hold the whole negro community responsible." The article pointed out that the same prejudice existed against Asians on the Pacific coast and had existed against ethnic Germans throughout the United States during the recent war.[71]

Overall the fate of Lincoln's African American population did not change radically between World War I and II, at least not overtly. Its population of 896 in 1920—1.6 percent out of a population of about 55,000—was nevertheless a 58 percent increase since 1904 brought on by the wartime labor needs of railroad companies.[72] By 1930 the Black population was close to one thousand, still insignificant compared to that of major cities in the North. Black people accounted for just 1.3 percent of Lincoln's population and was only a tenth as large as the Black population in Omaha. Black people were a bit more concentrated than they had been at the beginning of the century, with about 60 percent living in just three wards north of O Street and east of the university campus. They shared the area with other groups, and though congested, the area never acquired the reputation of being a slum. The small size of the Black community was seen as not sufficient to support Black professionals.[73]

What was not known, at least openly, was that these districts were being redlined and declared hazardous, thus codifying segregation and making it impossible for residents to establish equity. Likewise African Americans, as well as people of Chinese or Japanese ethnicity, could not purchase property outside these districts starting in 1916. Racial clauses were extended to the Brownbilt area south of Randolph School in 1924. During the 1930s "the 'Home Owners Loan Corporation' helped make loans more readily available to the working and middle class . . . except in hazardous areas marked in red or yellow deemed 'declining.'"[74]

Nevertheless African Americans continued to be well integrated in the city's public schools including Lincoln High School and in the Boy Scouts. However, Lincoln afforded "little incentive for Negro children to pursue higher education since the opportunities available to graduates were similar to those who have little or no education."[75] Black athletes did not attend the University of Nebraska because, as previously mentioned, the Missouri Valley Conference and its successor, the Big Six, excluded them because of the refusal of Missouri, Kansas, and Oklahoma to compete against teams with Black players. Indeed my father's Cornhusker yearbook of 1930 did not include a single Black face among the ten thousand students then attending the university.

Despite the relatively peaceful development of Lincoln's African American community, the Omaha lynching provided evidence that Nebraska had a race problem and helped give rise to the Ku Klux Klan in the Cornhusker State.[76] However, intimidation of minority groups was by no means limited to African Americans. Jews and Roman Catholics were also threatened, not only by organized hatred, but also by blackmail by the Nebraska Ku Klux Klan, which was organized in the fall of 1921. According to historian R. E. Dale, it defeated "some of the more useful officials in the state."[77]

The Klan originated in the Deep South during the era of Reconstruction after the Civil War. It enjoyed a revival owing to its glorification in *The Birth of a Nation* in 1915 and the militant nationalism aroused by the World War. After the war it spread beyond the South to the North and West, especially during the 1920s. The international ties of Roman Catholics and Jews made them logical targets of hyper-nationalism. The Klan insisted that it was not anti-Catholic but charged that the "Catholic Church had plans to undermine the Constitution of the United States. . . . The pope would end the separation of church and state and destroy religious freedom." As for Jews "they did not have the same values as Protestants making it impossible for them to be assimilated into American life."[78]

According to the Klan's national headquarters in Atlanta, Georgia, the Nebraska organization had some forty-five thousand members in 1923. Lincoln, with five thousand members, had the dubious distinction of being the state's oldest, largest, and most vocal "Klavern," followed by Omaha, Fremont, York, Grand Island, Hastings, North Platte, and Scottsbluff.[79] In 1925, when the Klan reached its peak popularity, it claimed between two and five million followers nationally.[80] One of the biggest demonstrations of the Klan's strength in Nebraska was their annual state meeting held in Lincoln in 1925, with 1,500 Klansmen parading down O Street in their white robes, masks, and pointed hats. A picnic sponsored by the Klan during state fair week attracted an estimated twenty-five thousand people, although many were merely onlookers.[81]

Klansmen insisted that they were attracted by the organization's fraternalism, although some were strong supporters of law enforcement. Others opposed the doctrine of evolution and objected to the foreign born—of whom there were nearly 150,000 in Nebraska—along with liberals, progressives, and radicals. Still others resisted changes in morals. These values, however, were by no means confined to Klansmen.[82]

The Klan began declining soon after reaching its zenith in 1925, in large part because of a hostile press, which charged that the "Klan promoted violence and that its leadership was corrupt and degenerate."[83] It also faced the stern opposition of influential leaders including Samuel Avery, chancellor of the University of Nebraska, who declared that the Klan's beliefs were incompatible with the university's values, which "should be characterized by a broad liberal spirit of fellowship. Learning knows no distinction on race or color." He added that "any student joining the Klan would be suspended."[84]

One of the supreme ironies of the interwar period is that Germans, who had been reviled during the First World War whether they lived in the United States or in Europe, emerged as one of the favored nationalities in the Immigration Act of 1924. Quotas were set at 2 percent of the population of various ethnic groups in 1890, a time when the number of Americans of German descent was at or near its zenith. By no accident immigration from southern and eastern Europe, including Italian, Greeks, Russians, and

Jews, had hardly even begun at that time. Immigration from Asia was effectively banned altogether by the new law.[85]

Perhaps the most unfortunate development to arise during the World War was indebtedness. Tempted by the high price of grain, many Nebraska farmers went into debt by purchasing land more suitable for grazing than it was for the growing of corn and wheat. If wartime prices were high for these products, the farmers prospered. Mortgage debts rose by more than 170 percent between 1910 and 1920, but profits were insufficient to pay for these purchases.[86] When prices fell for agricultural products, many such farmers lost their land. In many cases, particularly in western Nebraska and eastern Colorado, the buyers in these distress sales were the frugal Volga Germans.

One bright spot among the cloudy skies of the 1920s was the success of the Cornhusker football team. During the decade they won fifty-five games, lost eighteen, tied nine, and won three conference titles. Starting in 1920 reports about its games could be sent all over the state by wireless as they occurred.[87] Its game against perennial powerhouse Pittsburgh in 1921, won by Nebraska 10–0, may have been the first football game to be broadcast by radio in its entirety (although it was heard only in the Pittsburgh area). However, it was not until 1923 that a Nebraska station broadcast a Husker game and only in 1925 did Omaha station KFAB broadcast all home games.[88] Movie theaters showed clips of the games in their newsreels, an innovation that began during the war. Starting in 1924 Husker fans between the ages of ten and fifteen could attend the games by virtue of the Knothole Club, a privilege that I later happily exploited starting in 1948.[89]

11

Enduring Gains and Disappointing Setbacks

By 1920 Americans in general, and Lincolnites in particular, enjoyed a far higher standard of living than they had in 1890. Travel, both interurban and long distance, was vastly easier and faster. Cities as small as Fort Collins, Colorado, with a population around 11,500, had a streetcar system that would bring inhabitants from the out-ermost parts of town to the business and cultural center as well as a railroad station with regular service to every part of the country including the smallest villages.

Most people were healthier as well. The germ theory of disease was no longer controversial. Anesthesia was available in every modern hospital across the country. In 1925 Lincoln General Hospital opened its doors, joining St. Elizabeth Hospital, which had been established in 1889; Bryan Memorial Hospital had its start in 1926 on the Fairview property, which was a gift from the three-time presidential candidate. Meanwhile the number of hospitals in the United States had increased from 120 in 1872 to 6,000 in 1920.[1]

One of the consequences of the new and more modern hospitals is that the number of babies born—including your author—in Lincoln's hospitals rose rapidly. Nationally 75 percent of all births were in urban hospitals by 1939.[2] Lincoln and other modern American cities could already enjoy fresh fruits and vegetables brought from great distances by trains. Americans, except for some people in remote areas, had long been able to enjoy clean water and unspoiled meat, thanks to the Pure Food and Drug Act of 1906. Typhoid, diphtheria, influenzas and pneumonia, tuberculosis, and diarrhea all declined between 1900 and 1922, enabling life expectancy to increase from forty-nine to fifty-four years.[3] However, the trend resulted primarily from cleaner water and safer food and the nearness of hospitals in major cities.

Also important was the decline in the workweek from ten hours a day, six days a week in 1890, to closer to eight hours during a five-day week in 1920.[4] However, cancer, diabetes, and heart disease actually grew during the 1920s.[5] The likely causes were the rapid increase in cigarette smoking and a decline in physical activity. Walking or bicycling to work or school, or even to a streetcar stop, which were so popular between 1890 and 1920, were giving way to commuting by automobile. Walking for pure pleasure declined nationally, although that trend was partially offset by the growing popularity of golf (when golf carts had not yet been invented).[6]

By 1920 entertainment was cheaper and more available thanks first to vaudeville and increasingly to motion pictures. The conservative trend in politics did little to reverse prewar trends in entertainment. Likewise political conservatism did not stop the advance of secularism or disbelief in a literal hell, although there was a decline in atheism.[7] Indeed Richard Hofstadter, writing in broad generalities, maintains that "the clergy were probably the most conspicuous losers from the status revolution . . . and were hard hit in their capacity as moral and intellectual leaders by the considerable secularization that took place in American society and intellectual life. . . . Ministers now had to share a place with scientists and social scientists."[8] Sunday closing was still observed by stores, but dancing became more popular than ever after Lincoln's beautiful Antelope Park Pavilion was built. Headlines in the *Lincoln Star* claimed that the "Foxtrot Helps [the] Mind Recover from [the] Shock of War"; "Relaxation of Dance Aids in Restore[a-tion of] Reason to Insane, Says Superintendent of State Hospital."[9] Skirts grew steadily shorter for women during the 1920s. Although they were somewhat lower in the 1930s, ankle-length skirts never returned for everyday wear. Looser, more comfortable clothing became the main considerations in women's fashions.[10]

Cultural conservatism was very much still alive when Hollywood movies were subjected to the Motion Picture Production Code to avoid being threatened by local censors and boycotts and to prevent government censorship. It was fully enforced after 1934 and not eliminated until 1968, when it was replaced by a rating system. Until then couples were always shown sleeping in single beds separated by a nightstand, and even married couples were covered from

Look under the lid!

Be sure it is a Victrola you get for Christmas!

When you go into a store to purchase a Victrola, make sure the instrument you buy is a Victrola and not some other instrument masqueraded under that name.

The Victrola is the one instrument to which the most famous singers and instrumentalists have entrusted their art —an unanswerable proof of its merits. It is the one instrument and the only instrument specially made to play these artists' records. And, proud of our craftsmanship, we have placed our marks upon these products as an acceptance of our responsibility for them.

The word "Victrola" is our trademark as is also the picture "His Master's Voice." Protect yourself from substitution by the simple means we have provided.

LOOK UNDER THE LID!

Victor Talking Machine Company, Camden, New Jersey·

Victrola

REG. U.S. PAT. OFF.

41. "Look Under the Lid!" *Lincoln Star*, December 13, 1920, 3.

42. "June Is Dress Month." *Lincoln Star*, June 8, 1920, 3.

head to foot in nightclothes. Kisses were to lack passion and last no longer than two or three seconds. On the other hand, brawls, drunkenness, gun fights, chain smoking, and the massacre of Indians were perfectly acceptable.

It is doubtful that the quality of entertainment in Lincoln was better than it had been before the World War when top-rate opera and theater companies made the capital city one of their regular stops. German high culture—which included operas and compositions by Bach, Beethoven, Brahms, Hayden, and Mozart—together with its more plebian culture of beer gardens and popular drinking songs and music, never fully recovered their prewar popularity.[11] By the late 1920s, as previously noted, the radio was making it possible to be entertained without even leaving one's living room. This trend toward home entertainment was simply amplified by television, especially when it became colored and later in high definition.

More and more people sought high school and college education in Lincoln during the 1920s. Enrollment at the University of Nebraska grew from around seven thousand in 1920 to nearly twelve thousand in 1927, although state allocations did not keep up proportionately.[12] Enrollment declined throughout the first part of the Great Depression and again during the Second World War only to be followed by a postwar boom and another bust during most of the 1950s.[13] When I began my graduate studies at the university in 1959 there were just 8,500 students. Tuition was free from kindergarten through high school until 1923, when the University of Nebraska imposed a very modest $1 per credit hour for most courses but more for science and graduate courses.[14] It was to rise to a still very modest total of $150 per semester when I was studying for my master's degree.

Willa Cather, Nebraska's premier novelist during the whole period covered in this book and beyond and always a fearless critic, was not thrilled by the emphasis on jobs promising high salaries, which did little to cultivate the intellect. She also mourned the diminution or even extinction of the cultural influence of European immigrants. In an essay she wrote in 1923 titled "Nebraska: The End of a Cycle," she remarked that too much prosperity, too many moving picture shows, too much gaudy fiction have colored the tastes and manners of so many of these Nebraskans of the future. There, as elsewhere, one finds the frenzy to be showy; farmer boys who wish to be spenders before they are earners, girls who try to look like the heroines of the cinema screen, a coming generation which tries to cheat its aesthetics sense by buying things instead of making anything. There is even the danger that that fine institution, the University of Nebraska, may become a gigantic trade school. . . . The classics, the humanities, are having their dark hour. They are in eclipse. Studies that develop taste and enrich personality are not encouraged. . . . The generation now in the driver's seat hates to make anything, wants to live, and die in an automobile. They want to buy everything ready-made: clothes, food, education, music, pleasure. . . . The belief that snug success and easy money are the real aims of human life has settled down over our prairies, but as not yet hardened into molds and crusts.[15]

It is easy to sympathize with Cather's disappointment with the status of creativity in the arts and the women's rights movement during the interwar years. Her complaint was borne out by the declining enrollment in the College of Arts and Sciences, which fell by nearly 50 percent during the 1920s. According to historian Robert Knoll, students "and their parents believed that college training should prepare young people for good jobs and offer contacts." Meanwhile literary societies and subject-oriented clubs declined and were replaced by the fraternity system.[16]

However, most of the gains of the age of reform and progress from 1890 to 1920 remained in place and were not reversed. Some women did become college professors although most commonly in literature and only rarely in the natural or social sciences or technology. If their role in politics was modest during the interwar period, at least they had gained a foothold that would not be relinquished. Suffrage was seen by women as a vital step toward full equality with men.[17] Although prohibition was far from being a success and was repealed in 1933, it did allow states to continue the prohibition as well as the importation of alcoholic beverages. It is significant that the rate of alcoholism never resumed its pre-

43. Football fans pack uncompleted Memorial Stadium. RG 52-02, Archives and Special Collections, University of Nebraska–Lincoln Libraries.

war level even though drunkenness and disorderly conduct had increased by 41 percent during the prohibition era compared to the preceding years.[18]

The campaign against smoking was perhaps the most disappointing failure of the reform movement because both the sale and advertisement of cigarettes skyrocketed. Male movie stars were expected to smoke on the screen to look more masculine. Consequently many of them died prematurely, including Gary Cooper, Dean Martin, Yul Brenner, Robert Mitchum, and Steve McQueen, not to mention other celebrities like Walt Disney and the widely viewed television journalist Edward R. Murrow, just to cite a few examples. Nevertheless some people, including this author, took the warnings about cigarette smoking seriously and had a better chance of enjoying lifelong good health, at least in part, as a likely consequence. No one, least of all women themselves, can deny the benefits of electric lightbulbs, automatic washing machines, sewing machines, and vacuum cleaners. Middle- and upper-class women wanting family planning benefited in 1923 from the effective end of the Comstock Act of 1873, which had forbidden not only abortion but also the sale or mailing of birth control devices and information.

Meanwhile spectator sports became more popular than ever, and both men and women had the leisure time to enjoy them. Memorial Stadium was built by voluntary contributions from alumni, Lincoln businessmen, donors from all over the state, and even prisoners of the state penitentiary. It succeeded even though it occurred during a recession. With a capacity of around thirty-nine thousand, it was dedicated on October 26, 1923.[19] Even more impressive was the completion of the new state capitol in 1929, also funded by charitable donations; like the stadium it was dedicated to the servicemen and women of the Great War. Its unique architecture broke away from the stereotypical domed capitols of other states. Making the new capitol even more impressive was the removal of the Orpheum Theatre to create a mall stretching north to R Street.[20]

A new sense of patriotism emerged in Nebraska and around the country in the winter of 1941–42, this time not based on propaganda or a hatred of all things German but because of an actual attack on an American territory. Those of us who lived through that time could later remember the unity of purpose and willingness to sacrifice for the common good displayed by an overwhelming majority of Americans, and we have retained those memories to the present day.

Notes

1. Revisiting the Past

1. Nebraska is a particularly good example of how the lure of cheap farm-land virtually disappeared after 1890. Whereas the territory's population had been just 28,841 in 1860, it grew to 1,062,656 in 1890. During the next three decades, its population grew by only 230,000. Of this growth, around 180,000 was in Omaha and Lincoln.

2. Gordon, *The Rise and Fall*, 4.

3. *Nebraska State Journal*, January 5, 1913, 8.

4. Such quarrels about the location of capitals are quite common. Canberra became the capital of Australia because of the jealously between Sydney and Melbourne, Brasilia became the capital of Brazil because of disputes between Rio de Janeiro and São Paulo, and even Washington DC was a compromise between the free northern states and the slave-owning southern states.

5. Aldrich, *Spring Came on Forever*, 110.

6. Brown and McConnell, *75 Years in the Prairie Capital*, 27.

7. Olson and Naugle, *History of Nebraska*, 199; Hayes, *History of the City*, 12.

8. Brown, *The Prairie Capital*, 9.

9. *Lincoln Evening Call*, January 1, 1891, 12; Gordon, *The Rise and Fall*, 245.

10. Lincoln also remains the second largest city in the five-state Northern Great Plains region stretching from Nebraska to Montana.

11. *Lincoln Star*, October 21, 1905, 3.

12. Knoll, *Prairie University*, 51; Hickey, *Nebraska Moments*, 123.

13. Gordon, *The Rise and Fall*, 54.

14. Gordon, *The Rise and Fall*, 228.

15. *Lincoln Evening Call*, January 1, 1891, 1.

16. Douglass, *Oh Grandma*, 80; Brown and McConnell, *75 Years in the Prairie Capital*, 52.

17. Copple, *Tower on the Plains*, 67.

18. Brown, *The Prairie Capital*, 18.

19. McGerr, *A Fierce Discontent*, 12.

20. Brown and McConnell, *75 Years in the Prairie Capital*, 22. For an excellent article on Lincoln during the 1880s, see Dick, "Problems of the Post Frontier."

21. Slote, *The Kingdom of Art*, 6–7.

22. C. Pauley, "An Autobiography," 11; Copple, *Tower on the Plains*, 54.

23. Brown, *The Prairie Capital*, 18.

24. A rare example of a herdic carriage can be seen at Pioneer Village in Minden, Nebraska.

25. Jim McKee, "Horse Cars and Street Railways Common in Late 1800s Nebraska Towns," *Lincoln Journal Star*, April 6, 2014, https://journalstar.com /news/state-and-regional/nebraska/jim-mckee-from-horses-to-trolley-cars-in -nebraska-cities/article_98110ac1-6a8e-5081-a3a5-2cd68d54e523.html; McKay, *Tramways and Trolleys*, 11.

26. *Nebraska State Journal*, March 26, 1886, 8.

27. *Nebraska State Journal*, December 9, 1887, 8.

28. *Nebraska State Journal*, December 1, 1887, 8.

29. *Lincoln Star*, November 19, 1892, 7.

30. *Nebraska State Journal*, June 1, 1886, 5.

31. *Lincoln Star*, June 17, 1988.

32. *Lincoln Journal Star*, March 18, 2017.

33. Olson and Naugle, *History of Nebraska*, xiii.

34. Hayes, *History of the City*, 334.

35. Hayes, *History of the City*, 172–73.

36. It was originally used as a post office before being converted into the city hall in 1905. See Lincoln Chamber of Commerce, *Lincoln: Nebraska's Capital City*, 19.

37. Rader, *American Ways*, 151.

38. Fox, *The Mirror Makers*, 65.

39. Coletta, "Will the Real Progressive," 51.

40. *Nebraska State Journal*, September 30, 1926, 6. Bryan won more votes in the state of Nebraska when he ran against McKinley in 1896 and Taft in 1908 but succeeded in winning the vote in Lincoln and Lancaster County only in 1908. See Copple, *Tower on the Plains*, 88.

41. Hickey, *Nebraska Moments*, 175.

42. No other American politician had made such a trip in the middle of his career. Bryan paid for it by writing newspaper articles and giving speeches. See Kazin, *A Godly Hero*, 121, 128.

43. Kazin, *A Godly Hero*, 121, 245; Sellers, "Fairview Dedication," 344.

44. Kazin, *A Godly Hero*, 302, 304.

45. Coletta, "Will the Real Progressive," 51–52.

46. Kazin, *A Godly Hero*, 26.

47. See, for example, Coletta, "Will the Real Progressive," 15–57.

48. Hickey, *Nebraska Moments*, 173.

49. My paternal grandfather, L. H. Pauley, could not escape this requirement when he graduated from high school in Harvard, Nebraska, in 1902. His "recitation" was titled "The Door to Success Is Labeled 'Push,'" which the town's newspaper said was "well delivered and called forth hearty applause." See *Harvard Courier*, May 24, 1902, 5.

50. Kazin, *A Godly Hero*, 122.

51. Kazin, *A Godly Hero*, 108; Crichton, *America 1900*, 226.

52. Kazin, *A Godly Hero*, 150.

53. Crichton, *America 1900*, 285.

2. Electronic and Transportation Revolutions

1. *Nebraska State Journal*, January 15, 1890, 5 (author's emphasis).

2. *Nebraska State Journal*, January 15, 1890, 5.

3. Schlereth, *Victorian America*, 114.

4. *Lincoln Evening Call*, April 4, 1891, 1.

5. *Lincoln Herald*, December 13, 1890, 2.

6. *Lincoln Evening Call*, January 1, 1891, 4.

7. Schlereth, *Victorian America*, 114.

8. *Nebraska State Journal*, June 7, 1891, 1.

9. See, for example, an advertisement in the *Nebraska State Journal*, November 1, 1914, 9.

10. Gordon, *The Rise and Fall*, 121.

11. Muccigrosso, *Celebrating the New World*, 7.

12. *Lincoln Evening Call*, June 3, 1893, 1.

13. Nasaw, *Going Out*, 71.

14. Larson, *Devil in the White City*, 373.

15. For articles by Walter Wellman on the world's fair, see the *Lincoln Evening News* for "Fair Side Shows," May 12, 1893, 2; "Fair Finances," May 12, 1893, 7; "Foreign Exhibits," May 12, 1893, 3; *Nebraska State Journal*, May 1, 1893, 1.

16. Cullen, *American Dream*, ix–x.

17. Nasaw, *Going Out*, 82.

18. Nasaw, *Going Out*, 72.

19. *Nebraska State Journal*, May 2, 1893, 1.

20. *Lincoln Star*, May 17, 1893, 2.

21. The census of 1890 was notoriously inaccurate for both Omaha and Lincoln. Census takers in the two cities were eager to make their cities look "up and coming," which would attract more residents and businesses. See E. Palmer, "The Correctness of the 1890 Census," 259–67. For the fair's financial success, see Hickey, *Nebraska Moments*, 131.

22. *Nebraska State Journal*, February 15, 1898, 8.

23. *Nebraska State Journal*, February 14, 1898, 8.

24. *Lincoln Star*, October 1, 1890, 2.

25. Olson and Naugle, *History of Nebraska*, 257.

26. *Lincoln Star*, August 31, 1945, 4.

27. Gordon, *The Rise and Fall*, 122.

28. For an account of this incident as well as a close-up view of the Great Depression, see C. Pauley, "An Autobiography," 309–42.

29. *Nebraska State Journal*, July 3, 1891, 1.

30. Jim McKee, "Havelock Just a Trolley Car Ride Away," *Lincoln Journal Star*, November 15, 1998, 98.

31. Phillips, "Horsecar Days and Horsecar Ways," 18.

32. McKay, *Tramways and Trolleys*, 15.

33. Jim McKee, "Horse Cars and Street Railways," *Lincoln Journal Star*, April 6, 2014, https://journalstar.com/news/local/jim-mckee-horse-cars-and-street-railways/article_09fc3864-c8f7-5f87-b033-ede68e26791f.html.

34. McKay, *Tramways and Trolleys*, 25.

35. McKay, *Tramways and Trolleys*, 22.

36. Jim McKee, "When Electric Streetcars Traveled the Streets of Lincoln," *Lincoln Journal Star*, May 27, 2007, https://journalstar.com/online/newspaper-services/when-electric-streetcars-traveled-the-streets-of-lincoln-5-27-2007/article_e8f2b737-827f-57c9-bc48-d8a814e27cad.html.

37. McKay, *Tramways and Trolleys*, 6, 51.

38. Calhoun, *The Gilded Age*, 108; McKay, *Tramways and Trolleys*, 55, 58.

39. *Lincoln Evening Call*, January 1, 1891, 10.

40. Gordon, *The Rise and Fall*, 4; Jim McKee, "Peanut Vendors and Streetcar Rides," *Lincoln Star*, February 14, 1994, 16.

41. Phillips, "A History of Street Railways," 274.

42. Phillips, "A History of Street Railways," 290.

43. Phillips, "A History of Street Railways," 292.

44. Brown and McConnell, *75 Years in the Prairie Capital*, 145.

45. Phillips, "A History of Street Railways," 292.

46. Phillips, "A History of Street Railways," 324.

47. Phillips, "A History of Street Railways," 310.

48. "Streetcars in North America," Wikipedia, https://en.wikipedia.org/wiki/Streetcars_in_North_America. For a recent article about plans for a three-mile streetcar line in Omaha, see *Omaha World Herald*, January 23, 2022.

49. The peak year for bicycle sales was 1897. See *Lincoln Star*, February 18, 1907, 8.

50. *Nebraska State Journal*, July 24, 1892, 12.

51. "History of the Bicycle," Wikipedia, https://en.wikipedia.org/wiki/History_of_the_bicycle.

52. Piott, *Daily Life*, 90.

53. Muccigrosso, *Celebrating the New World*, 158.

54. Piott, *Daily Life*, 90.

55. *Lincoln Star*, February 18, 1907, 8.

56. *Nebraska State Journal*, February 14, 1902, 4.

57. *Nebraska State Journal*, July 6, 1915, 6.

58. *Lincoln Star*, September 22, 1913, 3.

59. *Nebraska State Journal*, March 8, 1896, 17.

60. C. Pauley, "An Autobiography," 9.

61. *New York Times*, November 10, 2019.

62. *Nebraska State Journal*, March 15, 1900, 3.

63. "Automobile History," History, updated August 21, 2018, https://www.history.com/topics/inventions/automobiles.

64. "v-8s and Chrome in America," Britannica, https://www.britannica.com /technology/automobile/V-8s-and-chrome-in-America.

65. Piott, *Daily Life*, 125.

66. Piott, *Daily Life*, 125.

67. See the interesting and amusing article by Thompson, "The Devil Wagon," 172–91. See also Sullivan, *Our Times*, 2:22; *Nebraska State Journal*, March 14, 1915, 2.

68. Schlereth, *Victorian America*, 26.

69. *Lincoln Star*, December 21, 1905, 5.

70. *Lincoln Star*, March 10, 1907, 1.

71. *Lincoln Evening News*, December 31, 1903, 3.

72. Koster, *A Story of Highway Development*, 13.

73. Gordon, *The Rise and Fall*, 151.

74. Brown and McConnell, *75 Years in the Prairie Capital*, 81, 121–22.

75. Angle, *Crossroads: 1913*, 38.

76. Faith, *The Progressive Era*, 402.

77. Gordon, *The Rise and Fall*, 155.

78. Piott, *Daily Life*, 124.

79. Angle, *Crossroads: 1913*, 38.

80. Sullivan, *Our Times*, 4:50.

81. *Nebraska State Journal*, March 31, 1907, 24.

82. *Nebraska State Journal*, March 22, 1905, 6; December 5, 1909, 19.

83. *Nebraska State Journal*, August 23, 1915, 6; September 13, 1915, 6.

84. "History of the Electric Vehicle," Wikipedia, https://en.wikipedia.org/wiki /History_of_the_electric_vehicle. To see an electric car with its high ceiling to accommodate ladies' hats, see Pioneer Village in Minden, Nebraska.

85. "The History of the Electric Car," Energy.gov, September 15, 2014, https:// www.energy.gov/articles/history-electric-car.

86. Warne, "The Acceptance of the Automobile in Nebraska," 223.

87. *Nebraska State Journal*, January 31, 1915, 1.

88. *Lincoln Star*, September 27, 1913, 4.

89. *Lincoln Star*, October 24, 1902, 3.

90. *Lincoln Star*, April 9, 1905, 15.

91. *Lincoln Star*, March 1908, 6.

92. Thompson, "The Devil Wagon," 226.

93. Douglass, *Oh Grandma*, 27.

94. *Nebraska State Journal*, December 5, 1909, 19.

95. Douglass, *Oh Grandma*, 28.

96. *Lincoln Daily News*, June 13, 1913, 5; *Sunday State Journal*, January 5, 1913, 8.

97. Jim McKee, "The Filling Station Comes to Lincoln," *Lincoln Journal Star*, August 7, 2005, 26.

98. Thompson, "The Devil Wagon," 175.

99. *Lincoln Star*, February 15, 1902, 3.

100. "Motor Vehicle Fatality Rate in U.S. by Year," Wikipedia, https://en .wikipedia.org/wiki/Motor_vehicle_fatality_rate_in_U.S._by_year.

101. *Nebraska State Journal*, August 31, 1913, 23.

102. *Nebraska State Journal*, November 28, 1906, 6.

103. The same speed was permitted for anyone riding or driving a horse or other animal pulling a wagon in downtown Lincoln as late as 1924. See *Lincoln Star*, February 1924, 6; *Nebraska State Journal*, June 14, 1912, 6.

104. *Lincoln Star*, June 17, 1918, 4.

105. *Lincoln Star*, July 6, 1908, 6.

106. *Nebraska State Journal*, September 21, 1907, 9.

107. *Lincoln Star*, July 3, 1912, 12.

108. *Nebraska State Journal*, June 9, 1908, 6; *Lincoln Star*, April 7, 1912, 37.

109. *Nebraska State Journal*, March 13, 1912, 7.

110. Grimes, "Establishing Nebraska's Highway System," 161.

111. Koster, *A Story of Highway Development*, 14.

112. *Lincoln Star*, February 15, 1902, 3.

113. Warne, "The Acceptance of the Automobile," 223; Bader, "The Curtailment of Railroad Service," 27.

114. Lynd and Lynd, *Middletown*, 256. "Middletown" was the fictitious name given by Robert and Helen Merrill Lynd to Muncie, Indiana, a town of about thirty thousand people, to illustrate social changes commonly occurring in mid-size towns throughout the United States during the 1920s.

115. *Nebraska State Journal*, January 31, 1915, 1.

116. Olson and Naugle, *History of Nebraska*, 299. See also McKee, "The Filling Station Comes to Lincoln."

117. *Nebraska State Journal*, June 4, 1911, 6.

118. Knelling, "A Thousand Mile Motor Trip," 22–27.

119. Gaster, "Nebraska's Changing Auto Culture," 180.

120. *Lincoln Star*, December 29, 1918, 13.

121. "Lincoln Highway," Wikipedia, https://en.wikipedia.org/wiki/Lincoln_Highway.

122. Bader, "The Curtailment," 199.

123. Ted Widmer, "1919: The Year of the Crack-Up," *New York Times*, December 31, 2018, https://www.nytimes.com/2018/12/31/opinion/1919-america.html?action=click&module=PackageItem&pgtype=Article&region=Header&action=click&m. Two men made an impromptu trip from New York City in 1911, but reports of the trip did not mention the number of days it took. My maternal grandfather, Fred Hulsebus, of Harlan, Iowa, must have been thrilled to hear that the trip had been made in a Hupmobile, a luxury brand he sold in his dealership. See *Lincoln Star*, October 22, 1911, 7.

124. C. Pauley, "An Autobiography," 12–13.

125. Gordon, *The Rise and Fall*, 240.

126. C. Pauley, "An Autobiography," 14.

127. See C. Pauley, "An Autobiography," 16.

128. *Nebraska State Journal*, January 31, 1915, 1.

129. Lynd and Lynd, *Middletown*, 46.

130. Rader, *American Ways*, 186.

131. Gordon, *The Rise and Fall*, 296–97.

132. "Automobile History," History, updated August 21, 2018, http://www
.history.com/topics/inventions/automobiles.

133. Lynd and Lynd, *Middletown*, 114.

134. Lynd and Lynd, *Middletown*, 255–59, 285.

3. The Athens of the West

1. Jim McKee, "Lincoln's Many Schools Earned Nickname 'Athens of the
West,'" *Lincoln Journal Star*, September 17, 1996, 17.

2. *Lincoln Star*, January 1, 1890, 7.

3. Brown and McConnell, *75 Years in the Prairie Capital*, 217.

4. Sawyer, *Lincoln the Capital City*, 219.

5. Lincoln Chamber of Commerce, *Lincoln: Nebraska's Capital City*, 10.

6. Manley, *Centennial History*, 89. Lincoln High School can certainly not be
criticized for having an inadequate curriculum in 1889. In addition to requiring
three years of Latin, Greek, and German, it had mandatory classes in chemistry,
physics, geology, commercial law, civil governments, English composition, elo-
cution, history, the development of English literature, and rhetoric. See Hayes,
History of the City, 230–31.

7. For an excellent article regarding Nebraska schools between 1890 and
1910, see Dudley, "Nebraska Public School Education." Rural scholars were
more likely to give farm children a shorter school year to allow them to help
around their family's farm.

8. Urban, Gaither, and Wagoner, *American Education*, 299.

9. Rader, *American Ways*, 91.

10. Dick, "Problems of the Post Frontier," 140.

11. Dudley, "Nebraska Public School Education," 66.

12. Olson and Naugle, *History of Nebraska*, 256–57.

13. Dudley, "Nebraska Public School Education," 72.

14. See B. Pauley, *Pioneering History*, 27.

15. Diner, *A Very Different Age*, 95.

16. Dudley, "Nebraska Public School Education," 68, 72.

17. Gordon, *The Rise and Fall*, 284.

18. See Wall, *Grinnell College*, 193.

19. Sawyer, *Lincoln the Capital City*, 220.

20. Knoll, *Prairie University*, 48.

21. Gordon, *The Rise and Fall*, 284–85.

22. Manley, *Centennial History*, 89, 91.

23. Quoted in Dudley, "Nebraska Public School Education," 79.

24. Dudley, "Nebraska Public School Education," 82, 86–87.

25. Dudley, "Nebraska Public School Education," 87.

26. For example in "Middletown," Indiana, the population was growing by three and a half times between 1890 and 1920, while the enrollment at the town's high school grew by nearly elevenfold. See Lynd and Lynd, *Middletown*, 182–83.

27. Schlereth, *Victorian America*, 248.

28. *Lincoln Evening Call*, December 31, 1892, 11.

29. *Lincoln Journal Star*, July 8, 2007, 20.

30. *Lincoln Journal Star*, July 8, 2007, 20; Hayes, *History of the City*, 235.

31. Sawyer, *Lincoln the Capital City*, 220.

32. McKee, *Lincoln, the Prairie Capital*, 112.

33. Veysay, *Emergence*, 630.

34. Cordery, "Women in Industrializing America," 23.

35. Cordery, "Women in Industrializing America," 45.

36. Hayes, *History of the City*, 239.

37. *Lincoln Star*, January 1, 1890, 2.

38. Knoll, *Prairie University*, 37.

39. Gappa, "Chancellor James Hulme Canfield," 392.

40. Larsen et al., *Upstream Metropolis*, 120.

41. Olson and Naugle, *History of Nebraska*, 235. In 1894, 13.54 inches of rain fell on Nebraska compared to an annual average of 21.73 inches. Eight Lincoln banks failed or closed between 1891 and 1896. See Copple, *Tower on the Plains*, 86–87.

42. Manley, *Centennial History*, 136.

43. Manley, *Centennial History*, 112.

44. Manley, *Centennial History*, 147.

45. Knoll, *Prairie University*, 27.

46. Knoll, *Prairie University*, 57; Manley, *Centennial History*, 148.

47. *Lincoln Star*, August 2, 1914, 77.

48. *Lincoln Star*, January 12, 1913, 1.

49. Manley, *Centennial History*, 158–59.

50. *Lincoln Star*, January 1, 1891, 1.

51. Manley, *Centennial History*, 193, 246; Copple, *Tower on the Plains*, 105.

52. Veysay, *Emergence*, 172. During the 1910s college enrollments increased by 68 percent. During the 1920s it rose by another 84 percent. See Snyder, *120 Years of American Education*, 65.

53. Urban, Gaither, and Wagoner, *American Education*, 187.

54. Veysay, *Emergence*, 25. Although the number of college women continued to grow during the 1920s, their percentage compared to men declined from 47 percent to 44 percent. See Snyder, *120 Years of American Education*, 65.

55. Deckard, *The Women's Movement*, 316.

56. *Omaha World Herald*, November 18, 2021, A11.

57. Deckard, *The Women's Movement*, 4, 272.

58. *Lincoln Star*, October 26, 1913, 16. See also Cordery, "Women in Industrializing America," 133; D'Emelio and Freedman, *Intimate Matters*, 190. Fear of a decline in the birthrate for college-educated women was particularly strong

among Viennese Jews before the First World War, when college enrollment was high for Jewish girls. See B. Pauley, *From Prejudice to Persecution*, 348.

59. Manley, *Centennial History*, 129.

60. Veysay, *Emergence*, 202–3.

61. Veysay, *Emergence*, 299.

62. W. Palmer, *From Gentlemen's Club to Professional Body*, 87–88, 116.

63. W. Palmer, *From Gentlemen's Club to Professional Body*, 125–31.

64. W. Palmer, *From Gentlemen's Club to Professional Body*, 384.

65. Rader, *American Ways*, 153.

66. See chapter 9, where it states that several University of Nebraska professors had studied at German universities.

67. Veysay, *Emergence*, 176–77.

68. Manley, *Centennial History*, 229.

69. *Lincoln Star*, January 1, 1908, 1.

70. *Lincoln Star*, January 1, 1908, 136.

71. Wiebe, *The Search for Order*, 113–22.

72. Knoll, *Prairie University*, 54.

73. Douglass, *Oh Grandma*, 84.

74. Rader, *Modern Ways*, 190.

75. Knoll, *Prairie University*, 257.

76. Manley, *Centennial History*, 241.

77. Manley, *Centennial History*, 281.

78. Manley, *Centennial History*, 262.

79. Moomaw, *A History of Cotner*, 23.

80. Moomaw, *A History of Cotner*, 22.

81. Moomaw, *A History of Cotner*, 12.

82. Moomaw, *A History of Cotner*, 199.

83. The exceptions were Oberlin College in Ohio, founded in 1833, and my alma mater, Grinnell College, in Iowa, founded in 1846.

84. *Lincoln Star*, January 1, 1991, 5.

85. Moomaw, *A History of Cotner*, 22.

86. Quoted in Moomaw, *A History of Cotner*, 25–26, 43.

87. Mickey, *Of Sunflowers*, 20.

88. *Lincoln Star*, March 23, 1898, 1.

89. Mickey, *Of Sunflowers*, 82.

90. *Nebraska State Journal*, September 25, 1898, 5.

91. Jim McKee, "Nebraska Wesleyan born at Osceola," *Lincoln Journal Star*, July 12, 1998, 88.

92. Hayes, *History of the City*, 235, 237.

93. Knoll, *Prairie University*, 94.

94. Cotner did acquire a gymnasium in 1906. Together with its stage equipment, it was used for dramatic, musical, and public entertainments. A girls' dormitory was built in 1920, and a boys' dorm was added later. The college also

eventually had a flood-lit athletic field and six tennis courts. See *Lincoln Star*, June 4, 1933, 25.

95. Moomaw, *A History of Cotner*, 23.

96. Moomaw, *A History of Cotner*, 40.

97. Manley, *Centennial History*, 251.

98. Mickey, *Of Sunflowers*, 159.

99. Manley, *Centennial History*, 159.

100. Manley, *Centennial History*, 43.

101. Manley, *Centennial History*, 152.

102. Hutches, "A History of Union College," 64.

103. Hutches, "A History of Union College," 76.

104. Hutches, "A History of Union College," 43–44.

105. Dick and Rees, *Union College*, 14–15.

106. Dick and Rees, *Union College*, 216.

107. Dick and Rees, *Union College*, 78–79, 81.

108. Dick and Rees, *Union College*, 154–55, 160.

109. Dick and Rees, *Union College*, 44–45.

110. Dick, "The Founding of Union College," 460.

111. Mickey, *Of Sunflowers*, 279.

112. Dick and Rees, *Union College*, 204.

113. Lincoln Chamber of Commerce, *Lincoln: Nebraska's Capital City*, 45.

114. Orad, *Reading Football*, 250.

115. *Lincoln Herald*, June 2, 1933, 1.

4. The New Woman

1. See Lynd and Lynd, *Middletown*, 117.

2. Gordon, *The Rise and Fall*, 195.

3. Dudley, "Nebraska Public School Education," 88.

4. Lynd and Lynd, *Middletown*, 127.

5. Women in Omaha around 1910 appear to have been more successful than Lincoln's women in gaining employment as bank officials, chemists, assayers, and metallurgists. See Larsen et al., *Upstream Metropolis*, 203.

6. Sullivan, *Our Times*, 1:26.

7. *Lincoln Star*, October 26, 1913, 19. See also B. Pauley, *From Prejudice to Persecution*, 90–92.

8. Anderson and Zinsser, *A History of Their Own*, 158.

9. Hunter, *How Young Ladies Became Girls*, 385.

10. *Lincoln Star*, June 16, 1916, 21.

11. *Lincoln Star*, September 10, 1914, 12. The column's subtitle was at first "If You Are in Doubt Ask Minerva" and later "Take Your Troubles to Minerva."

12. *Lincoln Star*, June 24, 1912, 54.

13. *Lincoln Star*, June 7, 1912, 8.

14. *Lincoln Star*, November 25, 1918, 10.

15. *Lincoln Star*, January 25, 1920, 17.

16. *Lincoln Star*, October 4, 1918, 8.

17. *Lincoln Star*, December 20, 1912, 21.

18. *Lincoln Star*, December 8, 1912, 16.

19. *Lincoln Star*, January 2, 1914, 10.

20. *Lincoln Star*, December 3, 1912, 10.

21. *Lincoln Evening Call*, December 15, 1890, 2.

22. *Lincoln Star*, January 7, 1898, 3.

23. International Association of Administrative Professionals, "History of the Secretarial Profession," 2–3.

24. Davis, *Women's Place*, 71.

25. Davis, *Women's Place*, 57, 59, 65.

26. Davis, *Women's Place*, 60–61.

27. *Nebraska State Journal*, August 30, 1885, 3.

28. *Nebraska State Journal*, July 7, 1890, 2.

29. *Lincoln Star*, May 25, 1906, 9.

30. Schlereth, *Victorian America*, 73.

31. *Lincoln Star*, July 28, 1918, 17.

32. Rader, *American Ways*, 186, 188.

33. C. E. Clark, *The American Family Home*, 140.

34. Schlereth, *Victorian America*, 74.

35. Schlereth, *Victorian America*, 141.

36. For a good general history of Lincoln's department stores, see Jim McKee, "Department Stores Rose—Then Fell," *Lincoln Journal Star*, November 17, 2013, 4.

37. *Nebraska State Journal*, June 4, 1898, 6.

38. Ford, *Dress Codes*, 126.

39. Anderson and Zinsser, *A History of Their Own*, 145.

40. Eubank and Tortora, *Survey of Historic Costume*, 349.

41. Schlereth, *Victorian America*, 166.

42. Anderson and Zinsser, *A History of Their Own*, 145.

43. "History of Corsets," Wikipedia, https://en.wikipedia.org/wiki/History_of_corsets.

44. Douglass, *Oh Grandma*, 49.

45. "History of Corsets," Wikipedia, https://en.wikipedia.org/wiki/History_of_corsets.

46. Ford, *Dress Codes*, 134.

47. Ford, *Dress Codes*, 133–34, 149.

48. Eubank and Tortora, *Survey*, 325.

49. Litwicki, "The Influence of Commerce," 198.

50. D'Emelio and Freedman, *Intimate Matters*, 190.

51. For an excellent article on this topic, see Wilke, "Physical Education for Women."

52. Wilke, "Physical Education," 198.

53. Wilke, "Physical Education," 198.

54. Knoll, *Prairie University*, 77.

55. Wilke, "Physical Education," 211.

56. Wilke, "Physical Education," 214.

57. Wilke, "Physical Education," 215.

58. Manley, *Centennial History*, 304.

59. Quoted in Mickey, *Of Sunflowers*, 264.

60. Horse and bar work involves riding a horse around a series of poles to improve the stride and rhythm of its gait. Trudy McElwee, in discussion with the author, June 28, 2021.

61. Mickey, *Of Sunflowers*, 264.

62. Dick and Rees, *Union College*, 64.

63. Mickey, *Of Sunflowers*, 484.

64. Mickey, *Of Sunflowers*, 487.

65. For an interesting article on porches, see Jim McKee, "Evolution of Porches as Top Summer Hot Spot," *Lincoln Journal Star*, May 18, 2003, 25.

66. C. Pauley, "An Autobiography," 2.

67. Schlereth, *Victorian America*, 122.

68. C. E. Clark, *The American Family Home*, 131.

69. Gordon, *The Rise and Fall*, 41.

70. Gordon, *The Rise and Fall*, 125.

71. Panati, *Extraordinary*, 200.

72. Panati, *Extraordinary*, 216.

73. Rader, *American Ways*, 140.

74. "Average Size of U.S. Homes, Decade by Decade," *Newser*, May 29, 2016, https://www.newser.com/story/225645/average-size-of-us-homes-decade-by -decade.html.

75. C. E. Clark, *The American Family Home*, 168.

76. C. E. Clark, *The American Family Home*, 167.

5. Feminine Reformers

1. Baker, "The Domestication of Politics," 624.

2. Anderson and Zinsser, *A History of Their Own*, 203.

3. See, for example, Hicks, "My Nine Years at the University of Nebraska."

4. Piott, *Daily Life*, 147.

5. *Nebraska State Journal*, January 17, 1919, 5.

6. Piott, *Daily Life*, 151.

7. Gordon, *The Rise and Fall*, 176.

8. Anderson and Zinsser, *A History of Their Own*, 85.

9. Burns, *1920*, 299.

10. Manley, *Centennial History*, 261.

11. Manley, *Centennial History*, 261.

12. Piott, *Daily Life*, 147.

13. *Nebraska State Journal*, August 18, 1885, 8.

14. *Lincoln Evening Call*, December 4, 1890, 3.

15. *Nebraska State Journal*, February 11, 1901, 6.

16. *Lincoln Star*, November 20, 1910, 7.

17. *Nebraska State Journal*, March 30, 1906, 4.

18. Kuzma, "Kicking the Habit," 96.

19. *Lincoln Star*, February 18, 1919, 6.

20. *Lincoln Star*, August 8, 1910, 1.

21. *Lincoln Star*, August 8, 1910, 1.

22. *Lincoln Star*, February 8, 1920, 1.

23. *Lincoln Star*, January 6, 1920, 1.

24. Burns, *1920*, 299.

25. See, for example, the nearly full-page article in the *Lincoln Star*, April 1919, 20.

26. Kuzma, "Kicking the Habit," 92.

27. McGerr, *A Fierce Discontent*, 110. See also Allerfeldt, *The Progressive Era*, 637.

28. Olson and Naugle, *History of Nebraska*, 91.

29. Cherny, *A Righteous Cause*, 22.

30. Anderson, "Lincoln, Nebraska, and *Prohibition*," 184–85.

31. Rader, *American Ways*, 168.

32. Schlereth, *Victorian America*, 226; Okrent, *Last Call*, 28.

33. Okrent, *Last Call*, 27.

34. Rader, *American Ways*, 200.

35. Flexner, *Century of Struggle*, 174.

36. Sullivan, *Our Times*, 5:25.

37. Sheldon, *Nebraska*, 1:366.

38. Burns, *1920*, 43.

39. Wenger, "The Anti-Saloon League in Nebraska," 288.

40. See, for example, Manley, *Centennial History*, 288; Mickey, *Of Sunflowers*, 44, 162–63.

41. Anderson, "Lincoln, Nebraska, and *Prohibition*," 184.

42. Okrent, *Last Call*, 34. See, for example, Manley, *Centennial History*, 288; Mickey, *Of Sunflowers*, 44, 162–63.

43. Anderson, "Lincoln, Nebraska, and *Prohibition*," 185.

44. Anderson, "Lincoln, Nebraska, and *Prohibition*," 180–85.

45. Sheldon, *Nebraska*, 1:5, 854, 856.

46. Sheldon, *Nebraska*, 1:1, 854, 856; Anderson, "Lincoln, Nebraska, and *Prohibition*," 199.

47. "The Battle," Nebraska Studies, https://nebraskastudies.org/en/1900-1924/prohibition-of-alcohol/the-bat-new/; Sheldon, *Nebraska*, 1:1, 913.

48. McGerr, *A Fierce Discontent*, 294.

49. "Eighteenth Amendment to the United States Constitution," Wikipedia, https://en.wikipedia.org/wiki/Eighteenth_Amendment_to_the_United_States_Constitution.

50. Sheldon, *Nebraska*, 1:949. Only one state senator out of thirty-two voted against the amendment. See Okrent, *Last Call*, 106.

51. *Nebraska State Journal*, January 17, 1919, 1.

52. *Nebraska State Journal*, January 17, 1919, 1.

53. *Commoner*, March 1, 1919, 3.

54. *Lincoln Star*, January 17, 1919, 8.

55. Burns, *1920*, 43, 47, 127, 135.

56. Burns, *1920*, 373.

57. See Hickman, "Thou Shalt Not Vote," 55–65.

58. Schlereth, *Victorian America*, 304.

59. *Nebraska State Journal*, July 13, 1914, 4.

60. *Lincoln Star*, October 21, 1914, 10.

61. *Lincoln Star*, October 21, 1914, 10.

62. Coulter, "Woman Suffrage in Nebraska," 62. In Douglas County (Omaha) there were 5,758 foreign born and 6,662 natives. In Lancaster County (Lincoln), just 2,838 were foreign born and 5,673 were natives.

63. Schlereth, *Victorian America*, 60.

64. First Lady Eleanor Roosevelt was also an early opponent of female suffrage, arguing that women could do better in the various organizations to which they belonged. See H. Evans, *The American Century*, 122.

65. Schlereth, *Victorian America*, 60.

66. Stevens, *A Dangerous Class*, 5.

67. *Nebraska State Journal*, November 25, 1900, 1.

68. Wilhite, "Sixty-Five Years Till Victory," 151.

69. Burns, *1920*, 60.

70. Sheldon, *Nebraska*, 1:267.

71. Sheldon, *Nebraska*, 1:452, 454, 457.

72. Cordery, "Women in Industrializing America," 127.

73. Wilhite, "Sixty-Five Years Till Victory," 151.

74. Bloomberg, "'Striving for Equal Rights for All,'" 86, 98.

75. Coulter, "Woman Suffrage in Nebraska," 52.

76. Bloomberg, "'Striving for Equal Rights for All,'" 98.

77. Stevens, *A Dangerous Class*, 14, 19.

78. Flexner, *Century of Struggle*, 241.

79. *Nebraska State Journal*, March 1, 1913, 2.

80. "Woman Suffrage Procession," Wikipedia, https://en.wikipedia.org/wiki/Woman_Suffrage_Procession; *Lincoln Star*, March 3, 1913, 7.

81. Seale, *The Imperial Season*, 190–91.

82. *Nebraska State Journal*, March 5, 1913, 6.

83. For an excellent article on the women's anti-suffrage movement in Nebraska, see Hickman, "Thou Shalt Not Vote."

84. Coulter, "Woman Suffrage in Nebraska," 111–13.

85. *Lincoln Star*, November 22, 1911, 10.

86. *Lincoln Star*, November 5, 1913, 8; *Lincoln Star*, June 17, 1914, 1.

87. Olson and Nagle, *History of Nebraska*, 199.

88. See, for example, *Nebraska State Journal*, March 13, 1913, 6; October 3, 1914, 17.

89. Coulter, "Woman Suffrage in Nebraska," 123.

90. Coulter, "Woman Suffrage in Nebraska," 133.

91. *Nebraska State Journal*, November 1, 1914, 18.

92. *Lincoln Star*, October 4, 1914, 7; *Lincoln Daily News*, October 21, 1914, 5.

93. *Lincoln Star*, October 21, 1914, 7; *Lincoln Star*, October 22, 1914, 10.

94. *Nebraska State Journal*, October 18, 1914, 15.

95. *Lincoln Star*, March 3, 1911, 3; *Lincoln Star*, March 30, 1914, 3.

96. *Lincoln Star*, November [n. d.], 1914, 13.

97. *Lincoln Star*, March 2, 1911, 3.

98. Sheldon, *Nebraska*, 1:892.

99. Coulter, "Woman Suffrage in Nebraska," 139; *Sunday World Herald*, November 15, 1914, 1.

100. Quoted in *Nebraska State Journal*, November 7, 1914, 4.

6. Amusements for All

1. Diner, *A Very Different Age*, 103.

2. Nasaw, *Going Out*, 4.

3. *Lincoln Star*, September 10, 1908, 4

4. Olson and Nagle, *History of Nebraska*, 253.

5. Johnson, *A History of the American People*, 535.

6. Gossage, "A History of the Funke Opera House," 6.

7. Ryan, "Hallo's Opera House," 323.

8. Ryan, "Hallo's Opera House," 324.

9. Ryan, "Hallo's Opera House," 328; Ehlers, "Second Floor," 5.

10. *Nebraska State Journal*, October 8, 1875, 3.

11. *Lincoln Star*, October 11, 1883, 8.

12. Gossage, "A History of the Funke Opera House," 9–11.

13. Slote, *The Kingdom of Art*, 9.

14. Levine, *Highbrow/Lowbrow*, 78.

15. Ehlers, "Second Floor," 3.

16. Brown and Raymond, *75 Years in the Prairie Capital*, 41.

17. Wolmar, *The Great Railroad Revolution*, 215.

18. Jennings, "Grand Opera," 2.

19. Levine, *Highbrow/Lowbrow*, 86.

20. Levine, *Highbrow/Lowbrow*, 34.

21. Sousa's performance in April 1891 produced the largest advance ticket sale in the history of entertainment in Lincoln. See Gossage, "A History of the Funke Opera House," 49; Levine, *Highbrow/Lowbrow*, 104.

22. Muccigrosso, *Celebrating the New World*, 170.

23. Muccigrosso, *Celebrating the New World*, 36.

24. Muccigrosso, *Celebrating the New World*, 65; Allen, "Art and Music's Growing Audience," 208.

25. *Nebraska State Journal*, December 13, 1900, 1.

26. *Lincoln Star*, February 27, 1908, 7; *Nebraska State Journal*, February 27, 1908, 10; *Nebraska State Journal*, March 4, 1908, 5.

27. Seymour, "Music in Lincoln," 37–38.

28. *Nebraska State Journal*, January 27, 1886, 5.

29. *Nebraska State Journal*, May 12, 1891, 5.

30. *Nebraska State Journal*, January 9, 1898, 6.

31. See Seymour, "The University of Nebraska School of Music," 399–418.

32. C. Pauley, "An Autobiography," 18–19.

33. C. Pauley, "An Autobiography," 17.

34. For a detailed history of minstrel shows, see "Minstrel Show," Wikipedia, https://en.wikipedia.org/wiki/Minstrel_show.

35. Gossage, "A History of the Funke Opera House," 76.

36. Walton, "A History of Professional Theater," 3–6.

37. For details about the Iroquois Theater fire, see *Lincoln Star*, December 31, 1904, 1, 5; *Lincoln Star*, January 1, 1903, 1; and *Lincoln Star*, January 2, 1903, 1.

38. Walton, "A History of Professional Theater," 2–6.

39. Gossage, "A History of the Funke Opera House," 68.

40. Walton, "A History of Professional Theater," 38–39. For the funding of the Temple Theater, see *Lincoln Journal Star*, January 25, 2009, 25.

41. Walton, "A History of Professional Theater," 38.

42. Walton, "A History of Professional Theater," 65.

43. Eckman, "Respectable Leisure," 19; Dulles, "The Chautauqua," 96.

44. Dulles, "The Chautauqua," 95.

45. Eckman, "Promoting an Ideology of Culture," 18–23.

46. Eckman, "Respectable Leisure," 21.

47. *Nebraska State Journal*, July 4, 1891, 4.

48. Eckman, "Respectable Leisure," 28.

49. Eckman, "Culture as Entertainment," 246; Dulles, "The Chautauqua," 95.

50. For interesting articles by Jim McKee describing Epworth Park, see *Lincoln Star*, June 1, 1993, 19; and *Lincoln Journal Star*, March 14, 1999; August 15, 2004, 30; June 10, 2007, 22.

51. *Lincoln State Journal*, September 19, 1943, 25.

52. Kazin, *A Godly Hero*, 34, 131, 136; Jim McKee, "Bryan a Natural for Chautauqua," *Lincoln Journal Star*, June 10, 2007, 22. In his last years, Bryan emphasized his fundamentalist belief in the literal translation of the Bible as was seen in his role in the Scopes "Monkey" Trial of 1925. Spencer Tracy starred in the film *Inherit the Wind*, which depicted the trial.

53. Holter, *Flames on the Plains*, 231–32, 391.

54. Rader, *American Ways*, 194; Ashby, *With Amusement for All*, 107.

55. Calhoun, *The Gilded Age*, 192; Nasaw, *Going Out*, 56.

56. Nasaw, *Going Out*, 226; Ashby, *With Amusement for All*, 216.

57. Douglass, *Oh Grandma*, 43–44.

58. Schlereth, *Victorian America*, 204. For a defense of the desire of young people to go to the movies as well as municipal dance halls, see *Lincoln Star*, October 19, 1912, 4.

59. Gordon, *The Rise and Fall*, 198.

60. Piott, *Daily Life*, 120.

61. Gordon, *The Rise and Fall*, 49.

62. *Nebraska State Journal*, December 24, 1905, 10; January 16, 1906, 7.

63. Sorlin, "Cinema and the Memory of the Great War," 6.

64. Nasaw, *Going Out*, 202.

65. Advertisement in the *Lincoln Star*, January 9, 1916, 32.

66. "*The Birth of a Nation*," Wikipedia, https://en.wikipedia.org/wiki/The_Birth_of_a_Nation; Schuyler, "The Ku Klux Klan in Nebraska," 234.

67. Walton, "A History of Professional Theater," 56.

68. *Lincoln Star*, January 9, 1916, 30.

69. Walton, "A History of Professional Theater," 32.

70. *Lincoln Star*, January 20, 1916, 5.

71. *Lincoln Star*, January 21, 1916, 12.

72. Nasaw, *Going Out*, 238.

73. Lynd and Lynd, *Middletown*, 137.

74. Nasaw, *Going Out*, 238, 241.

75. Nasaw, *Going Out*, 224.

76. Ashby, *With Amusement for All*, 186.

77. *Lincoln Star*, June 1, 1916, 9.

78. *Lincoln Star*, December 26, 1920, 15.

79. Piott, *Daily Life*, 102.

80. Manley, *Centennial History*, 262.

81. *Nebraska State Journal*, January 6, 1918, 36.

82. *Lincoln Star*, February 25, 1976, 9. The turnpike burned to the ground in 1976 and was not rebuilt.

83. Manley, *Centennial History*, 101.

84. *Nebraska State Journal*, July 3, 1917, 8.

85. *Lincoln Star*, March 22, 1913, 1.

86. Cantor and Werthman, *The History of Popular Culture*, 55.

87. Valentine, "Evangelist," 209.

88. Valentine, "Evangelist," 225.

89. *Nebraska State Journal*, October 13, 1915, 3.

90. *Nebraska State Journal*, October 13, 1915, 3.

91. *Lincoln Star*, April 15, 1918, 29.

92. *Daily Nebraskan*, October 18, 1915, 1; *Lincoln Star*, October 15, 1915, 1.

93. Manley, *Centennial History*, 262.

94. Mickey, *Of Sunflowers*, 245.

95. *Lincoln Star*, October 19, 1904, 4.

96. *Lincoln Star*, December 11, 1902, 3.

97. Johnson, *A History of the American People*, 540.

98. *Nebraska State Journal*, October 20, 1890, 5; Wolmar, *The Great Railroad Revolution*, 190.

99. *Lincoln Star*, December 25, 1908, 3.

100. Wolmar, *The Great Railroad Revolution*, 190.

101. Douglass, *Oh Grandma*, 61, 92; *Lincoln Star*, June 9, 1914, 6.

102. *Lincoln Star*, June 9, 1914, 6; *Lincoln Star*, June 12, 1914, 13.

103. Schlereth, *Victorian America*, 30–31.

104. "Amusement Park," Wikipedia, https://en.wikipedia.org/wiki/Amusement _park.

105. *Lincoln Star*, April 26, 1959, 11.

106. *Lincoln Evening Call*, December 31, 1892, 11.

107. *Nebraska State Journal*, July 4, 1908, 3.

108. *Lincoln Star*, July 2, 1910, 12.

109. *Lincoln Star*, July 1, 1912, 6.

110. *Nebraska State Journal*, July 4, 1914, 5.

111. Rader, *American Ways*, 193–94.

112. *Lincoln Journal Star*, October 26, 1997, 89.

113. Janet M. Davis, "America's Big Circus Spectacular Has a Long and Cherished History," *Smithsonian Magazine*, March 22, 2017, https://www.smithsonian mag.com/history/americas-big-circus-spectacular-has-long-and-cherished-history -180962621.

114. Douglass, *Oh Grandma*, 12.

115. Brown and McConnell, *75 Years in the Prairie Capital*, 39.

116. *Nebraska State Journal*, June 6, 1890, 4.

117. *Lincoln Star*, July 12, 1908, 9.

118. *Lincoln Star*, September 1, 1901, 1; *Lincoln Star*, September 26, 1901, 14.

119. *Nebraska State Journal*, September 3, 1908, 1.

120. The failure was caused by my grandmother not having an exact recipe as well as attempting to bake in Laramie, Wyoming, with its elevation of 7,200 feet rather than in Lincoln, which is only 1,200 feet above sea level.

121. Larson, *Devil in the White City*, 250.

122. "Buffalo Bill," Wikipedia, https://en.wikipedia.org/wiki/Buffalo_Bill.

123. Hickey, *Nebraska Moments*, 29.

124. "Buffalo Bill," Wikipedia, https://en.wikipedia.org/wiki/Buffalo_Bill.

125. It is possible today to travel by train from Nebraska to Florida by Amtrak, but it requires a major detour through Washington DC, rather than using a more direct route through St. Louis as was usually done in the past. It would also require boarding a train in Lincoln or Omaha at inconvenient hours.

7. College Football

1. *Lincoln Evening Call*, November 28, 1890, 8.

2. *Lincoln Star*, October 18, 1980, 13,

3. *Nebraska State Journal*, November 24, 1889, 8.

4. Veysay, *Emergence*, 269.

5. *Nebraska State Journal*, November 19, 1993, 16.

6. *Nebraska State Journal*, September 25, 1910, 26.

7. "American College Football," University of Wisconsin, http://homepages .cae.wisc.edu/~dwilson/rsfc/RuleChanges.txt (page discontinued).

8. "Drop Kick," Wikipedia, https://en.wikipedia.org/wiki/Drop_kick.

9. *Lincoln Star*, October 19, 1954, 13.

10. Of 555 cities in the United States in 1905, 432 of them had high school football teams. See Orad, *Reading Football*, 132.

11. *Lincoln Evening Call*, October 3, 1897, 4; *Lincoln Star*, September 8, 1989, 41.

12. *Lincoln Star*, November 30, 1924, 13.

13. *Nebraska State Journal*, December 2, 1900, 13.

14. *Lincoln Evening News*, December 14, 1895, 8. See also "Hedding College," Lost Colleges, https://www.lostcolleges.com/hedding-college.

15. *Nebraska State Journal*, October 30, 1898, 14.

16. *Lincoln Star*, February 3, 1906, 5.

17. *Lincoln Star*, March 12, 1907, 10.

18. *Lincoln Star*, October 20, 1908, 6.

19. *Lincoln Herald*, January 26, 1906, 6.

20. *Lincoln Star*, November 16, 1903, 2.

21. *Lincoln Star*, February 2, 1910, 10.

22. *Lincoln Star*, October 30, 1897, 1.

23. *Lincoln Star*, February 15, 1913, 5.

24. *Lincoln Star*, March 12, 1907, 10.

25. Watterson, *History of Football*, 64–65, 79, 108.

26. *Lincoln Star*, September 8, 1912, 7.

27. Watterson, *History of Football*, 64–65, 79, 108; *Nebraska State Journal*, March 25, 1906, 27.

28. *Nebraska State Journal*, February 9, 1908, 11.

29. *Nebraska State Journal*, September 11, 1910, 30.

30. *Lincoln Star*, November 30, 1924, 13.

31. *Nebraska State Journal*, October 2, 1910, 26.

32. *Nebraska State Journal*, September 25, 1910, 26.

33. *Nebraska State Journal*, March 25, 1906, 25.

34. *Lincoln Star*, October 12, 1915, 8.

35. *Sunday State Journal*, October 26, 1907, 1.

36. *Nebraska State Journal*, November 28, 1911, 1–2.

37. Watterson, *History of Football*, 104–5.

38. Orad, *Reading Football*, 132.

39. *Lincoln Star*, November 1909, 9.

40. *Lincoln Star*, December 9, 1915, 9.

41. "History of the Football Helmet," Wikipedia, https://en.wikipedia.org /wiki/History_of_the_football_helmet.

42. "History of the Football Helmet," Wikipedia, https://en.wikipedia.org /wiki/History_of_the_football_helmet.

43. *Nebraska State Journal,* January 20, 1906, 2.

44. *Nebraska State Journal,* November 15, 1899, 8.

45. *Lincoln Star,* October 20, 1908, 6.

46. *Nebraska State Journal,* May 14, 1910, 2; *Lincoln Star,* November 30, 1924, 13.

47. Watterson, *History of Football,* 133.

48. Orad, *Reading Football,* 38.

49. Orad, *Reading Football,* 39.

50. *Nebraska State Journal,* February 22, 1891, 9.

51. *Nebraska State Journal,* November 19, 1893, 16.

52. *Lincoln Star,* November 7, 1892, 4.

53. *Nebraska State Journal,* November 25, 1892, 2.

54. *Nebraska State Journal,* December 7, 1894, 6.

55. Ware and McBride, *Fifty Years of Nebraska Football,* 14.

56. "History of Nebraska Cornhuskers Football," Wikipedia, https://en .wikipedia.org/wiki/History_of_Nebraska_Cornhuskers_football.

57. *Lincoln Star,* November 17, 1895, 5.

58. Orad, *Reading Football,* 38–39.

59. *Lincoln Star,* November 25, 1992, 4–5.

60. *Nebraska State Journal,* November 19, 1893, 16.

61. *Nebraska State Journal,* November 19, 1893, 1.

62. *Nebraska State Journal,* October 28, 1894, 2.

63. *Nebraska State Journal,* October 6, 1893, 6.

64. *Lincoln Star,* September 9, 1899, 5.

65. *Lincoln Star,* September 20, 1899, 5.

66. *Lincoln Star,* November 3, 1909, 8.

67. *Lincoln Star,* September 29, 1900, 5.

68. *Lincoln Star,* October 1903, 14.

69. *Lincoln Star,* December 13, 1900, 5.

70. *Lincoln Star,* April 27, 1901, 1.

71. *Lincoln Star,* April 27, 1901, 1.

72. During Booth's twenty-four-game winning streak, his team gave up only eleven points. However, his unscored-upon team in 1901 did not come close to establishing a collegiate record. The University of Michigan won fifty-eight games without giving up a score starting in 1901. See Watterson, *History of Football,* 80.

73. *Lincoln Star,* January 12, 1903, 5.

74. *Lincoln Star,* November 24, 1902, 5.

75. *Lincoln Star,* November 22, 1902, 1.

76. *Lincoln Star,* November 11, 1911, 2.

77. *Nebraska State Journal,* October 19, 1913, 1 (author's emphasis).

78. *Nebraska State Journal,* October 19, 1913, 1.

79. *Lincoln Star,* October 19, 1914, 29.

80. *Nebraska State Journal,* October 25, 1915, 1.

81. For example, see *Lincoln Star*, October 16, 1920, 3.

82. *Nebraska State Journal*, December 9, 1915, 8.

83. *Lincoln Star*, October 30, 1913, 1.

84. *Lincoln Star*, October 17, 1944, 19; January 8, 1948, 12; April 12, 1949, 11.

85. *Lincoln Star*, December 9, 1915, 8.

86. See, for example, *Lincoln Star*, December 17, 1916, 9; January 10, 1922, 9.

87. *Lincoln Star*, August 2, 1914, 29.

88. Larsen et al., *Upstream Metropolis*, 173.

89. See, for example, *Lincoln Star*, December 1918, 13.

90. *Lincoln Star*, November 18, 1895, 1.

91. *Nebraska State Journal*, October 31, 1897, 6.

92. *Lincoln Star*, November 2, 1904, 5.

93. *Lincoln Star*, November 26, 1903, 1.

94. *Lincoln Star*, October 22, 1911, 2.

95. *Nebraska State Journal*, December 2, 1900, 13; March 23, 1914, 3.

8. Minorities and Immigrants

1. The two students worked under the direction of the American History Department with aid from the Department of Sociology. For an excellent summary of the Davies and Marsh dissertation, see *Nebraska State Journal*, June 26, 1904, 18.

2. Davies and Marsh, "A Study of the Negro in Lincoln," 56.

3. Morris, *American History Revised*, 107.

4. *Nebraska State Journal*, May 24, 1915, 4.

5. Larsen et al., *Upstream Metropolis*, 206.

6. Davies and Marsh, "A Study of the Negro in Lincoln," 191–93.

7. The absence of African Americans lasted for a long time. My father's *Cornhusker* yearbook for 1930 does not show a picture of a single Black person out of a student body of around ten thousand.

8. Davies and Marsh, "A Study of the Negro in Lincoln," 153.

9. Davies and Marsh, "A Study of the Negro in Lincoln," 186.

10. Davies and Marsh, "A Study of the Negro in Lincoln," 163.

11. Davies and Marsh, "A Study of the Negro in Lincoln," 166.

12. Davies and Marsh, "A Study of the Negro in Lincoln," 179.

13. Davies and Marsh, "A Study of the Negro in Lincoln," 187.

14. Davies and Marsh, "A Study of the Negro in Lincoln," 175.

15. Davies and Marsh, "A Study of the Negro in Lincoln," 215.

16. Davies and Marsh, "A Study of the Negro in Lincoln," 212–13.

17. Davies and Marsh, "A Study of the Negro in Lincoln," 218.

18. Davies and Marsh, "A Study of the Negro in Lincoln," 220

19. Davies and Marsh, "A Study of the Negro in Lincoln," 221.

20. Hildebrand, "The New Negro Movement," 166–89.

21. Hildebrand, "The New Negro Movement," 168.

22. Hess, "The Negro in Nebraska," 56.

23. "Nuremberg Laws," Wikipedia, https://en.wikipedia.org/wiki/Nuremberg_Laws.

24. "Anti-Miscegenation Laws in the United States," Wikipedia, https://en.wikipedia.org/wiki/Anti-miscegenation_laws_in_the_United_States.

25. *Lincoln Star*, July 2, 1919, 5.

26. See, for example, *Lincoln Star*, October 16, 1964, 13.

27. Hildebrand, "The New Negro Movement," 169; Larsen et al., *Upstream Metropolis*, 218. For an interesting study of why Lincoln's Black population did not pursue higher education or understand what they needed to do to enter a professional field like medicine or law, see Collins, "A Survey." For a discussion of school integration in Lincoln and Omaha in the 1880s, see Trowbridge, "'A Double Mixture,'" especially 150.

28. Larsen et al., *Upstream Metropolis*, 216.

29. *Lincoln Star*, June 10, 1909, 1.

30. Lynd and Lynd, *Middletown*, 47.

31. For an excellent article on the subject, see Ishikawa, "The Desegregation."

32. *Die Welt-Post*, March 9, 1925, 7.

33. Kinbacher, *Urban Villages*, 54–55. See also Kinbacher's article "Life in the Russian Bottoms."

34. Alexander, *Daily Life in Immigrant America*, 27.

35. *Lincoln Star*, April 25, 1904, 1.

36. *Lincoln Star*, June 6, 1914, 1.

37. Jim McKee, "Rock Island Arrives in Lincoln—Belatedly," *Lincoln Journal Star*, March 5, 1996, 20; Jim McKee, "There's a History of Building in Lincoln's Flood Plain," *Lincoln Journal Star*, January 27, 2008, 36.

38. Martin, *A Nation of Immigrants*, 52.

39. Janssen, *Von Zarenreich*, 74.

40. Hickey, *Nebraska Moments*, 109.

41. Janssen, *Von Zarenreich*, 112.

42. Williams, *The Czar's Germans*, 3–4. Other Germans from Russia, including those who had been living near the Black Sea, settled mostly in the plains between Kansas and North Dakota, as well as in Manitoba, Saskatchewan, and Alberta. Some of them even went to Argentina and Chile.

43. Williams, "The History of the German-Russian Colony," 82.

44. Kinbacher, *Urban Villages*, 54–55.

45. Janssen, *Von Zarenreich*, 232.

46. Williams, "The History of the German-Russian Colony," 95–96.

47. Jansen, *Von Zarenreich*, 222.

48. Kinbacher, *Urban Villages*, 178.

49. For information about Volgers being called derogatory names, I am indebted to Dr. Kenneth Rock, a retired specialist in Volga German history at Colorado State University in Fort Collins, Colorado.

50. Luebke, *Immigrants and Politics*, 46.

51. Williams, "A Social Study of the Russian Germans," 8.

52. Schwabenland, "German-Russians," 101–2.
53. Jones, *American Immigration*, 158.
54. See Larsen et al., *Upstream Metropolis*, 209–16.
55. Martin, *A Nation of Immigrants*, 51.
56. Kinbacher, *Urban Villages*, 58; Hickey, *Nebraska Moments*, 110.
57. Nancy Deer Borrell, in discussion with the author, August 27, 2021.
58. Janssen, *Von Zarenreich*, 170.
59. See, for example, *Lincoln Star*, January 22, 1911, 3.
60. Williams, "The History of the German-Russian Colony in Lincoln," 94–95.
61. Williams, "The History of the German-Russian Colony in Lincoln," 64.
62. Kinbacher, *Urban Villages*, 8, 82–83.

9. World War

1. Farwell, *Over There*, 48.
2. Sullivan, *Our Times*, 4:11–12.
3. *Lincoln Star*, August 3, 1914, 6.
4. Strachan, *The First World War*, 101.
5. Strachan, *The First World War*, 115.
6. C. Clark, *The Sleepwalkers*, 358.
7. *Lincoln Star*, August 4, 1914, 3.
8. Tate, *Modernism, History*, 5.
9. Tate, *Modernism, History*, 41–42.
10. *Lincoln Star*, October 8, 1918, 3.
11. C. Clark, *The Sleepwalkers*, 553.
12. Barry, *The Great Influenza*, 206.
13. Keegan, *The First World War*, 69.
14. Brands, *Woodrow Wilson*, 56–57.
15. H. Evans, *The American Century*, 144.
16. Farwell, *Over There*, 24–25.
17. *Nebraska State Journal*, May 8, 1915, 6.
18. *Nebraska State Journal*, May 15, 1915, 6.
19. Farwell, *Over There*, 25.
20. *Lincoln Star*, June 9, 1915, 1.
21. C. E. Clark, *The American Family Home*, 173–74. See also *Nebraska State Journal*, June 9, 1915, 1.
22. *Nebraska State Journal*, June 12, 1915, 6.
23. Kennedy, *Profiles in Courage*, 182.
24. In addition to Senator Norris, there were three members of the House of Representatives from Nebraska who opposed American entry into the war, which was fully one-half of the six-member Nebraska House delegation. Harl Dalstrom, in discussion with the author, March 15, 2021.
25. *Lincoln Star*, October 4, 1918, 5.
26. *Lincoln Star*, October 4, 1918, 4.
27. *Lincoln Star*, October 4, 1918, 1.

28. *Lincoln Star*, November 8, 1918, 8.

29. Kennedy was given extensive help by a Lincolnite and graduate of the University of Nebraska, Ted Sorenson, who was a close friend of my uncle Gordon Pauley.

30. *Lincoln Star*, May 2, 1918, 15.

31. Rader, *American Ways*, 217.

32. Sullivan, *Our Times*, 4:489–90.

33. *Lincoln Star*, September 30, 1918, 8.

34. Ninety percent of charges of sedition proved to be false. See Sullivan, *Our Times*, 4:412.

35. *Lincoln Star*, June 10, 1918, 1.

36. The three references to Huns in 1914 were to Attila the Hun, the fifth-century invader of the Roman Empire.

37. *Lincoln Star*, October 19, 1918, 4.

38. Sorlin, "Cinema and the Memory," 13, 15.

39. Reeves, "Official British Film Propaganda," 45.

40. *Lincoln Star*, September 9, 1918, 5.

41. *Lincoln Star*, August 23, 1918, 5.

42. Farwell, *Over There*, 124, 127.

43. *Lincoln Star*, January 27, 1918, 1.

44. Farwell, *Over There*, 130. For additional information about Hoover's food policies, see Leuchtenburg, *Herbert Hoover*, 34–37.

45. Dale, "Back to Normal," 201–2; Coulter, "Woman Suffrage in Nebraska," 13.

46. *Omaha Daily Bee*, December 20, 1918, 14.

47. Dale, "Back to Normal," 201–2.

48. Farwell, *Over There*, 51.

49. Farwell, *Over There*, 60–61, 63.

50. *Nebraska State Journal*, September 13, 1918, 3.

51. Olson and Naugle. *History of Nebraska*, 278. See also Schach, "German-Language Newspapers," 84–107, especially 85; Diner, *A Very Different Age*, 254.

52. Kinbacher, *Urban Villages*, 58.

53. Kinbacher, *Urban Villages*, 59. Deer Borrell, discussion, August 27, 2021.

54. Kinbacher, *Urban Villages*, 60.

55. See, for example, "Drive the Germans from our Schools," *Nebraska State Journal*, January 14, 1918, 1.

56. *Lincoln Star*, April 10, 1919, 1.

57. *Lincoln Star*, December 26, 1919, 1.

58. Douglass, *Oh Grandma*, 77.

59. "German Language in the United States," Wikipedia, https://en.wikipedia.org/wiki/German_language_in_the_United_States. See also Rodgers, "The Foreign Language Issue," 10–13.

60. C. Pauley, "An Autobiography," 10.

61. *Lincoln Star*, October 31, 1921, 1.

62. *Nebraska State Journal*, December 22, 1920, 3.

63. Copple, *Tower on the Plains*, 128, 131.

64. *Lincoln Star*, May 27, 1918, 8.

65. Manley, "The Nebraska Sate Council of Defense," 231.

66. Barry, *The Great Influenza*, 308.

67. *Lincoln Star*, April 6, 1918, 1.

68. *Lincoln Star*, May 27, 1918, 6.

69. Manley, "The Nebraska State Council," 232.

70. *Lincoln Star*, April 19, 1918, 1.

71. On the same day, a representative of the Deutsche Geseilige Verein denied that it had been meeting in secret and maintained that it had consulted with both students and faculty, learning that opinion was divided about the club. Nevertheless its members voted to disband for the duration of the war. See *Daily Nebraskan*, April 18, 1918, 1.

72. Quoted in *Lincoln Star*, April 19, 1918, 5.

73. *Daily Nebraskan*, April 26, 1918, 1; Manley, *Centennial History*, 214–15.

74. *Lincoln Star*, May 20, 1918, 6.

75. *Lincoln Herald*, May 31, 1918, 4.

76. Manley, *Centennial History*, 215.

77. *Lincoln Star*, June 30, 1918, 18.

78. Manley, *Centennial History*, 224.

79. *Nebraska State Journal*, June 24, 1918, 4.

80. Knoll, *Prairie University*, 67.

81. Olson and Naugle, *History of Nebraska*, 279.

82. A long out-of-print centennial history of Lincoln did devote eight lines to the pandemic in Lincoln. See Copple, *Tower on the Plains*, 114.

83. Barry, *The Great Influenza*, 238.

84. Bristow, *American Pandemic*, 3. Bristow puts the number of American dead at five hundred thousand above the number of people who died of other diseases (*American Pandemic*, 4).

85. Bristow, *American Pandemic*, 52.

86. Bristow, *American Pandemic*, 209, 220–21.

87. Barry, *The Great Influenza*, 6, 82.

88. Brands, *Woodrow Wilson*, 75.

89. Barry, *The Great Influenza*, 308

90. Barry, *The Great Influenza*, 206.

91. Bristow, *American Pandemic*, 87, 129, 131.

92. Christine Hauser, "The Mask Slackers of 1918," *New York Times*, August 3, 2020, https://www.nytimes.com/2020/08/03/us/mask-protests-1918.html.

93. Bristow, *American Pandemic*, 42–43.

94. *Lincoln Journal*, November 16, 1918, 3; Traxel, *Crusader Nation*, 331.

95. Barry, *Great Influenza*, 460.

96. *Lincoln Star*, January 4, 1916, 1.

97. *Lincoln Star*, September 20, 1918, 2.

98. *Lincoln Star*, October 1, 1918, 2.

99. *New York Times*, December 26, 2020.

100. *Nebraska State Journal*, November 4, 1918, 11. See also Barry, *The Great Influenza*, 355.

101. *Lincoln Star*, October 8, 1918, 1.

102. *Lincoln Star*, October 8, 1918, 13.

103. *Lincoln Star*, October 12, 1918, 1, 7.

104. *Daily Nebraskan*, October 1, 1918, 1; October 14, 1918, 1; November 4, 1918, 1.

105. *Lincoln Star*, December 8, 1918, 3.

106. *Lincoln Star*, November 1918, 5.

107. *Lincoln Star*, December 27, 1918, 3.

108. Aldrich, *Spring Came on Forever*, 218.

109. Copple, *Tower on the Plains*, 114.

110. Copple, *Tower on the Plains*, 114.

111. *Lincoln Star*, November 19, 1918, 5.

112. *Lincoln Star*, January 8, 1919, 4.

113. *Lincoln Star*, July 10, 1913, 10.

114. *Lincoln Star*, November 11, 1918, 1–2.

115. Douglass, *Oh Grandma*, 79.

116. Dale, "Back to Normal," 180.

117. *Lincoln Star*, December 15, 1918, 17. The suffering was alleviated to some degree for ninety-eight families "through the medium of 'Minerva's Helping-Hand,'" sponsored by the *Lincoln Star*. See *Lincoln Star*, December 25, 1918, 1.

10. Reaction, Prosperity, and Depression

1. *Lincoln Star*, December 15, 1918, 17.

2. For an overview of the peace conference and its consequences, see B. Pauley, *The Habsburg Legacy*, especially 68–99.

3. *New York Times*, August 33, 2021; Piott, *Daily Life*, 214, 219.

4. *Nebraska State Journal*, May 22, 1919, 7.

5. Johnson, *A History of the American People*, 646.

6. Sullivan, *Our Times*, 1:114, 383.

7. Sullivan, *Our Times*, 1:117; Seale, *The Imperial Season*, 206.

8. *Omaha World Herald*, September 9, 1919, 2.

9. Brand, *Woodrow Wilson*, 119–24.

10. Hickey, *Nebraska Moments*, 180.

11. Leuchtenburg, *Herbert Hoover*, 41–43n, 46–47.

12. Leuchtenburg, *Herbert Hoover*, 6–47.

13. Leuchtenburg, *Herbert Hoover*, 11–12.

14. *Lincoln Star*, November 1, 1920, 1.

15. H. Evans, *The American Century*, 180; Deckard, *The Women's Movement*, 301.

16. Burns, *1920*, 273.

17. McElvaine, *The Great Depression*, 18.

18. Knoll, *Prairie University*, 92.

19. *Lincoln Star*, June 25, 1925, 3.

20. *Nebraska State Journal*, August 30, 1925, 22.

21. Warne, "The Acceptance of the Automobile," 235.

22. *Lincoln Star*, May 14, 1930, 1.

23. *Nebraska State Journal*, February 26, 1927, 1.

24. *Nebraska State Journal*, January 25, 1931, 35.

25. *Lincoln Star*, August 10, 1923, 9.

26. *Lincoln Star*, December 15, 1926, 18.

27. *Lincoln Star*, November 1, 1928, 22.

28. *Lincoln Star*, April 26, 1926, 12.

29. *Nebraska State Journal*, November 28, 1926, 27.

30. *Lincoln Star*, July 8, 1923, 20.

31. *Lincoln Star*, July 11, 1924, 8.

32. *Lincoln Star*, November 7, 1924, 24.

33. Gordon, *The Rise and Fall*, 290. Buying on the installment plan began in Lincoln at least as early as 1908. See an advertisement in the *Nebraska State Journal*, October 8, 1908, 21. See also Rader, *American Ways*, 186.

34. Sullivan, *Our Times*, 1:385.

35. In 1930 only 8 percent of American homes owned electric refrigerators. By 1930 that percentage had risen to 40. See Gordon, *The Rise and Fall*, 121.

36. Burns, *1920*, 11; Cozens and Stumpf, "Mass Media," 151.

37. In 1940 almost a quarter of American homes were still without electricity. Only 54 percent had indoor plumbing, which would include running water, a private bath, and a flush toilet. See Brokaw, *The Greatest Generation*, 205.

38. Schlereth, *Victorian America*, 196.

39. Dalstrom, discussion, March 30, 2021.

40. Gordon, *The Rise and Fall*, 193; Nasaw, *Going Out*, 203.

41. *Nebraska State Journal*, October 20, 1912, 2.

42. Sullivan, *Our Times*, 1:34.

43. Burns, *1920*, 6.

44. Diner, *A Very Different Age*, 263.

45. Hofstadter, *The Age of Reform*, 288.

46. Allen, "The Red Scare," 231; "First Red Scare," Wikipedia, https://en .wikipedia.org/wiki/First_Red_Scare.

47. An Equal Rights Amendment was drafted by the National Women's Party in 1923, but it required the support of thirty-eight states to be approved by no later than 1972. Kentucky's belated approval in 2020 left the status of the amendment still in doubt.

48. R. Evans, *The Feminists*, 209.

49. Deckard, *The Women's Movement*, 315.

50. D'Emelio and Freedman, *Intimate Matters*, 160, 199.

51. Deckard, *The Women's Movement*, 301, 309.

52. Deckard, *The Women's Movement*, 309–10.

53. For an excellent account of the campaign against cigarette smoking in Nazi Germany, see Proctor, *The Nazi War on Cancer*.

54. This policy was in force at the College of Wooster (Ohio), where I was an instructor of history in 1964–65, even if the husband and wife applied to teach in different departments.

55. For details, see B. Pauley, *Pioneering History*, 186–87.

56. Trains carried a record 1.2 billion passengers in 1920 not counting commuters. By the end of the decade, however, the number of passengers had fallen by more than 40 percent. See Wolmar, *The Great Railroad Revolution*, 200.

57. For an excellent article on Nebraska railroads during the interwar years, see Bader, "The Curtailment," especially 41–42.

58. McGerr, *A Fierce Discontent*, 294.

59. *Lincoln Star*, December 14, 1967, 8.

60. Sullivan, *Our Times*, 1:155.

61. Bader, "The Curtailment," 41–42.

62. Dale, "Back to Normal," 180, 183–84, 206.

63. Deckard, *The Women's Movement*, 180.

64. Deckard, *The Women's Movement*, 186.

65. Copple, *Tower on the Plains*, 115.

66. "Lynching in the United States," Wikipedia, https://en.wikipedia.org/wiki/Lynching_in_the_United_States.

67. Menard, "Tom Dennison," 157–58.

68. Larsen et al., *Upstream Metropolis*, 220.

69. For details, see Menard, "Tom Dennison"; *Lincoln Star*, September 29, 1919, 1–2; *Lincoln Star*, September 30, 1919, 2.

70. Menard, "'Lest We Forget,'" 163.

71. *Nebraska State Journal*, October 6, 1919, 6.

72. Hildebrand, "The New Negro Movement," 168.

73. Mihelich, "The Formation," 64–65. See also Schuyler, "The Ku Klux Klan," 243.

74. *Omaha World Herald*, October 23, 2021.

75. Mihelich, "The Formation," 66.

76. Schuyler, "The Ku Klux Klan," 244.

77. Dale, "Back to Normal," 204.

78. Schuyler, "The Ku Klux Klan," 240.

79. Schuyler, "The Ku Klux Klan," 235, 238.

80. Schuyler, "The Klux Klan," 235.

81. Schuyler, "The Ku Klux Klan," 236.

82. Schuyler, "The Ku Klux Klan," 242.

83. Schuyler, "The Ku Klux Klan," 253.

84. Schuyler, "The Ku Klux Klan," 246.

85. "Immigration Act of 1924," Wikipedia, https://en.wikipedia.org/wiki/Immigration_Act_of_1924.

86. Olson and Naugle, *History of Nebraska*, 287.

87. *Lincoln Star*, November 25, 1920, 1.
88. *Omaha World Herald*, November 15, 2021.
89. *Lincoln Star*, September 1924, 9.

11. Gains and Setbacks

1. Gordon, *The Rise and Fall*, 228.
2. Felder, *Century of Women*, 17.
3. Sullivan, *Our Times*, 1:308.
4. Gordon, *The Rise and Fall*, 255.
5. Sullivan, *Our Times*, 1:380.
6. For example, see Lynd and Lynd, *Middletown*, 260.
7. Sullivan, *Our Times*, 1:219; Veysay, *Emergence*, 280.
8. Hofstadter, *The Age of Reform*, 150–51.
9. *Lincoln Star*, December 26, 1920, 15.
10. Lynd and Lynd, *Middletown*, 67.
11. Daniels, "The Immigrant Experience," 98.
12. Knoll, *Prairie University*, 69.
13. Copple, *Tower on the Plains*, 149–50.
14. Knoll, *Prairie University*, 69.
15. Willa Cather, "Nebraska: The End of a Cycle," *Nation*, September 4, 1923.
16. Knoll, *Prairie University*, 72, 75.
17. Coulter, "A History of Woman Suffrage," 2.
18. Sullivan, *Our Times*, 4:219. See also Burns, *1920*, 127.
19. Fagan, "'Give Till It Hurts,'" 179, 185–86.
20. The mall was the brainchild of the capitol's architect, Bertram Goodhue. See Douglass, *Oh Grandma*, 41.

Bibliography

Ahlgren, Carol, and David Anthone. "Bad Roads and Big Hearts: Nebraska and the Great Race of 1906." *Nebraska History* 73 (Winter 1992): 173–79.

Aldrich, Beth Streeter. *Spring Came on Forever*. Lincoln: University of Nebraska Press, 1935.

Alexander, June Granatir. *Daily Life in Immigrant America, 1870–1920*. Westport CT: Greenwood Press, 2007.

Alfers, Kenneth Gerald. "Triumph of the West: The Trans-Mississippi Exposition." *Nebraska History* 53 (Fall 1972): 313–29.

Allen, Frederick Lewis. "Art and Music's Growing Audience." In *The History of Popular Culture since 1815*, edited by Norman Cantor and Michael S. Werthman. New York: The Macmillan Company, 1968.

———. *The Big Change: America Transforms Itself, 1900–1939*. East Lansing: Michigan University Press, 1952.

———. "The Red Scare." In *The History of Popular Culture since 1815*, edited by Norman Cantor and Michael S. Werthman. New York: The Macmillan Company, 1968.

Allerfeldt, Kristofer, ed. *The Progressive Era in the USA: 1890–1921*. London: Routledge, 2007.

Anderson, Bonnie S., and Judith P. Zinsser. *A History of Their Own*. Vol. 2, *Women in Europe from Prehistory to the Present*. Rev. ed. New York: Oxford University Press, 2000.

Anderson, John. "Lincoln, Nebraska, and *Prohibition*: The Election of May 4, 1909." *Nebraska History* 70 (1989): 184–200.

Angle, Paul M. *Crossroads: 1913*. Chicago: Rand McNally & Company, 1963.

Arnold, Catharine. *Pandemic 1918: Eyewitness Accounts from the Greatest Medical Holocaust in Modern History*. New York: St. Martin's Press, 2018.

Ashby, LeRoy. *With Amusement for All: A History of American Popular Culture since 1830*. Lexington: University of Kentucky Press, 2006.

Bader, Robert E. "The Curtailment of Railroad Service in Nebraska, 1920–1941." *Nebraska History* 36 (1955): 27–42.

Baker, Paula. "The Domestication of Politics: Women and American Politics." In *The Progressive Era in the USA: 1890–1921*, edited by Kristofer Allerfeldt, 620–47. London: Routledge, 2007.

Barr, William M. O. "A Brief History of Advertising in America." *Advertising Society Review* 6, no. 3 (2005): 41.

Barrows, Roger G. "Urbanizing America." In *The Gilded Age: Perspectives on the Origins of Modern America*, edited by Charles W. Calhoun, 100–118. 2nd ed. Lanham MD: Rowman & Littlefield, 2007.

Barry, John M. *The Great Influenza: The Story of the Greatest Pandemic in History*. New York: Penguin Books, 2018.

Beam, Patrice L. "The Last Victorian Fair: The Trans-Mississippi International Exposition." *Journal of the West* 33 (January 1944): 10–23.

Bergquist, James M. *Daily Life in Immigrant America, 1820–1870*. Westport CT: Greenwood Press, 2008.

Bertuca, David J., Donald K. Hartman, and Susan M. Neumeister. *The World's Columbian Exposition: A Centennial Bibliographic Guide*. Westport CT: Greenwood Press, 1996.

Bloomberg, Kristin Mapel. "'Striving for Equal Rights for All': Woman Suffrage in Nebraska, 1855–1882." *Nebraska History* 90 (2009): 84–103.

Brands, H. W. *Woodrow Wilson*. New York: Henry Holt & Company, 2003.

Bristow, Nancy K. *American Pandemic: The Lost Worlds of the 1918 Influenza Epidemic*. New York: Oxford University Press, 2012.

Brokaw, Tom. *The Greatest Generation*. New York: Random House, 1998.

Brown, E. P. *The Prairie Capital*. Lincoln: Miller & Paine, 1930.

Brown, E. P., and Raymond A. McConnell. *75 Years in the Prairie Capital*. Lincoln: Miller & Paine, 1955.

Brown, Jeremy. *Influenza: The Hundred-Year Hunt to Cure the Deadliest Disease in History*. New York: Touchstone, 2018.

Burns, Eric. *1920: The Year That Made the Decade Roar*. New York: Pegasus Books, 2015.

Cable, Mary. *American Manners and Morals*. New York: American Heritage Press, 1969.

Calhoun, Charles W., ed. *The Gilded Age: Perspectives on the Origins of Modern America*. 2nd ed. Lanham MD: Rowman & Littlefield, 2007.

Cantor, Norman F., and Michael S. Werthman, eds. *The History of Popular Culture since 1815*. New York: The Macmillan Company, 1968.

Carlson, W. Bernard. "Technology and America as a Consumer Society, 1870–1899." In *The Gilded Age: Perspectives on the Origins of Modern America*, edited by Charles W. Calhoun, 39–52. 2nd ed. Lanham MD: Rowman & Littlefield, 2007.

Cherny, Robert W. *A Righteous Cause: The Life of William Jennings Bryan*. Norman: University of Oklahoma Press, 1994.

———. "William Jennings Bryan and the Historians." *Nebraska History* 77 (1996): 184–93.

Chudacoff, Howard P. *Mobile Americans: Residential and Social Mobility in Omaha, 1880–1920*. New York: Oxford University Press, 1972.

Clark, Christopher. *The Sleepwalkers: How Europe Went to War in 1914*. New York: Harper Collins, 2017.

Clark, Clifford Edward, Jr. *The American Family Home, 1890–1960*. Chapel Hill: University of North Carolina Press, 1986.

Clements, Kendrick A. "Secretary of State William Jennings Bryan." *Nebraska History* 77 (1996): 167–76.

Coletta, Paolo E. "A Question of Alternatives: Wilson, Bryan, Lansing, and America's Intervention in World War I." *Nebraska History* 63 (Spring 1982): 33–57.

———. "William Jennings Bryan's Plan for World Peace." *Nebraska History* 58 (Summer 1977): 197–213.

———. "Will the Real Progressive Stand Up? William Jennings Bryan and Theodore Roosevelt to 1909." *Nebraska History* 65 (1984): 15–57.

Collins, Talma Ree Bell. "A Survey of the Present Educational and Vocational Status of the Negro Youth in Lincoln, Nebraska." Master's thesis, University of Nebraska–Lincoln, 1951.

Copple, Neale. *Tower on the Plains: Lincoln's Centennial History, 1859–1959*. Lincoln: Lincoln Centennial Commission Publishers, 1959.

Cordery, Stacey A. "Women in Industrializing America." In *The Gilded Age: Perspectives on the Origins of Modern America*, edited by Charles W. Calhoun, 119–42. 2nd ed. Lanham MD: Rowman & Littlefield, 2007.

Coulter, Thomas Chalmer. "A History of Woman Suffrage in Nebraska, 1856–1920." PhD diss., Ohio State University, 1967.

Cozens, Frederick W., and Florence S. Stumpf. "Mass Media Sports Fans." In *The History of Popular Culture since 1815*, edited by Norman F. Cantor and Michael S. Werthman, 181–85. New York: The Macmillan Company, 1968.

Crichton, Judy. *America 1900: The Turning Point*. New York: Henry Holt & Company, 1998.

Cullen, Jim. *The American Dream: A Short Story of an Idea That Shaped a Nation*. Oxford: Oxford University Press, 2004.

Dale, R. E. "Back to Normal." *Nebraska History* 38 (1957): 179–206.

Daniels, Roger. "The Immigrant Experience in the Gilded Age." In *The Gilded Age: Perspectives on the Origins of Modern America*, edited by Charles W. Calhoun, 75–100. 2nd ed. Lanham MD: Rowman & Littlefield, 2007.

———. *Not Like Us: Immigration and Minorities in America, 1890–1934*. Chicago: Ivan R. Dee, 1997.

Davies, Mary, and E. Genevieve Marsh. "A Study of the Negro in Lincoln." Master's thesis, University of Nebraska, 1904.

Davis, Margery W. *Women's Place Is at the Typewriter: Office Work and Office Workers*. Philadelphia: Temple University Press, 1982.

DeBauche, Leslie Midkiff. "The United States' Film Industry and World War One." In *The First World War and Popular Cinema, 1914 to the Present*, edited by Michael Paris, 138–62. New Brunswick NJ: Rutgers University Press, 2000.

Deckard, Barbara Sinclair. *The Women's Movement: Political, Socioeconomic, and Psychological Issues*. 2nd ed. New York: Harper & Row, 1979.

D'Emelio, John, and Estelle B. Freedman. *Intimate Matters: A History of Sexuality in America*. Chicago: University of Chicago Press, 1988.
Derks, Scott, ed. *The Value of the Dollar: 1860–1999*. Millerton NH: Grey House, 1999.
Dick, Everett. "The Founding of Union College, 1890–1900." *Nebraska History* 68 (1970): 447–70.
———. "Problems of the Post Frontier Prairie City as Portrayed by Lincoln, Nebraska, 1880–1890." *Nebraska History* 28 (1947): 132–43.
Dick, Everett, and David D. Rees. *Union College: Fifty Years of Service*. Lincoln: Union College Press, 1941.
Diner, Steven. *A Very Different Age: Americans of the Progressive Era*. New York: Hall and Wong, 1998.
Donahue, Neoma M. "Public Parks in the Recreation Movement in Nebraska with Special Reference to Lincoln, 1890–1935." Master's thesis, University of Nebraska, 1935.
Douglass, Gladys S. *Oh Grandma, You're Kidding: Memories of 75 Years in Lincoln*. Lincoln: J & J Lee, 1983.
Dudley, Richard E. "Nebraska Public School Education, 1890–1910." *Nebraska History* 54 (1973): 64–90.
Dulles, Foster Rhea. "The Chautauqua: Entertainment and Self-Improvement." In *The History of Popular Culture since 1815*, edited by Norman F. Cantor and Michael S. Werthman, 95–96. New York: The Macmillan Company, 1968.
Eckman, James P. "Culture as Entertainment: The Circuit Chautauqua in Nebraska, 1904–1924." *Nebraska History* 75 (1994): 244–53.
———. "Promoting an Ideology of Culture: The Chautauqua Literary and Scientific Circles in Nebraska, 1878–1900." *Nebraska History* 73 (1992): 18–24.
———. "Regeneration through Culture: Chautauqua in Nebraska, 1882–1925." PhD diss., University of Nebraska, 1989.
———. "Respectable Leisure: The Crete Chautauqua, 1882–1897." *Nebraska History* 69 (1988): 19–29.
Ehlers, D. Layne. "Second Floor, Brick Block: Nebraska's Opera Houses." *Nebraska History* 72 (1991): 3–20.
Eubank, Keith, and Phyllis B. Tortora. *Survey of Historic Costume: A History of Western Dress*. 3rd ed. New York: Fairchild Publications, 1998.
Evans, Harold. *The American Century*. New York: Alfred A. Knopf, 1998.
Evans, Richard J. *The Feminists*. New York: Barnes & Noble, 1955.
Fagan, Michele. "'Give Till It Hurts': Financing Memorial Stadium." *Nebraska History* 79 (1998): 179–91.
Faith, Jaycox. *The Progressive Era*. New York: Facts on File, 2005.
Farwell, Byron. *Over There: The United States in the Great War, 1917–1918*. New York: W. W. Norton & Company, 1999.
Felder, Deborah G. *Century of Women: Most International Event in Twentieth Century Women's History*. Syracuse NY: Pinecone Press Book, 1999.

Fitsche, S. D. "The Fight for Prohibition in Nebraska." *Nebraska History* 6 (1923): 81–88.

Flexner, Eleanor. *Century of Struggle: The Women's Rights Movement in the United States*. Cambridge: Harvard University Press, 1996.

Ford, Richard Thompson. *Dress Codes: How the Laws of Fashion Made History*. New York: Simon and Schuster, 2021.

Fox, Stephen. *The Mirror Makers: A History of American Advertising and Its Creators*. New York: William Morrow & Company, 1984.

Gappa, Lavon Mary. "Chancellor James Hulme Canfield: His Impact on the University of Nebraska, 1891–1895." *Nebraska History* 66 (1985): 392–410.

Gaster, Patricia. "Nebraska's Changing Auto Culture, 1900–1930." *Nebraska History* 73 (1992): 180–85.

Gordon, Robert. *The Rise and Fall of American Growth: The U.S. Standard of Living since the Civil War*. Princeton: Princeton University Press, 2016.

Gossage, Forest Donald. "A History of the Funke Opera House in Lincoln, Nebraska, 1884–1902." Master's thesis, University of Nebraska, 1961.

Gould, Lewis L. *America in the Progressive Era, 1890–1914*. London: Longman, 2014.

Grimes, Mary Cochran. "Establishing Nebraska's Highway System, 1915–1934." *Nebraska History* 73 (1992): 160–72.

Harkins, Michael J. "Public Health Nuisances in Omaha, 1870–1900." *Nebraska History* 56 (1975): 471–92.

Harvard History Book Committee. *Harvard, Nebraska 100 Years + 2*. Harvard NE, 1973.

Hayes, Arthur B. *History of the City of Lincoln, Nebraska, with Brief Historic Sketches of the State and Lancaster County*. Lincoln: State Journal Company Printers, 1889.

Hess, Eldora F. "The Negro in Nebraska." Master's thesis, University of Nebraska–Lincoln, 1932.

Hickey, Donald R. *Nebraska Moments: Glimpses of Nebraska's Past*. Lincoln: University of Nebraska Press, 1992.

Hickman, Laura McKee. "Thou Shalt Not Vote: Anti-Suffrage in Nebraska, 1914–1920." *Nebraska History* 80 (1999): 55–65.

Hicks, John D. "My Nine Years at the University of Nebraska." *Nebraska History* 46 (March 1967): 1–27.

———. "'Then (1891)' and 'Now (1961)': Some Comparisons." *Nebraska History* 47 (1966): 139–55.

Hildebrand, Jennifer. "The New Negro Movement in Lincoln, Nebraska." *Nebraska History* 91 (2010): 166–89.

Hofstadter, Richard. *The Age of Reform: From Bryan to FDR*. New York: Vintage Books, 1955.

Holter, Don W. *Flames on the Plains: A History of United Methodism in Nebraska*. Nashville TN: Parthenon Press, 1983.

Hunter, Jane H. *How Young Ladies Became Girls: The Victorian Origins of Modern Girlhood*. New Haven: Yale University Press, 2002.

Hutches, George E. "A History of Union College and College View." Master's thesis, University of Nebraska, 1936.

Illies, Florian. *1913: The Year Before the Storm*. Brooklyn: Melville House, 2013.

International Association of Administrative Professionals. "History of the Secretarial Profession." 1998. Updated January 7, 2022.

Ishikawa, Jesse S. "The Desegregation of the Lincoln Municipal Swimming Pool." *Nebraska History* 99 (Fall 2018): 159–66.

Janssen, Sussanne. *Von Zarenreich in den amerikanischen Westen: Deutchen in Russland und Russlanddeutsche in den USA (1871–1928): Die kulturelle Adaption einer ethnischen Grupppe in Kontakt zweier Staaten*. Münster: LIT, 1997.

Jeffery, Mary Louise. "Young Radicals of the Nineties." *Nebraska History* 38 (1957): 25–41.

Jennings, Harlan. "Grand Opera in Nebraska in the 1890s." *Nebraska History* 78 (1997): 2–13.

Johnson, Paul. *A History of the American People*. New York: Harper Collins, 1997.

Jones, Maldwyn Allen. *American Immigration*. 2nd ed. Chicago: University of Chicago Press, 1960.

Kazin, Michael. *A Godly Hero: The Life of William Jennings Bryan*. New York: Anchor Books, 2007.

Keegan, John. *The First World War*. New York: Alfred A. Knopf, 1999.

Kennedy, John F. *Profiles in Courage*. New York: Harper & Brothers, 1956.

Kinbacher, Kurt E. "Life in the Russian Bottoms. Community Building and Identity Transformation among Germans from Russia, 1876, 1926." *Journal of American Ethnic History* 76, no. 2 (Winter 2007): 27–57.

———. *Urban Villages and Local Identities: Germans from Russia, Omaha Indians, and Vietnamese in Lincoln, Nebraska*. Lubbock: Texas Tech University Press, 2015.

King, David C., Mariah Marvin, David Weitzman, and Toni Dwiggins. *United States History*. Pres. ed. Menlo Park CA: Addison-Wesley Publishing Company, 1986.

Knelling, Jill Marie, ed. "A Thousand Mile Motor Trip through Western Nebraska, 1916." *Nebraska History* 78 (1997): 22–27.

Knoll, Robert. *Prairie University: A History of the University of Nebraska*. Lincoln: University of Nebraska Press, 1995.

Koster, George E. *A Story of Highway Development in Nebraska*. Lincoln: Department of Roads, 1997.

Kuzma, Michael. "Kicking the Habit: Nebraska's 1905 Anti-Cigarette Law." *Nebraska History* 86 (2005): 92–96.

Larsen, Lawrence H., Harl A. Dalstrom, Kay Calamé Dalstrom, and Barbara Cottrell. *Upstream Metropolis: An Urban Biography of Omaha and Council Bluffs*. Lincoln: University of Nebraska Press, 1995.

Larson, Erik. *The Devil in the White City: Murder, Magic, and Madness at the Fair That Changed America*. New York: Knopf Doubleday, 2004.

Laver, James. *Manners and Morals in the Age of Optimism, 1848–1914*. New York: Harper & Row, 1966.

Leuchtenburg, William F. *Herbert Hoover*. New York: Henry Holt & Company, 2009.

Levine, Lawrence. *Highbrow/Lowbrow: The Emergence of Cultural Hierarchy in America*. Cambridge: Harvard University Press, 1988.

Lincoln Chamber of Commerce. *Lincoln: Nebraska's Capital City, 1867–1923*. Lincoln, 1923.

Litwicki, Ellen M. "The Influence of Commerce, Technology, and Race on Popular Culture in the Gilded Age." In *The Gilded Age: Perspectives on the Origins of Modern America*, edited by Charles W. Calhoun, 187–210. 2nd ed. Lanham MD: Rowman & Littlefield, 2007.

Luebke, Frederick C. "The German-American Alliance in Nebraska, 1910–1917." *Nebraska History* 49 (1968): 165–85.

———. *Immigrants and Politics: The Germans of Nebraska, 1880–1900*. Lincoln: University of Nebraska Press, 1969.

———. *Nebraska: An Illustrated History*. Lincoln: University of Nebraska Press, 1995.

Lynd, Robert S., and Helen Merrell Lynd. *Middletown: A Story in Modern American Culture*. San Diego: Harvest/HBJ, 1929.

Manley, Robert N. *Centennial History of the University of Nebraska*. Vol. 1, *Frontier University (1868–1919)*. Lincoln: University of Nebraska Press, 1969.

———. "Language and Liberty: The Nebraska State Council of Defense and the Lutheran Churches (1917–1918)." *Concordia Historical Institute Quarterly* 37 (April 1964): 17.

———. "The Nebraska Sate Council of Defense and the Nonpartisan League, 1917–1918." *Nebraska History* 43 (1962): 229–52.

Martin, Susan F. *A Nation of Immigrants*. Cambridge, UK: Cambridge University Press, 2001.

McDonough, Judith. "Women Reformers in the Progressive Era." *Social Education* 63 (September 1999): 315–19.

McElvaine, Robert S. *The Great Depression: America, 1929–1941*. New York: Times Books, 1984.

McGerr, Michael. *A Fierce Discontent: The Rise and Fall of the Progressive Movement in America*. New York: First Harper Perennial, 2010.

McKay, John P. *Tramways and Trolleys: The Rise of Urban Mass Transport in Europe*. Princeton: Princeton University Press, 1976.

McKee, James L. *Lincoln, the Prairie Capital: An Illustrated History*. Lincoln: J & J Lee, 1964.

Menard, Orville D. "'Lest We Forget': The Lynching of Will Brown, Omaha's 1919 Race Riot." *Nebraska History* 91 (2010): 152–65.

———. "Tom Dennison, the *Omaha Bee*, and the 1919 Race Riot." *Nebraska History* 68 (1987): 152–65.

Mickey, David H. *Of Sunflowers, Coyotes, and Plainsmen*. Lincoln: Augstums Printing Company, 1992.

Mihelich, Dennis N. "The Formation of the Lincoln Urban League." *Nebraska History* 68 (1987): 63–87.

Mintz, Steven A. *Prison of Expectations: The Family in Victorian Culture*. New York: New York University Press, 1983.

Moomaw, Leonidas. *A History of Cotner University, Including the Early Religious and Educational Movement of the Christian Church in Nebraska*. Bethany NE, 1916.

Morris, Edmund. *Theodor Rex*. New York: Random House, 2002.

Morris, Seymour, Jr. *American History Revised: 200 Startling Facts That Never Made It into the Textbooks*. New York: Broadway Books, 2010.

Muccigrosso, Robert. *Celebrating the New World: Chicago's Columbian Exposition of 1893*. Chicago: Ivan R. Dee, 1993.

Nasaw, David. *Going Out: The Rise and Fall of Public Amusements*. New York: Basic Books, 1993.

Okrent, Daniel. *Last Call: The Rise and Fall of Prohibition*. New York: Scribner, 2010.

Olson, James C., and Ronald Naugle. *History of Nebraska*. 3rd ed. Lincoln: University of Nebraska Press, 1997.

Orad, Michael. *Reading Football: How the Popular Press Created American Spectacle*. Chapel Hill: University of North Carolina Press, 1993.

Ozment, Steven. *A Mighty Fortress: A New History of the German People*. New York: Harper Collins Publishers, 2004.

Palmer, Edgar Z. "The Correctness of the 1890 Census of Population in Nebraska Cities." *Nebraska History* 32 (December 1951): 259–67.

Palmer, William. *From Gentlemen's Club to Professional Body: The Evolution of the History Department in the United States, 1940–1980*. New York: Booksurge, 2008.

Panati, Charles. *Extraordinary Origins of Everyday Things*. New York: Harper & Row, 1987.

Paris, Michael, ed. *The First World War and Popular Cinema, 1914 to the Present*. New Brunswick NJ: Rutgers University Press, 2000.

Paul, Andrea I. "A Bully Show: Theodore Roosevelt's 1900 Campaign Tour through Nebraska." *Nebraska History* 73 (1992): 138–43.

Pauley, Bruce F. *From Prejudice to Persecution: A History of Austrian Anti-Semitism*. Chapel Hill: University of North Carolina Press, 1992.

———. *The Habsburg Legacy, 1867–1939*. Malabar FL: Robert E. Krieger, 1987. First published 1972 by Holt, Rinehart & Winston (New York).

———. *Pioneering History on Two Continents: An Autobiography*. Lincoln: University of Nebraska Press, 2014.

Pauley, Carroll R. "An Autobiography." Unpublished manuscript, 1976. Love Library, University of Nebraska–Lincoln.

Peiss, Kathy. *Cheap Amusement: Working Women and Leisure in Turn-of-the-Century New York*. Philadelphia: Temple University Press, 1986.

Phillips, Elmo Bryant. "A History of Street Railways in Nebraska." Master's thesis, University of Nebraska–Lincoln, 1944.

———. "Horsecar Days and Horsecar Ways in Nebraska." *Nebraska History* 29 (March 1948): 16–32.

Piott, Steven L. *Daily Life in the Progressive Era*. Santa Barbara CA: Greenwood, 2011.

Potter, James E. "'Barkley vs. Pool': Woman Suffrage and the Nebraska Referendum Law." *Nebraska History* 69 (1988): 11–18.

Price, John Roy. *The Last Liberal Republican: An Insider's Perspective on Nixon's Surprising Social Policy.* Lawrence: University Press of Kansas, 2021.

Proctor, Robert N. *The Nazi War on Cancer.* Princeton: Princeton University Press, 1999.

Rader, Benjamin. *American Ways: A Brief History of American Cultures.* Belmont CA: Wadsworth, 2001.

Reeves, Nicholas. "Official British Film Propaganda." In *The First World War and Popular Cinema, 1914 to the Present,* edited by Michael Paris, 27–50. New Brunswick NJ: Rutgers University Press, 2000.

Rodgers, Jack. "The Foreign Language Issue in Nebraska, 1918–1923." *Nebraska History* 39 (1958): 1–22.

Ryan, Pat M. "Hallo's Opera House: Pioneer Theatre of Lincoln." *Nebraska History* 45 (1964): 323–30.

Rydell, Robert. *All the World's a Fair: Visions of Empire at America's International Expositions.* Chicago: University of Chicago Press, 1984.

Sawyer, Andrew J. *Lincoln the Capital City and Lancaster County.* Chicago: S. J. Clarke, 1916.

Schach, Paul. "German-Language Newspapers in Nebraska, 1860–1890." *Nebraska History* 65 (1984): 84–107.

Schlereth, Thomas J. *Victorian America: Transformations in Everyday Life, 1876–1915.* New York: Harper Perennial, 1992.

Schudsen, Michael. *Discovering the News: A Social History of American Newspapers.* New York: Basic Books, 1978.

Schuyler, Michael W. "The Ku Klux Klan in Nebraska, 1920–1930." *Nebraska History* 66 (1985): 234–56.

Schwabenland, Emma D. "German-Russians on the Volga and the United States." Master's thesis, University of Colorado, 1929.

Seale, William. *The Imperial Season: America's Capital in the Time of the First Ambassadors, 1893–1918.* Washington DC: Smithsonian Books, 2013.

Sellers, James L. "Fairview Dedication." *Nebraska History* 45 (1964): 343–46.

Seymour, Margaret R. "Music in Lincoln, Nebraska, in the 19th Century: A Study of Musical Culture of a Frontier Society." Master's thesis, University of Nebraska, 1973.

———. "The University of Nebraska School of Music, 1876–1904." *Nebraska History* 54 (1973): 399–418.

Sheldon, Addison E. *Nebraska: The Land and the People.* 3 vols. Chicago: Lewis Publishing Company, 1931.

Sherman, Richard G. "Charles G. Dawson, a Nebraska Businessman, 1887–1894: The Making of an Entrepreneur." *Nebraska History* 46 (1965): 193–207.

Shortridge, James R. "The Emergence of the Middle West as an American Regional Label." *Annals of the Association of American Geographers* 74, no. 2 (June 1984): 209–20.

Slote, Bernice. *The Kingdom of Art: Willa Cather's First Principles and Critical Statements, 1893–1896.* Lincoln: University of Nebraska Press, 1966.

Snyder, Thomas D., ed. *120 Years of American Education: A Statistical Portrait.* Washington DC: National Center for Educational Statistics, 1993.

Sorlin, Pierre. "Cinema and the Memory of the Great War." In *The First World War and Popular Cinema, 1914 to the Present*, edited by Michael Paris, 5–26. New Brunswick NJ: Rutgers University Press, 2000.

Stead, W. I. *The Americanization of the World: The Trend of the Twentieth Century.* New York: Hoover Marklay, 1901.

Stevens, Betty. *A Dangerous Class: A History of Suffrage in Nebraska and the League of Women Voters of Nebraska.* Self-published, 1995.

Strachan, Hew. *The First World War.* Vol. 1 of *To Arms.* Oxford: Oxford University Press, 2001.

Sullivan, Mark. *Our Times: The United States, 1900–1925.* 6 vols. New York: Charles Scribner's Sons, 1930–36.

Tannenbaum, Edward R. *1900: The Generation Before the Great War.* Garden City NY: Anchor Press, 1976.

Tate, Michael, comp. *Nebraska History: An Annotated Bibliography.* Westport CT: Greenwood Press, 1995.

Tate, Trudi. *Modernism, History, and the First World War.* New York: St. Martin's Press, 1998.

Thompson, Tommy R. "The Devil Wagon Comes to Omaha: The First Decade of the Automobile, 1900–1910." *Nebraska History* 61 (1980): 173–91.

Traxel, David. *Crusader Nation: The United States in Peace and the Great War, 1898–1920.* New York: Knopf, 2007.

Trowbridge, David J. Peavler. "'A Double Mixture': Equality and Economy in the Integration of Nebraska Schools, 1858–1883." *Nebraska History* 91 (2010): 136–51.

Urban, Wayne J., Milton Gaither, and Jennings L. Wagoner Jr. *American Education: A History.* Boston: McGraw Hill, 2000.

Valentine, Leslie R. "Evangelist Billy Sunday's Clean-up Campaign: Local Reaction to His 50-Day Revival, 1915." *Nebraska History* 64 (1983): 209–27.

Veysay, Laurence. *The Emergence of the American University.* Chicago: University of Chicago Press, 1970.

Wall, Joseph Frazier. *Grinnell College in the Nineteenth Century: From Salvation to Service.* Ames: Iowa State University Press, 1997.

Walton, James H. "A History of Professional Theater at 'The Oliver' in Lincoln, Nebraska (1897–1918)." Master's thesis, University of Nebraska, 1956.

Ware, Frederick, and Gregg McBride. *Fifty Years of Nebraska Football.* Omaha: Omaha World Herald, 1940.

Warne, Clinton Lee. "The Acceptance of the Automobile in Nebraska." *Nebraska History* 37 (September 1956): 222–35.

Watterson, John. *History of Football: History, Spectacle, Controversies.* Baltimore: Johns Hopkins University Press, 2000.

Wawro, Geoffrey. *A Mad Catastrophe: The Outbreak of World War I and the Collapse of the Habsburg Empire*. New York: Basic Books, 2014.

Wenger, Robert E. "The Anti-Saloon League in Nebraska, 1898–1910." *Nebraska History* 52 (1971): 267–92.

Wiebe, Robert H. *The Search for Order, 1877–1920*. New York: Hill and Wang, 1967.

Wilhite, Ann L. "Sixty-Five Years Till Victory: A History of Women's Suffrage in Nebraska." *Nebraska History* 49 (1968): 149–63.

Wilke, Phyllis Kay. "Physical Education for Women at the University of Nebraska, 1879–1923." *Nebraska History* 56 (Summer 1975): 193–220.

Williams, Hattie Plum. *The Czar's Germans: With Particular Reference to the Volga Germans*. Edited by Emma S. Haynes, Phillip B. Legler, and Gerda S. Walker. Lincoln: American Historical Society of Germans from Russia, 1975.

———. "The History of the German-Russian Colony in Lincoln." Master's thesis, University of Nebraska, 1909.

———. "The Road to Citizenship: A Study of Naturalization in a Nebraska County." Edited by Anne Polk Diffendal. *Nebraska History* 68 (1987): 166–82.

———. "A Social Study of the Russian Germans." PhD diss., University of Nebraska, 1916.

Wolmar, Christian. *The Great Railroad Revolution: The History of Trains in America*. New York: Public Affairs, 2012.

Yost, Nellie Snyder. "Nebraska's Scholarly Athlete: Louise Pound, 1872–1958." *Nebraska History* 64 (1983): 477–90.

Zinn, Howard. *A People's History of the United States, 1492–Present*. New York: Harper Collins, 2003.

Index

Page numbers in italics refer to illustrations.

AAA. *See* American Automobile Association (AAA)
abolition of slavery, 101
academic freedom, 64, 217
Academy of Music, 125
advertisements: for automobiles, 39; for bicycles, *35*; for birth control, 100; for celebrations, 147, *148*; for cigarettes, 103, 106–7, *106*, 240; for circuses, 149; for clothing, *88*, 89, *251*; for cosmetics, 235; for dance classes, *141*; for movies, 136–37, *137*, *139*; for opera, 127; political, 207–8; racism in, 185, *186*; by railroad, *144*, 145, 185; regulation of, 223; revenue from, 102, 103, 223; for talking machines, *250*; for war bonds, 202, *203*
African Methodist Episcopal Church, 138, 181
Aggies (Kansas State), 173
Aida (Verde), 128
airplanes, 5, 237–38
alcohol consumption. *See* prohibition; temperance movement; Women's Christian Temperance Union (WCTU)
Aldrich, Bess Streeter, 6–7, 224–25
Aldrich, Chester, 121
Alexander II, Czar, 190, 195
Allen, Gracie, 135
Allied Powers, 201–2, 204, 205
Alone in London (play), 125
American Automobile Association (AAA), 46
American Historical Association, 64
American Historical Society of Germans from Russia, 198

American History Department (University of Nebraska), 277n1
American History Revised (Morris), 220
amusement parks, 33, 133–34, 146–48
amusements. *See* entertainment
Andrews, Benjamin, 61–62, 155–56, 162
Antelope Park, 141, 249
Anti-Saloon League, 71, 110, 111–12
appliances, household, 24, 97–98, 123, 236–37
Army, U.S., 204, 215
Asians, discrimination against, 182, 244
assassinations, 200–201, 205
Association of American Universities, 61
Atchison, Topeka, and Santa Fe Railroad, 146
Attila the Hun, 280n36
Australia, 116
Austria, 64, 189
Austria-Hungary, 200, 202, 204, 205, 221, 228
Automobile Club (Lincoln NE), 46, 47
Automobile Magazine, 38
automobiles, *40*, *43*, *47*; consequences of use of, 4, 5, 47, 49–50, 232–34; dangers of, 44–46; in distance travel, 47–49, 262n123; electric, 41–42; European-manufactured, 39; French influence on, 38; numbers of, 46–47; physicians on, 43; prices of, 39, 41, 42; public transportation replaced by, 34, 241; reactions to, 42–44; sales of, dropping, 236; status of owning, 44; voter turnout helped by, 120
Autry, Gene, 136

Avery, Samuel, 121, 173, 174–75, 217, 224, 246

backyards, 94, 96, 97
banks and banking, 191, 264n41
Baptist Church, 28, 101, 181
barbed wire in war, 200
Barkley, Edna M., 91
Barnum, P. T., 148–49
Barret, S. H., 149
Barry, John, 220, 222
Barsby, John, 125
basketball, 90–92, *91*, 170–71
bathrooms, 93, 95–96, 97, 179
Battle of the Somme (movie), 210
Bearg, Ernest, 175
The Beast of Berlin (movie), 210
beets in Volga German culture, 193–94
Belgium in First World War, 201–2
Ben-Hur (movie), 136
Benny, Jack, 135
Berenson, Senda, 90
Berg, Edith Hart O., 87
Berle, Milton, 135
Bess (milk cow), 94
Bessey, Charles E., 103, 162
Bible, 68, 107–8, 272n52
bicycles and bicyclists, 35–38, *35*, 46–47, 85, 260n49
Big Nine Conference, 156, 168, 169–70
Big Six Conference, 170, 174, 245
Binney, Constance, 105
birth control, 100, 239, 254–55
The Birth of a Nation (movie), 136–38, *137*, 245
birthrate, 63, 76, 97, 100, 181, 187, 248, 264n58
Bittenbender, Ada, 121
blackface, 130, 135, 137, 185
Blacks, *183–84, 186*; attitudes toward, 20–21, 181–82, 185; demographics of, 178–79, 244; and education, 179, 181, 185–87, 245, 277n7; in entertainment, 130, 134–35, 185; as football players, 164, 173–74; home ownership denied to, 244–45; as inventors, 81; and Ku Klux Klan, 245; in military, 229; movie portrayals of, 137–38; political views of,

181; violence against, 138, 243–44; voting rights for, 114; whites compared to, 181; work of, 180–81, 182; in world fairs, 29
Bloomer, Amelia, 84–85, 116
bloomers, 84–85
Board of Regents, 66, 90, 91, 153, 168, 217–19
Bolshevism, fear of, 227, 238
Booth, Walter C. "Bummy," 166, 167–68, 169–70, 175, 276n72
Boy Scouts, 118, 133, 245
Branch, A. Edwin, 166–67
Brasilia, Brazil, 257n4
Breakers Hotel, 144
breakfast rooms, 95
Brenner, Yul, 254
Britain and the British, 119, 201–2, 204–6, 208, 210, 229
Brown, Francis, 45–46
Brown, Joshua Purdy, 148
Brown, William, 243
Bryan, Mary Elizabeth, 14
Bryan, William Jennings, *12*; about, 11, 17–20, 133; donations of, 248; family life of, 14; on First World War, 206–7; as fundamentalist, 272n52; political career of, 22, 258n40; on prohibition, 112; on suffrage, 114; travels of, 258n42
Bryan Memorial Hospital, 248
Buffalo Bill's Wild West Show, 150–51
Bugeaters, 165–67
Burckhardt, O. J., 138
Burlington and Missouri Railroad, 8–9, 190–91
Burlington Beach, 33, 147
Burlington Railroad, 133, 145–46, 176, 192–93
Burns, George, 135
Bushman, H. M., 155
Butler, Frank, 150
Butte Athletic Club, 165
Butte College, 162

Cadet Band, 129, *129*
Cadillacs, 236
California, 138, 143, 145
Camel cigarettes, *106*, 107

Canberra, Australia, 257n4
Canfield, James Hulme, 60–61, 90, 102, 163
Capital Beach, 33, 147–48, *148*
capitals, selection of, 5–6, 257n4
capitol buildings, 6–7, 7, 10, 14, 23, 255
Carnegie, Andrew, 17
Carnegie Library (Lincoln NE), 17, *18*, 67
carriages, horse-drawn, 13, 39–41, 42, 43, 258n24
cars, electric, 41–42
cartoons, *43*, *183–84*, 185, *212*, *218*, *228*
Caruso, Enrico, 133
Castle School for Dancing, *141*
Cather, Willa, 215, 252–53
Catherine the Great, 189, 190
Catholic Church, 105, 111, 114, 132, 245
census: (1870), 81; (1880), 9, 114; (1890), 59, 66–67, 178, 259n21; (1910), 178–79; (1920), 4; (1930), 237
Centennial (opera house), 126
Central Powers, 205
Chapman, C. F., 223–24
charity ball (1890), 22
Chautauqua, 126, 131–34, 149–50
Chicago Daily News, 209
Chicago Great Western Railway, 146
Chicago IL, 25
Chicago World's Fair (Columbian Exposition, 1893), 24, 25–27, 150
children, 16, 52, 53, 75, 194, 196, 263n7
Chinese Americans, 244
Christians and Christianity, 28, 59, 68–69, 73, 101, 142, 151, 155
churches: and alcohol consumption, 30–31, 109, 111, 113; Blacks involved in, 181; and Chautauqua, 132; on dancing, 141–43; on football, 156; in Lincoln NE, 14; nationalists targeting, 245; and permissiveness, 242; on racist film, 137–38; and suffrage, 114; in university life, 66, 67, 69, 70–71; Volga German heritage in, 196, 197–98; and world fairs, 28
cigarettes and cigarette smoking, 103–7, *106*, 113, 240, 254
cigars and cigar smoking, 103, 104–5
circuses, 147–49, 150
city hall (Lincoln NE), 15, 258n36

Civil War as predictor, 199–200
The Clansman (Dixon), 138
The Clansman (movie). See *The Birth of a Nation* (movie)
Clausewitz, Carl von: *On War*, 200
clerical work, 78–79, 80
Cleveland, Grover, 25–26
clothing and fashion, 82–89, *86*, *87*, *88*, 249, *251*
clubs: automobile, 46, 47; of city residents, 100–101, 128, 222, 242; and reform movement, 114; university, 66, 177, 217–18, 247
Cody, William "Bill," 150–51
Cole, W. C. "King," 159, 170, 175
College of Agriculture (University of Nebraska), 61–62
College of Arts and Sciences (University of Nebraska), 253
College of Literature, Science, and Arts (University of Nebraska), 56
College of Wooster, 284n54
colleges and universities, 57–58; about, 74; beginnings of, 56, 59–60; buildings of, 69–70; changes in, 62–65; enrollment of, 264n52; factors affecting, 66–67, 72–73; purpose of, 59; religious affiliations of, 67–69; student life at, 70–72, 73; women attending, 16–17. *See also* Cotner College; Nebraska Wesleyan University; Union College; University of Nebraska
College View NE, 32–33, 72–73
Colliers, 96
Colorado, 116–17
Columbian Exposition. *See* Chicago World's Fair (Columbian Exposition, 1893)
Commager, Henry Steele: *The Growth of the American Republic*, 220
Comstock Act (1873), 254–55
Coney Island, 146
Congregational Church, 101, 109
conscription, 189, 190, 204, 211–13
conspiracy theories, 201, 205
contraception, 100, 239, 254–55
Coolidge, Calvin, 232
Cooper, Gary, 254
Cornhusker (yearbook), 245, 277n7

Cornhuskers: in Big Nine Conference, 169; coaches of, 170, 176; during First World War, 213; as team nickname, 165, 167; win-loss record of, 167, 168–69, 171–72, 174, 247
corsets, 85–87, *86*
cosmetics, 234–35
Cotner College, 51, *58*, 59, 67–69, 70, 74, 102, 265n94
COVID-19 pandemic, 37, 222, 237
Cowan, J. W., 156
Crawford, Frank, 164, 165
crinolines, 85
Crystal Palace Exhibition (London, 1851), 24, 96
Cugnot, Nicolas-Joseph, 38

Daily Nebraskan, 103, 143, 216, 217–19, 224, 240
dancing, 71, 125, 140–43, 149
Davies, Mary E., 178–82, 185–86, 277n1
deaths, 100, 160–61, 233–34, 254
debt, 49, 74, 247
democracy, 227–29, *228*
Democrats, 17–20, 22, 117, 181, 231
Denver Athletic Club, 162–63
Department of American History (University of Nebraska), 217
Department of Sociology (University of Nebraska), 277n1
depressions, economic, 11, 27, 61, 147, 242–43. *See also* Great Depression
Deutsche Geseilige Verein, 217–18, 281n71
Devaney, Bob, 177
Die Welt-Post, 187, 196, 213–14
dining rooms, 96
diphtheria, 194
Disciples of Christ, 67
Disney, Elias, 25
Disney, Walt, 25, 254
divorce, 76, 115, 119, 239
Dix, Dorothy, 137
Dixon, Thomas: *The Clansman*, 138
Doane College, 166
Donizetti, Gaetano: *Lucia de Lammermoor*, 128
Douglas County NE, 121, 179, 211, 270n62

draft. *See* conscription
Drais, Karl von, 35
drought, 67, 125–26, 144–45
Du Bois, W. E. B., 229
Durante, Jimmy, 135
Dust Bowl, 242

Edison, Thomas, 23, 26, 93, 102
Ed Sullivan Show, 135
Eiffel Tower, 25
Eighteenth Amendment, 109, 111–13, 239, 241
electricity, 4–5, 22–24, 25–26, 27, 29–30, 70, 236, 283n37. *See also* lights, electric; streetcars, electric
elevators, 81, 82, 235
Eliot, Charles William, 155
Elizabeth II, Queen, 42
Ellinwood, Charles, 69
English Grand Opera Company and Orchestra, 128
entertainment: about, 151; amusement parks as, 146–48; beaches as, 146–48; changes in, 249, 252; Chautauqua as, 131–34; circuses as, 148–49; dancing as, 140–43; diversity of, 126, 128–30; leisure time for, 123–24; movies as, 131, 135–38; racism in, 182–85; radio as, 237; state fairs as, 149–50; travel as, 143–46; at universities and colleges, 66, 71; vaudeville as, 134–36; venues for, 124–26, 130–31; wild west shows as, 150–51
Epworth Park, 133–34
Equal Rights Amendment, 283n47
escalators, 81, 82
espionage, laws against, 209
Espionage Act (1918), 214
Eubank, Keith, 84
evangelicals, 101, 141–42
Evans, Jarvis G., 155

fabric, *87*
Fairview (Bryan house), 19
farmers and farming, 42, 49, 123, 150, 191–92, 193, 227, 247, 257n1, 263n7
fashion. *See* clothing and fashion
Faust (Gounod), 128
Federal Aid Road Act (1916), 48

Federal Trade Commission, 223
Federation of Nebraska Churches, 156
Finland, 116
First World War, *218*; about, 199; academic freedom during, 64; airplanes used in, 5; American involvement in, 199–200, 205–6; anti-German sentiment during, 208–11, 213–15; beginnings of, 200–201; casualties of, 161–62; confusion about, 53; conscription for, 211–13; consequences of, 140, 227–30, *228*, 241, 242, 245, 247; end of, 225–26; and hunger, *212*; and immigrants, 211; metal reused in, 87; opposition to, 206–8, 279n24; and prohibition movement, 109; reactions to, 202, 204–5; recognition of soldiers in, 255; and smoking, 105, 107; and Spanish flu, 219–20, 221, 225–26; and war spirit, 215–19
Flagler, Henry Morrison, 144
flappers, 89, 234
Fling, Fred, 169, 217
Flippin, George, 164
floods, 134, 188
Florida, 143–45, *144*
food prices, 242
food shortages, 205, 231
football, *158*, *161*, *171*, *254*; attitudes toward, 154–57; changes in, 157–63, 171–72, 242; conference affiliations in, 169–70; deaths from, 160–61; injuries from, 154–55, 156–57, 160–62, 177; leagues in, 153; and military draftees, 213; racism in, 173–74; and school spirit, 63, 66; success of, 175–77; suffrage campaign helped by, 121; as suspicious activity, 151. *See also* University of Nebraska football
Ford, Henry, 39, 41, 102
Ford, Richard, 89
Ford cars, 41
foreign language study, 53, 64, 73, 213–15
Foster, Amos, 170
Fowler, W. K., 104
France, 201–2, 204–5
Franco-Prussian War (1870), 200, 204
Franz Ferdinand (Austrian archduke), 200

Franz Joseph (Austro-Hungarian emperor), 42
Friedens Lutheran Church, 197–98
Frothingham, Landon, 163
Fulmer, Clark A., 68–69
fundamentalism, 18, 19, 272n52
Funke, Frederick, 126
Funke Opera House, 126, 128–30

gardens, 96
gasoline, 41, 42
Gehrke, Edward, 48
Gehrke, May, 48
General Federation of Women's Clubs, 114
George, Mrs. A. J., 114
German-American Alliance, 202
German Americans: immigration quotas for, 246; and prohibition, 17, 108, 111–12; and Selective Service, 212; settlement area of, 278n42; social events for, 22; Volga Germans compared to, 196–98; war sentiment against, 111–12, 208–11, 213–15, 217–19, 226, 241, 244; and women's suffrage, 114, 121–22. *See also* Volga Germans
German Dramatic Club, 217–18
German Empire, 112, 122
Germania Maennerchor, 22
German language, 64, 188, 196–97, 213–15
German Russians, 187–88, 191, 192. *See also* Volga Germans
Germany, 64, 182, 201–2, 204–7, 208, 229, 230, 240
Gillette, King, 96
girls: clothing of, 86–87; education of, 54, 55, 68, 73, 75, 76; employment for, 193; expectations for, 77, 143; physical education for, 91–92; as sports fans, 155, 177. *See also* women
Girls' Rooters Club, 177
Glacier National Park, 146
Goodhue, Bertram, 285n20
Gophers. *See* Minnesota football
Gounod, Charles: *Faust*, 128
Graduate School of Education (University of Nebraska), 217
Graham, Ralph, 174

Grant, Cary, 135
Great Britain. *See* Britain and the British
Great Depression: automobile sales affected by, 233; bicycle use during, 37; cigarette smoking during, 106; domestic products affected by, 236; higher education affected by, 68, 74, 252; population growth slowed by, 242; recreation affected by, 134, 143
Great Northern Express, 146
Grinnell College, 166, 265n83
The Growth of the American Republic (Morison, Commager, and Leuchtenburg), 220

Hadley, Arthur, 162
Hagenbeck-Wallace Circus, 149
hair, 3, 84, 161
Hallo's Opera, 125, 128
Harding, Warren G., 231–32
Harvard High School and Harvard School District, 52, 63
Harvard University, 53, 165
Hayes, Alan, 59
health, public. *See* public health
helmets, football, 161
Heppner, Amanda, 143
herdic carriages, 13, 21, 258n24
high schools, 9, 52–53, 54–55, 63, 264n26. *See also* Lincoln High School
highways, 46, 48
Hildebrand, Jennifer, 182
History of Nebraska (Olson), 219
A History of the American People (Johnson), 220
Hitler, Adolf, 240
hobble skirts, 87, 89
Hofstadter, Richard, 238, 249
Homestead Act (1862), 190
Hoover, Herbert, 226, 231, 232
horses, 11, 13, 31–32, 40–41, 42, 43, 92, 268n60
hospitals, 9–10, 12–13, 248
House of Representatives, U.S., 20–21, 22, 112, 240, 279n24
housing, 70, 93–98, 179–80, 242
Hulsebus, Fred, 100, 236, 262n123
"Huns," Germans as, 202, 208, 209–10, 227
The Hun Within (movie), 210

Hupmobiles, 236, 262n123
Huskers, 160, 167, 168, 170, 175, 176–77, 247. *See also* Cornhuskers
Husker Theatre, 136

immigrants: conscription of, 211–13; education of, 53, 55, 76; entertainment for, 134; German, 204; German Russian, 278n42; influence of, 252; numbers of, 270n62; and progressivism, 17; and prohibition, 108–9; quota system for, 246–47; voting rights of, 211. *See also* Volga Germans
income tax, 110
Industrial Revolution, 2–3
Inherit the Wind (movie), 272n52
Iroquois Theater, 130
Ishikawa, Jesse, 187
Italian Grand Opera Company, 128

Japanese Americans, 187, 244
Jayhawks, 173
Jeffrey, T. W., 137–38
Jewel Theatre, 135–36
Jews, 182, 245, 264n58
Jim Crow laws, 20–21, 182
Johns Hopkins University, 64
Johnson, Paul: *A History of the American People*, 220
Joseph II, Emperor, 146
Joyo theater, 131
joy riding, 43, 44
The Jungle (Sinclair), 16

The Kaiser (movie), 210
Kansas City Grau Opera Company, 128
Kansas State University, 173, 174, 176
KDKA (radio station), 237
Kennedy, John F., 42, 280n29; *Profiles in Courage*, 208
KFAB (radio station), 247
kinetoscope, 27
King, Mrs. D. G., 121
kitchens, 93–94, 95, 97
Knoll, Robert, 61, 253; *Prairie University*, 219
Knothole Club, 247
Kosmet Club, 66
Ku Klux Klan, 137–38, 245–46

Ladies Home Journal, 16

LaFollette, Robert M., 133
Lancaster County NE, 120–21, 178–79, 270n62
Lancaster NE (later Lincoln NE), 5
League of Nations, 230–31, 232
The Leisure Class (Veblen), 10
Leuchtenburg, William E.: *The Growth of the American Republic*, 220
Liberty Bonds, 202, *203*, 214–15
libraries, 17, *18*, 67
Liechtenstein, 116
Life, 96
lights, electric, 22–24, 27, 81, 93, 131
Lincoln, Abraham, 181
Lincoln Chamber of Commerce, 241
Lincoln Choral Union, 128
Lincoln City Council, 143
Lincoln Commercial Club, 222
Lincoln Council of Churches, 242
Lincoln Daily News, 200
Lincoln Evening Call, 22–23, 78, 104, 153
Lincoln General Hospital, 248
Lincoln Glee Club, 128
Lincoln Herald, 23, 219
Lincoln High School, 55, 56, 186–87, 214, 245, 263n6
Lincoln Highway, 44
Lincoln Journal, 92–93
Lincoln NE, *6*, *21*, *30*; about, 248–49, 252; beginnings of, 5–10; changes in, 1, 2, 10–15; planning of, 10–11; population of, 175–76, 257n10, 259n21; reform movements in, 15–21, 108, 110–11; and university sites, 72
Lincoln Oratorical Society, 128–29
Lincoln Park Restaurant, 133
Lincoln Philharmonic Orchestra, 128, 129
Lincoln Star: advice column in, 282n117; on automobiles, 39, 40, 43–44; on *The Birth of a Nation*, 137; on coaches, 167–68; on dancing, 140, 249; on driving, 45, 46; on education, 67–68; and First World War, 200–201, 202, 207–8, 216, 217, 219, 226; on football, 156, 160–61, 162, 164, 166–67, 174, 177; on immigrants, 188; on petting, 234; on prohibition, 112; on Prussia, 209; on racism, 186; on railroad, 124; on "regular" flu, 222; on smoking, 105; on Spanish flu,

223, 224; on student employment, 176; and suffrage, 114, 119; on University of Nebraska, 61–62; on Warren G. Harding, 231–32; on world fairs, 26, 27
Lincoln Telephone Exchange, 14
Lincoln Traction Company, 34
Lincoln Women's Club, 242
Lindbergh, Charles, 238
Lindell Hotel, 23
literacy, 179, 191–92, 212–13
Little Black Sambo (comic strip), 130, *184*, 185
living conditions, 1–5, 11–14
Lohengrin (Wagner), 128
Louisville and Nashville Railroad, 145
Louis XIV, 189
Lucia de Lammermoor (Donizetti), 128
Lucky Strike cigarettes, 107
Lusitania, 205–6
Lutheran Church, 197–98
Lynch, Mac, 125
lynchings, 138, 208, 243–44, 245
Lynd family, 262n114

machine guns, 199–200
Madam Butterfly (Puccini), 128
magazines, 102, 103
mail, 97, 238
mall near capitol building, 255, 285n20
marriage, 76, 77, 182
Marsh, Genevieve, 178–82, 185–86, 277n1
Martin, Dean, 254
Marx Brothers, 135
masks as health measure, 221, 222, 225
Maurer, Dorothy, 28
McCrann, W. J., 224
McKinley, William, 17, 20, 27, 94, 258n40
McQueen, Steve, 254
meatpacking industry, 16, 243
Medical College (Omaha NE), 65
medical education, 65, 68
Melbourne, Australia, 257n4
Memorial Stadium, 166, *175*, 254, 255
men: alcohol use by, 108; clothing for, 83–85; education of, 63; historical prominence of, 75; as secretaries, 79; and smoking, 104–5, 254; and suffrage, 15, 116–18, 121; traditional role of, 99–100; women kept separate from, 71–72

Messiah (Handel), 128–29
Methodist Church: and alcohol consumption, 30–31, 101, 107–8, 109, 111, 113; Chautauqua founded by, 132; on dancing, 142; evangelist preacher in, 143; on racist film, 137–38; in social life, 181; in university life, 67
Methodist Episcopal Church, 69
Metropolitan Opera, 208
"Middletown" IN, 46–47, 49, 138, 262n114, 264n26
Miles, Alexander, 81
Miller, Elizabeth Smith, 84
Miller & Paine, 81–82, *82*
Minerva (columnist) and "Minerva's Mail," 76–78, 80, 143, 209, 234, 235, 266n11, 282n117
Ministerial Association of Lincoln, 138, 156
Minnesota football, 157, 168–69, 171–72, 176–77
minstrel shows, 129–30, 185
missionaries and missionary work, 68–69, 73
Mississippi Valley Historical Association, 65
Missouri Pacific Railroad, 145
Missouri Valley Conference (MVC), 163, 170, 171, 174, 245
Mitchum, Robert, 254
Model T Ford, 39, 41
morality concern(s): alcohol use as, 107–8; clothing as, 86; entertainment as, 140–43; and football, 155, 162; mingling of sexes as, 36; and movies, 249, 252; Sunday events as, 27–29; in university life, 59, 62; and women's changing role, 114–15
Morison, Samuel Eliot: *The Growth of the American Republic*, 220
Mormons, 116
Morris, Seymour, Jr.: *American History Revised*, 220
Morrison, Lydia Hoffman, 1–2
motorcycles, 37
Mount Zion Baptist Church, 181
movies: advances in, 237; beginnings of, 135–36; and morality concerns, 249, 252; and patriotism, 210; performances

replaced by, 126, 131, 134; racism encouraged by, 136–38, 245
Muncie IN. *See* "Middletown" IN
Murrow, Edward R., 254
MVC. *See* Missouri Valley Conference (MVC)

National Association for the Advancement of Colored People (NAACP), 137
National Broadcasting Company, 237
National Guard, 204
national parks, 47, 48, 146
National Women's Party, 283n47
National Women's Suffrage Association (NWSA), 116, 119, 120
Nazi Germany, 182, 229
Nebraska, 6, *8*; and automobiles, 41–42, 46–48, 49; capital selection for, 5–6; farming in, 257n1; postwar, 227, 229, 241–44, 245–47, 252–53, 255; prohibition in, 109–10, 112; and women's suffrage, 115–17, 119–20
Nebraska Airplane Flying School, 238
Nebraska Christian University. *See* Cotner College
Nebraska City NE, 5
Nebraska Conference of the Methodist Church, 69
Nebraska Constitution, 116, 211
Nebraska Field (stadium), 171
Nebraska Hall (University of Nebraska), 57
Nebraska Sports Hall of Fame, 92–93
Nebraska State Council of Defense, 215–16, 217, 219
Nebraska State Fair, 62, 149–50
Nebraska State Journal: on automobile accident deaths, 234; on automobiles, 38; on aviation, 237; on Blacks, 164, 244; on charity ball, 22; on football, 155, 163, 166, 172; on *Lusitania* sinking, 206; on prohibition, 112; on Spanish flu, 223; on street conditions, 13; on suffrage movement, 118; on war opposition, 207, 208, 219; on women workers, 79–80
Nebraska Wesleyan University, 57; beginnings of, 51; buildings of, 69; economics affecting, 68; enrollment of, 74; and football, 156; housing at, 70; moral concerns of, 30–31, 59, 143; reform backed

by, 102; religious affiliation of, 67, 68–69; during Spanish flu, 222, 224; student life at, 70–71; and women students, 89, 91–92

New Deal, 19

"new down," *158*

Newman Methodist Episcopal Church, 181

newspapers: about, 102; and cigarettes, 103, 106; on expositions, 26; during First World War, 202, 209, 213–14; influence of, 16; and prohibition, 112; racism in, 182, 185; on Spanish flu, 221, 222–23; on voting rights, 116–17. *See also specific newspapers*

New York Times, 16, 37–38, 102, 200

New Zealand, 116

Nicholas II, Czar, 195

night schools, 55, 76

Nineteenth Amendment, 16, 115, 239

Norris, George W., 207–8

North and South Bottoms (neighborhood), 187, 188–89, 192–93, 197–98, 214

Northern Pacific Railroad, 146

North Platte NE, 151

Northwestern Line, 25

North Western Railroad, 146

Norway, 116

Notre Dame football, 172–73

Nuremburg Laws, 182

NWSA. *See* National Women's Suffrage Association (NWSA)

Oakley, Annie, 150

Oberlin College, 265n83

Official Road Book of the Nebraska State Automobile Association, 45

"Old Main" (Nebraska Wesleyan University), 69

Oliver Theater, 71, 126, 128, 130–31, 136, 137

Olson, James: *History of Nebraska*, 219

Omaha Bee, 121, 243

Omaha NE, *28*, 59; automobile drivers in, 45; Blacks in, 179, 185, 243–44; breweries in, 68, 109, 111; and capital city choice, 5–6; immigrants in, 195; population of, 257n2, 259n21; as railroad station, 6, 31; and university location

choice, 60, 153; women in, 266n5; and women's suffrage, 114, 121; and world fairs, 24–25, 27–28

Omaha Weekly Tribune and Republican, 115

Omaha YMCA football team, 152–53, 177

omnibuses, 13, 31

On War (Clausewitz), 200

operas and opera houses, 124–28, *127*, 208

oratory, 20, 70, 258n49

O Street, 10, 13, *21*, *82*, 146

Othello (Shakespeare), *127*

outhouses, 94

Panic (1893), 27, 59, 67, 68, 144–45

Pankhurst, Emmeline, 119

Paris Peace Conference (1919), 227, 229

Paris world's fair (1889), 25

parlors, 94–95

Passion's Playground (movie), *139*

Pauley, Albertina, 1, 48–49, 95–96, 150

Pauley, Alice, 97

Pauley, Bruce: about, 1; on alcohol use, 113; on Blacks, 186–87; education of, 215, 252; family history of, 93–94; and football, 177, 247; heritage of, 196, 197–98, 211; as historian, 1–2, 79, 240–41; memories of, 9, 81–82, 83, 95–98, 133, 136, 188

Pauley, Carroll, *47*; in childhood, 95; education of, 129; as farm owner, 193; and First World War, 214–15; as lumberyard owner, 29–30, 124; memories of, 94, 148, 151; on road trip, 48–49

Pauley, Conrad, 94–95, 100, 192

Pauley, Elizabeth Ross, 93

Pauley, Gordon, 280n29

Pauley, Heinrich, 93, 190–92

Pauley, L. H., *47*; bicycle use of, 37; death of, 96; education of, 52, 54, 125, 192, 258n49; family of, 100; as lumberyard owner, 49, 95, 192; national identity of, 214–15; on road trip, 48

Pauley, Marianne, 1, 93

Pauley, Reon, 141

Pauley Lumber Company, 1, 49, 56, 124, 141, 188, 192, 214–15

Pauli, Christian, 191

Paulÿ, Philipp Jacob, 189

Paxton Hotel, 164

payment plans, installment, 39, 49–50, 236, 283n33

Peony Park, 148

A People's History of the United States (Zinn), 220

Pershing, John J., 202, 231

Pershing's Crusaders (movie), 210

petting (sexual behavior), 234

Philbrick, Inez, 120–21

pipes for smoking, 104–5

pneumonia, 160

Ponce de Leon Hotel, 144

Populist Party, 17

porches, 94

Pound, Louise, 92–93, 216–17

Pound, Olivia, 92

Pound, Roscoe, 92

Praeger, Robert, 208

Prairie University (Knoll), 219

Prater (amusement park), 146

pregnancies, 100, 239

Presbyterian Church, 101, 109, 111

Princeton University, 152

professors, 63, 64–65, 119, 156

Profiles in Courage (Kennedy), 208

Progressive Era, 99

progressivism, 15–20, 238

prohibition: consequences of, 112–13, 241–42, 253–54; hopes for, 227; and immigrants, 17, 108–9, 111, 197; laws enforcing, 239; support for, 15, 18, 19, 107, 109–12; women's role in, 16, 75, 108, 109; women's suffrage linked with, 117. *See also* temperance movement; Women's Christian Temperance Union (WCTU)

propaganda, 202–4, 205, 208–10, 229, 230

Protestants, 74, 113, 132, 142

Prussia, 64, 200, 209

The Prussian Cur (movie), 210

public health, 9–10, 16, 221–25, 248–49

Puccini, Giacomo: *Madam Butterfly*, 128

Pulitzer Prize, 208

Pullman, George, 145

Pullman cars, 145, 185

Pure Food and Drug Act (1906), 16, 248

racism, *183–84, 186*; in education, 185–87; in elected government positions, 20–21;

by Ku Klux Klan, 245–46; and lynching, 243–44; in military, 229; in movies, 137–38; in newspapers, 182, 185; against performers, 130, 134–35, 182, 185; in property ownership opportunities, 244–45; in sports, 164, 173–74, 245; at swimming pool, 187; in voting rights, 114

Radford, B. J., 68

radio, 106, 134, 143, 236–37, 247, 252

railroad, *8, 144, 186*; activists benefiting from, 120; colleges benefiting from, 67; decline of, 241, 284n56; as employer, 182, 185, 192–93, 244; importance of, 29, 124, 126; and leisure time, 130, 131, 133, 143–46, 148–49; as long-distance transportation, 190–91, 274n125; and mail delivery, 238; standard time influenced by, 146; stations for, 5–6, 7–9, 25, 248

rainfall, 14, 61, 67, 264n41

record players, *250*

Red Scare, 238

Red Summer, 227

refrigerators, 29–30, 236, 283n35

Republicans, 117, 181, 230–32

Reserve Officers Training Corps Band, 129, *129*

Rialto Theatre, *139*, 210

Richard III (Shakespeare), *127*

Richmond VA, 32

Righter, Lena, 96

Ringling Brothers Circus, 149

Rio de Janeiro, Brazil, 257n4

road shows, 126

Robinson, E. N., 166

Robinson, Seth, 56

Rock Island Railroad, 8, 145–46, 176

Rockne, Knute, 172, 173

Rockwell, Norman, 96

Rogers, Roy, 136

Rogers, Will, 135

Roosevelt, Eleanor, 270n64

Roosevelt, Franklin, 19, 231

Roosevelt, Theodore, 17, 42, 71, 133, 157, 231

Ross, Clinton, 173

Russia, 187–88, 189–91, 192, 195–96, 201, 204–5

Russian Bolshevik revolution, 238
Rutgers University, 152

Sabbatarians, 27, 140
Saint Paul Methodist Church, 143
salesclerks, 80–81
saloons, 101, 108–9, 110–12
Salt Creek, 6, 133, 188
Salt-Wahoo Watershed Association, 188
"Sambo's Soliloquy," *184*
São Paulo, Brazil, 257n4
Saturday Evening Post, 96, 102
Schlieffen, Alfred von, and Schlieffen
  Plan, 205
schoolhouses, 52
school spirit, 63, 153
Scopes "Monkey" Trial (1925), 272n52
Second World War, 37, 211, 227, 229,
  252, 255
secretaries, 78–79, 80
secularism, 68, 131–32, 150, 249
sedition, 209, 280n34
segregation, 20–21, 134–35, 164, 179,
  187, 229, 244–45. *See also* racism
Selective Service Act, 211–13
Sells Brothers, 148–49
Senate, U.S., 112, 207, 230
servants, 80, 89, 97
Seventh Day Adventists, 33, 67
Seven Years' War, 189
Seward, William Henry, 79
Shakespeare, William, 126; *Othello*, 127;
  Richard III, 127
shaving and razors, 25, 96
Shaw, Anna Howard, 120
Sherman, Charles "Cy," 165
sidewalks, 9, 13–14
Siman Act (1919), 214, 215
Sinclair, Upton: *The Jungle*, 16
Sixteenth Amendment, 110
Skelton, Red, 135
slavery, 101, 178, 181
sleeping cars, *186*
smallpox, 194
Smith, Edward, 243
snowball fight, 73
Social Science Service Board (Omaha NE),
  142

soldiers: depictions of, 204, 209, 210; and
  Germans, 230; honors for, 227, 255;
  in offense role, 201–2; segregation of,
  229; and smoking, 105, 107; Spanish flu
  affecting, 220, 222
Sorenson, Ted, 280n29
Sousa, John Philip, 128, 271n21
South Bottoms. *See* North and South Bottoms (neighborhood)
Spanish flu: casualties of, 161, 224, 225,
  281n84; course of, 220–21, 224–25; in
  memory, 224–25; and parade (Philadelphia PA, 1918), 220–21; response to,
  213, 219–24, 281n82
speed limits, 41, 45–46, 233, 262n103
The Spirit of '76 (movie), 210
standard railroad time, 146
state fairs, 62, 149–50
St. Augustine FL, 144
steamships, 24, 195
St. Elizabeth Hospital, 9, 248
Stephens, W. L., 104
Stiehm, Ewald O. "Jumbo," 170–72, 173–75
stores, retail, 80–82, *82*, 224
streetcars, electric: automobile sales affecting, 38, 241; controversy over, 33–34;
  cost of, 71; demise of, 34; impact of, 22–
  23, 30–31, 32–33, 66, 81, 124, 148, 248;
  relevance of, 34–35, 37; and university
  life, 72; and world fairs, 25, 146–47
streetcars, horse-drawn, 31–32, 38, 66
streets, 12–14, 21, 44–45, *82*, 130–31
strikes, labor, 11, 34, 238, 243
suffrage, women's: factors affecting, 122;
  legislation about, 16, 115–17, 121;
  opponents to, 113–15; parade as turning
  point for, 117–19; supporters of, 113,
  117, 119–21, 253; worldwide, 116
suffragettes, 117–18, 119, 120–21
suitings (fabric), *87*
suits, 83, *88*
Sullivan, Mark, 209
Sunday, Billy, 133, 142–43, 202
Supreme Court, Nebraska, 214
Supreme Court, U.S., 211, 215
Switzerland, 116
Sydney, Australia, 257n4

Taft, William Howard, 17, 133, 258n40
teachers, 52–53, 54, 73, 185, 194
technology in everyday life, 2–5, 18–19, 32
telephones, 9, 14, 236
television, 96, 252
temperance movement, 14, 84, 101, 108, 110. *See also* prohibition; Women's Christian Temperance Union (WCTU)
Temple theater, 131
theater as entertainment, 126, 128, 131, 142
theaters as venue, 71, 125–26, 130, 135–36, 138, 210
Thomas, Charles, 165, 166
time, standard, 146
Title IX, 91
Tivoli Gardens, 146
To Hell with the Kaiser (movie), 210
toilets, 95–96
Tompkins, E. N., 142
Tortora, Phyllis, 84
Tracy, Spencer, 272n52
trains. *See* railroad
trams, 31–32, 66. *See also* streetcars, electric; streetcars, horse-drawn
Trans-Mississippi and International Exposition (Omaha, 1898), 24, 27–29, *28*
transportation, public, 7–8, 11–12, 30–35, 124, 241, 248
travel, transatlantic, 189–90, 194–95
trees, 6, 14
tricycle, steam-powered, 38
Turnpike (dance hall), 141, 273n82
The Two Orphans (play), 125
typing and typewriters, 17, 78–80

Union College, 51, *58*, 59, 67–69, 71–74, 92, 102
Union Pacific Railroad, 5–6, 146, 147
Union Station (Omaha NE), 241
United States: changes in, 248–49, 252–55; education in, 52, 53, 64; in First World War, 199, 200, 204–9; and peacekeeping, 230–31; population of, 4–5; suffrage movements in, 116; transportation in, 39; as world power, 232–33
University Athletic Board (University of Nebraska), 169, 171

University Hall (University of Nebraska), 56, 69–70
University of Nebraska, 57, *91*, 129, *171*; alumni of, 177; beginnings of, 12, 56, 59–60; buildings of, 69–70; curriculum of, 41, 53–54; dancing forbidden by, 140–41; and denominational colleges, 67; enrollment of, 15, 21, 60–61, 252; faculty workload of, 63; German influence in, 216–17; graduate education in, 65, 277n1; and high schools, 54–55, 56; Japanese American students at, 187; and Ku Klux Klan, 246; morality concerns of, 62; music school in, 129; physical education at, 89–90, 213; physical expansion of, 10, 61–62; racism in, 185–86, 245; reform backed by, 102; reputation of, 51; smoking opposed by, 103–4; during Spanish flu, 222, 224; student life at, 66, 73–74, 143; war spirit in, 215–19; and women athletes, 90–91, 92–93
University of Nebraska football, *171*; advantages for, 175–77; attitudes toward, 155–56, 162–63; beginnings of, 152–53; and Blacks, 173, 274; coaches for, 163–64, 166–68, 170–71, 174–75; game history of, 171–73, 276n72; game locations of, 163; growth and development of, 165–66, 168–70; media covering, 247; supporters of, 177; and team nicknames, 165
University of Oklahoma, 174
University of Wyoming, 241
University Place NE, 30–31, 70
U.S. Customs, 206
Utah, voting rights in, 116

vacations, 143–46
vaccines, 52, 194
vaudeville, 126, 131, 134–36, 143, 185, 237, 249
Veblen, Thorstein: *The Leisure Class*, 10
velocipedes, 35–36
Verde, Giuseppe: *Aida*, 128
Victoria, Queen, 100, 235
Victorian era, influence of, 62, 96–97, 99–100, 114, 131–32, 234, 235
Victrolas, *250*

Vienna world exhibition (1873), 146
Volga Germans, *193*; education of, 194; European migration of, 189–91; independent spirit of, 195–98; land purchases by, 247; language of, 188, 192, 197; overseas migration of, 190–92, 204; and prohibition, 111; and Reich Germans, 188, 196–97; settlement area of, 187–89; war sentiment against, 213–14; work of, 192–94

Wagner, Richard, 208; *Lohengrin*, 128
Walt Disney World (Orlando FL), 25, 148
war bonds, 202, *203*, 214–15
Washington, Booker T., 133
Washington DC, 80, 105, 117–18, 257n4
Washington Naval Conference (1921–22), 231, 239
WCTU. *See* Women's Christian Temperance Union (WCTU)
Webster, John, 114
Western Independent University Football Association, 170
wets (anti-prohibitionists), 108, 111
White, Laura Amanda, 241
White City exposition. *See* Chicago World's Fair (Columbian Exposition, 1893)
wild west shows, 150–51
Williams, Hattie Plum, 193–94
Williams, John Sharp (senator), 185–86
Williams, J. S. (coach), 163
Wilson, Woodrow, *228*; and *The Birth of a Nation*, 136; colleagues of, 17–18; education promoted by, 64; and First World War, 205, 206–7, 211, 221, 227; in international affairs, 227, 230–31; and Spanish flu, 221
Winter Garden variety house, 125
women, *86–88*, *251*; and alcohol reform, 108, 109, 111; and birthrate, 264n58;

changes for, 4, 75–76, 239–41, 253, 254–55, 283n47; and cigarette use, 103, 105, 107; clothing for, 83–87, 89, 91–92, 249; as consumers, 81–82; and domestic surroundings, 93, 97–98; education of, 60, 61, 63, 74, 264n58; and electric cars, 41; employment of, 78–81, 240–41, 266n5, 284n54; and exercise, 36, 37, 85, 89–93; as football fans, 177; Jewish, 264n58; leisure time of, 123–24; marriage as goal of, 76–78; masculinity in, 113–14, 239; men compared to, 99–100; men kept separate from, 71–72; in reform movements, 15–17, 100–102; traditions challenged by, 234–35; world fairs representing, 26–27. *See also* girls; suffrage, women's
Women's Christian Temperance Union (WCTU), 30–31, 71, 101, 104, 234, 235. *See also* prohibition
Wonderland (motion picture theater), 131, 136
Wood, William, 186
World Bicycle, *35*
world fairs, 24–29, 146
World War I. *See* First World War
World War II. *See* Second World War
Wright, John, 223–24
Wright, Orville, 237
Wright, Wilbur, 237
Wyoming, 16, 116
Wyuka Cemetery, 100, 224

Yellowstone National Park, *47*, 48, 146
YMCA, 105, 152–53, 177, 234
Yost, Fielding H., 166
YWCA, 234

Zehrung, Frank C., 130
Zinn, Howard: *A People's History of the United States*, 220

Printed in the USA
CPSIA information can be obtained
at www.ICGtesting.com
LVHW041205151223
766489LV00003B/234